Hiding from History

Hiding from History

POLITICS AND PUBLIC IMAGINATION

Meili Steele

Cornell University Press Ithaca and London

Some material from this book has been published elsewhere in somewhat different versions. A revised version of "Hiding from History: Habermas's Elision of Public Imagination," *Constellations* 12 (2005): 409–436, appears as chapter 1. Parts of "Ricoeur versus Taylor on Language and Narrative," *Metaphilosophy* 34 (2003):224–246, appear in revised form in chapters 2 and 3. A section of "Three Problematics of Linguistic Vulnerability: Gadamer, Benhabib, and Butler," *Feminist Interpretations of Hans-Georg Gadamer*, ed. Lorraine Code (University Park: Pennsylvania State University Press, 2003), 335–366, appears in revised form in chapter 2. The essay "Ellison versus Arendt on Little Rock: The Role of Language in Political Judgment," *Constellations: A Journal of Critical and Democratic Theory* 9 (2002): 184–206, has been revised as chapter 4.

First published 2005 by
Cornell University Press

Printed in the United States of America

Library of Congress Cataloging-in-Publication Data

Steele, Meili, 1949–
 Hiding from history : politics and public imagination / Meili Steele.
  p. cm.
 Includes bibliographical references and index.
 ISBN-13: 978-0-8014-4385-5 (cloth : alk. paper)
 ISBN-10: 0-8014-4385-7 (cloth : alk. paper)
 1. Public history. 2. Historiography. 3. History—Philosophy. I. Title
 D16.163.S84 2005
 901—dc22
                    2005016120

FOR LAURA

Contents

Acknowledgments

I have many people to thank for their help with this book.
At Cornell University Press, I would like to thank Bernie
Kendler, Candace Akins, and the two readers of the manu-
script. For their excellent copyediting, I want to thank Kay
Scheuer and Brittany Powell. For research support, I would
like to thank Robert Newman and Steve Lynn, who served as
my department chairs during the book's gestation. I tested
early versions of the ideas for the book in Prague at the
annual meetings of the Philosophy and Human Sciences
group. I give special recognition to Alessandro Ferrara,
Linda Alcoff, Maeve Cooke, Martin Sauter, and Johanna
Meehan. I also greatly benefited from an NEH seminar on
French philosophy run by Thomas Pavel, then at Princeton
University. At the University of South Carolina, I want to
thank the Walker Institute and Don Puchala for inviting me
to participate in colloquia on international relations and Peter
Sederberg and the Honors College for asking me to develop a
new course on inquiry in the humanities. Larry Rhu, Naeem
Inyatullah, Kate Brown, Greg Forter, Nina Levine, Chris
Tollefson, Pascal Michon, and Eduardo Mendietta took the
time to read sections of the book and offer invaluable feed-
back. John McGowan put his finger on several crucial
ambiguities in my exposition and gave me the opportunity to
lay out the entire argument of the book before an audience at
the University of North Carolina, Chapel Hill. Michael
Halberstam has given me years of challenging conversation
on every aspect of this book. His insight and encouragement
have been indispensable to me. My wife, Cassie Premo Steele,
has read every word and offered the stylistic advice that only a
writer can offer.

Hiding from History

The common life on which a liberal order depends [. . .]
must be the life of a people united by what they have
learned together from the things that once came to divide
them.—Charles Larmore, *Morals and Modernity* (1996, 144)

Introduction
The History Debates as
a Crisis for Liberalism

Six years ago I was reading the local newspaper in Columbia, South Carolina, and discovered that the state legislature was proposing to put the public understanding of history to a referendum.[1] The focus of the referendum was whether the flying of the Confederate battle flag over the statehouse was a fitting memorial to past traditions or a symbol of the legacy of racism. The legislature had raised the flag over the statehouse in 1962 at the beginning of the Civil Rights movement;[2] however, now that the flag's presence had become controversial, many legislators wanted to avoid a public stand. By calling for a referendum on the flag, the legislators hid from what properly should have been a public debate by appealing to democratic procedures.

The ensuing discussion revealed that this interpretive vacuum was not an isolated example of political cowardice but part of the state's educational philosophy. Public school teachers, like legislators, tried to ignore the interpretive issues surrounding the flag.[3] For many legislators, educators, and the Chamber of Commerce, the controversy was an annoying distraction from the problems of the present. Education meant instruction in the basic skills and facts necessary for the global market along with the inculcation of respect for the law. The certainty of moral education could be divorced from historical ambiguity. Citizens did not need cultural or historical orientation for deliberation about their public lives. According to this way of thinking, there was no reason to get bogged down in the subjective self-understandings of individuals who could decide for themselves which interpretation of history to believe. If history were to go beyond facts, then this matter should be privatized—individuals could seek out their own interpretations, just as they could decide what novels to read or movies to watch.

When public pressure mounted—including an effective boycott by the NAACP—it became obvious that the flag issue was not going away and that business would be hurt by its continued presence. Then many of the legislators who had previously wanted to forget the flag started working to take it down for the same reasons that they had earlier wanted to ignore it—to get it out of the way of business. A compromise was finally worked out. The flag was to be moved from the top of the capitol dome to a place on the statehouse grounds, and an African American memorial monument was to be constructed on another part of the grounds.

The widespread satisfaction at resolving the debate helped everyone ignore the model of public deliberation that was dramatized. According to this model, conflicting historical interpretations should not raise questions about how a democracy should interpret its past; rather, the resolution of public disputes should be the result of a compromise among competing interest groups.4 Cultural difference and history were merely politically sensitive issues that needed to be handled strategically rather than through discussion about how citizens should reason. By giving each side its own memory site, the state tried to neutralize not only the conflict but history itself. Schoolteachers could thus continue their practice of giving a version of the past that had no conflicted legacies, that offered no interpretive political concerns for the present.

In coming to this resolution, South Carolina was not taking a peculiarly Southern path. Rather, this resolution is typical of a liberal understanding of democratic discussion. We can begin to connect the flag debate to political philosophy by looking at liberalism's historical narrative of the transition to modern democracy in which its citizens draw a lesson that transforms their political self-understanding. Charles Larmore articulates this narrative well: "Liberal democracy builds upon the memory of past conflict and the hard-won knowledge that many of the ideals that used to shape political life now form the object of reasonable disagreement [. . .]. [Citizens] feel united in what they have learned together from the things that once divided them. This shared memory is itself sustained, of course, by a common allegiance to constitutional principles of equal freedom and respect" (1996, 213). There are two parts to this statement: the emergence of shared ideals that trump and frame all others; the emergence of a common horizon of history and meaning. The effect of them together is to drive history out of politics.

The shared ideals of the new polity, equal freedom and respect, command a consensus unlike that of other values, and the consensus is usually backed up by a special argument for the necessity of these values as well as by an appeal to empirical traditions.[5] The reason liberals argue for necessity is that they want to put these values, and the consensus they command, beyond politics and historical contingency. This consensus does not ask atheists and Baptists, Kantians and Catholics, Buddhists and Muslims, environmentalists and Exxon executives to take on a new worldview; rather, they need only affirm democratic principles from their own frameworks.[6] Thus, Larmore claims, "ours is a form of life, which, permeated by the modern experience of reasonable disagreements about the goods, rests on the conviction that we can nonetheless agree upon a core morality" (1996, 58).

With this pressure to find common principles comes the pressure to establish a common horizon of meaning and history. If the synchronic problem of politics is the diversity of views, there is the diachronic good news that historical tradition provides continuity.[7] For political purposes, citizens' differences can be treated as if they do not problematize the language of public conversation. Both Larmore and John Rawls ground the identity of political community in empirical assertions of commonality. While Larmore speaks of the binding power of a shared history, Rawls says that a liberal community shares "the facts of common sense political sociology" (1993, 193).[8] Here we see substantive historical beliefs put beyond the reach of political debate as the common background. This continuity of meaning joins with the core morality to make conflicted historical meanings mere background noise in public reasoning.

Even though the parties in the flag debate do not invoke liberal political philosophers, they do exhibit liberal thinking. The principal goal for many concerned was to get away from a politics that engages the languages and meanings of public discussion. In the liberal vision, the two monuments on the statehouse grounds represent the triumph of equal respect for difference. In the view I will present, the two monuments not only perpetuate a long-standing division in American public life; they represent the failure of political philosophy to address questions of historical meaning. From 1865 onward there has been a division in American public memory of the Civil War, in which the African American public spheres remembered differently than "white" public spheres.[9] This division produced different linguistic and cultural expressions so as to form alternative historical traditions. The two monuments on the grounds of the statehouse of South Carolina continue these traditions of conflicted memory. While liberalism wants to define differences about the "good" individually and synchronically and then contain them with a common medium of tradition, this example shows that politics must attend to the medium of meanings and their histories. Although dialogues of professional historians are not always of immediate concern to public political reasoning, such reasoning depends upon implicit historiographical claims.[10]

This local conflict over the flag resonates with the recent national debates over history in the United States, Germany, and France. In most parts of the United States, the source of controversy has been not the Civil War but multiculturalism and patriotism (Nash 1997). In Germany, we find the "Historians' Debate" over how to give a proper account of the Holocaust (Baldwin 1990). In France, we find debates over the commemoration of 1789 and how to understand a multiethnic state (Kaplan 1995). However, the resonance of this local example does not stop here; it extends to the international debates about how to understand the ways that different societies negotiate cultural and political "transitions to modernity"— or, more precisely, to modern democratic culture.[11] All these issues ask us to bring together what Western modernity has tried to keep apart—the explanatory work of social and cultural history and the philosophical work of practical reason.

DIVIDING THE TASKS OF REASON, OCCLUDING PUBLIC IMAGINATION

The locus classicus for the split between theoretical and moral reasoning is the Kantian distinction between the noumenal moral (judicial) world and the scientific world of phenomena, including the vagaries of history. In the noumenal world, we think of ourselves as free moral agents according to the principles of practical reason. Moral meaning is itself abstracted from history and defined according to ahistorical rules.[12] In the phenomenal world, on the other hand, we are simply objects of nature to be explained by theoretical reason. In both cases, however, we are to think through universalizable, ahistorical rules, not through inherited historical meanings and their social imaginaries. Thus, the explanatory concerns of historians are separated from the reasoning through principle that concerns judges and legislators.[13] From Kant's era to the present, there has been continuous pressure on this philosophical framework to make concessions to history, as the recent works of both Larmore and Rawls show; however, there has been little engagement by philosophers of practical reason with the historical meanings that concern those who offer the most prominent contemporary challenge to liberalism's philosophy of meaning, constructivists.

The constructivist approaches to meaning, such as we see in Benedict Anderson's *Imagined Communities* or Edward Said's *Orientalism,* do not study historical institutions for their contribution to public reasoning, as we find in liberal appeals to tradition. Attacking the idealist approach to meaning found in philosophies of practical reason, constructivists treat meaning as the product of unacknowledged historical, ideological, and economic forces. Principles cannot be defined apart from particular histories, and these histories cannot be reduced to a shared tradition. Anderson's work, for instance, describes the constitutive roles that the novel and the newspaper played in shaping public imagination during the historical transition from religious cultures and dynastic regimes to secular cultures and national regimes. Modern citizens cannot simply isolate liberal moral lessons about the significance of reasonable disagreement; rather, they must recognize how new forms of language and temporality structure reason and identity from the ground up. Anderson, like other constructivist thinkers, takes up the role of the historian seeking to explain how the imagination is shaped rather than the perspective of the citizen and philosopher who asks how we can reason through these "imagined communities." In other words, these constructivist thinkers never deal with the question of how we should think about public reason after their critiques, contenting themselves with talking about public meanings from the outside. In doing so, they simply reinforce the split between a concern with explanatory or constructivist critique that turns citizens and meanings into objects and a concern with the principles of reasoning that ignores the historical institutions of meaning and social forces that inform these principles.[14]

Can we develop a conception of public imagination that enables us to bring into the same deliberative space these contrasting approaches to the question of meaning? The key to overcoming this split is to bring together what they share: a philosophical hostility to the historical languages of everyday life. Cultural theorists usually treat these languages as objects to be explained structurally or causally. Or, they can eschew explanation altogether and objectify these languages through a withering, immanent critique that deprives them of any purchase on the world—for example, Said's unmasking of the Western discourses on the Orient.[15] The disciplinary boundaries separating sociology, history, and literary theory relieve them of the task of connecting their critiques to any account of public reasoning.[16]

Normative philosophers approach the languages of everyday life differently. Instead of objectifying them, political philosophers evaporate these languages by a paradoxical move. On the one hand, the core morality has to be sufficiently distant from the languages of everyday life so as to provide a standard against which these languages can be measured; thus, the definition of morality relies on a device such as the original position, which asks citizens to think outside of historical particularity. On the other hand, the morality must already be in the particular languages of everyday life in an unproblematic way, so we find an appeal to abstract tradition that does not engage actual languages. For both normative and cultural theorists, the languages of the world serve only to obscure proper reasoning.[17] To bring these languages back into our understanding of political reason, we need some new concepts.

PUBLIC IMAGINATION AND INSTITUTIONS OF MEANING

"Public imagination"—a phrase I will use interchangeably with "social imaginary"—is a broad term for talking about the historical meanings of a political culture. By this phrase, I mean not only the explicit concepts of a culture but also the images, plots, symbols, and background practices through which citizens imagine their lives. Hence, the social imaginary includes normative languages and assumptions about personhood, history, language, rights, and the like.[18] Public imagination transforms the opposition between historical objects and principled subjects, by blocking the moves of philosophers in the liberal tradition of practical reason who isolate normative principles from their social imaginaries and opening a new space for public reasoning. In opposing the universality of principles to the infinite particularity of context, philosophers of practical reason run together two ideas of context—empirical context, which is infinitely variable, and semantic context or social imaginary, which is not. The shapes of public imagination are not universal, but they are historically generalizable constituents of public mind.[19] Thus, when citizens confront an innovative situation or text, they are not simply applying principles but recontextualizing beliefs, concepts, and images—that is, reasoning through the social imaginary. Even if we objectify features of the social imaginary as historians or sociologists, rather than as philosophers of language and practical reason, we are nonetheless drawing on other dimensions of this shared imaginary background, which can never be fully thematized. The term "public imagination" signals that meaning and imagination are not confined to the mental functioning of individuals, but effective and consequential in the world as historical forces. Such a conceptualization will help get us beyond the division of subjective and objective approaches to the question of meaning that divides the disciplines.[20]

I will develop my conception of social imaginary by looking first at the broadest institution of meaning, that is, language, and the transcendental arguments that are made about it, such as those of Jürgen Habermas, Judith Butler, and Charles Taylor.[21] However, I will also look at other representative figures from philosophy, literary theory, and history to show how different disciplines engage the question of public imagination. Transcendental arguments about language cut across disciplinary boundaries, and they can have complementary or critical relationships to the self-understandings of particular institutions of meaning. For example, a transcendental argument for a hermeneutic philosophy of language, such as Taylor's, can challenge the understanding of art as subjective expression. By contrast, Habermas's philosophy of language dovetails with the self-understandings of the law.

I will be making a philosophical argument for how we should understand the deliberative subject's relationship to historical institutions of meaning and then developing a conception of practical reason that follows from this understanding. In doing so, I will link everyday political dialogue to political philosophy, historical change, and literature. We can get a sense of what this will entail by looking quickly at the work of Martha Nussbaum, who has sought to overcome the narrowness of liberal thinking by drawing on one of the important resources of public imagination, literature.

In *Poetic Justice: The Literary Imagination and Public Life*, she attacks the narrow, rule-bound thinking that dominates both the Kantian and utilitarian traditions of moral reasoning. Instead, she urges us to draw on literature in order to get a detailed account of what it means to lead a life different from our own. "My central subject is the ability to imagine what it is like to live the life of another person who might, given changes in circumstances, be oneself or one of one's loved ones" (1995, 5). Literature, for Nussbaum, is not a private but public matter, for she wants us to consider "the literary as a public imagination" (3). Her imagination is one "that will steer judges in their judging, legislators in their legislating, policy makers in measuring the quality of life of people near and far" (3). Nussbaum makes several important moves here. She opens the boundary between literature, everyday speech, law, and philosophy. Literary texts are not sealed off in an aesthetic realm or relegated to the extraordinary. Rather, literature explores and tests the ethical potential in everyday language. Moreover, literary texts do not simply provide examples for philosophical and legal reasoning; rather, the language of literature (and everyday life) is often more perspicuous than the language of philosophy on matters of public concern. But while I applaud this move to consider literature as public imagination, I reject Nussbaum's understanding of the relationship of citizens to the institutions of meaning—that is, to language, literature, and the court—and their historicity.

For Nussbaum, "public imagination" provides access to an alternative life, a subject-to-subject conception that is synchronic, individualistic, and phenomenological: literary texts offer a kind of specificity and emotional richness missing from both universalizing normative theory and the social sciences. Nussbaum's ethical framework brackets the problems of historical distance between text and reader, the explanatory concerns of cultural historians, and the interpretive dilemmas posed by the linguistic differences of text and interpreter. For Nussbaum, literature's relationship to history does not require us to consult modern philosophies of history but Aristotle: "Literature focuses on the possible, inviting readers to wonder about themselves" (5). Hence, it is not surprising that she does not see her view as incompatible with that of sensitive Kantians: "My own preferred version of the ethical stance derives from Aristotle, but everything I say here could be accommodated by a Kantianism modified so as to give the emotions a carefully demarcated cognitive role" (xvi).

For cultural and literary theorists, Nussbaum's idealized and dehistoricized approach to literature as a resource for reasoning is naive. Literature does not give us unproblematic access to the world but is bound up with the society's mechanisms of ideological production.[22] Literature is obfuscating as well as clarifying. Cultural theorists treat literature and culture as objects for constructivist analysis—for instance, the institutions of the canon—but, as we've said, they do not come back to Nussbaum's question of how culture informs their own conceptions of reason and action. As she says, "once we give up on good reasons for action, we are left with causes of action that may move us with necessitating force" (135).

What Nussbaum leaves out is that literature is arguing with the languages of the social imaginary. Literature is providing not just empirical specificity or context for norms but a comprehensive engagement with public imagination.[23] Literature's argumentative dimension is most obvious in philosophical literary texts such Swift's *Gulliver's Travels* or Proust's *A la recherche du temps perdu.* In these texts we find not only claims about epistemology, morality, politics, and time but also reasoning through the presentation of characters, description, and other elements. Such texts provide accounts of how we are in the world and seek to discredit other accounts found in the literature, philosophy, and social science of the time. (This is not to say that such texts are right, of course.) Public imagination provides an inescapable common argumentative terrain not just for literature and philosophy, of course, but also for other disciplines, such as history, as the current debates about memory illustrate so well. Moreover, arguments about the shapes of the social imaginary are not limited to professional debates or such obviously philosophical texts as those of Swift and Proust; they can be also found in other media. The popular film *Forrest Gump,* for instance, offers a powerful conservative political reading of America in the 1960s, in which the political movements of the time are trivialized or demonized.[24]

The argumentative dimension of literature (and film) brings to the surface the speculative dimension of everyday speech and points to the possibility of a richer kind of public reasoning than we have seen in normative philosophy.[25] Normative philosophy limits the speculative dimension of language to such narrow operations as "original position" or the inescapable presuppositions of speech, as we find in Rawls and Habermas. Such moves isolate normative concepts from their historical imbrication with other concepts, including images, plots, and symbols. Literature brings to the surface the speculative dimension of everyday speech and shows us that the configurations of meaning are not mere assertions but complex arguments that depend on more than abstract moral presuppositions. The imaginative configurations in which normative concepts appear are not merely secondary contingent or contextual variables; rather, they are an opening into a different conception of reasoning.

In sum, what is important about the current disciplinary debates is that they point to a failure in democratic political philosophy—and the social or cultural theory that often accompanies it—to theorize properly the relationship of citizens to historical institutions of meaning or public imagination. The phrase "hiding from history" in my title refers to the complex ways that our democratic institutions and intellectual disciplines avoid the historical character of practical reason and also avoid its dependence on public imagination. My solution is to develop a conception of public imagination that is philosophically and historically satisfying.

My concern here is not with the sociological and historical question about the "invention of traditions" or nations but with how political philosophy and cultural theory drive out public imagination as a resource for rationality as well as an object of critique.[26] This is not to say that explanatory concerns have no place. On the contrary, citizens and educators must inevitably take sides in debates about the causes of modern problems. My point is that we cannot divorce public practical reason from positions on history. For instance, even though local school boards in the United States have not taken an announced position on the intentional/functionalist debate surrounding the Holocaust—whether to explain the Holocaust through the intentions of the historical actors or the systems of modernization—programs of instruction in history and literature have clearly lined up in the intentionalist camp, leaving out any interrogation of the liberal economic and political systems. In this and other ways, citizens are inevitably drawn into issues of philosophy of history.[27]

In my view, public imagination, our inherited historical meanings, is thus a site of reasoning and not only an object of study.[28] The distinctiveness of my argument for placing reason inside as well as outside the changing shapes of cultural history can be seen if we note that my thesis provides a point of agreement among political thinkers who strongly disagree with each other. What Michel Foucault, Jürgen Habermas, Edward Said, and Samuel Huntington all agree about is that we cannot reason through the changing shapes of cultural history.[29] Foucault and Huntington analyze how the shaping force of historical cultural practices problematizes the question of rationality. Habermas and Said defend the moral ideals of political reason by placing them outside cultural history. My book will show that reasoning through cultural history, through public imagination, is inescapable, but that it cannot be done on the terms of what these thinkers take culture, history, and reason to be.

THE STRUCTURE OF THE BOOK

I begin by showing some of the ways that competing schools of philosophy and cultural theory hide from historical public imagination. In the first chapter, I look at liberal and deliberative theory, Western democracy's most fully developed theory of practical public reason. While democracy does and ought to alter the shape of citizens' self-understandings, what modern political theory does is to preshape the space of deliberation by blocking out public imagination as having a constitutive role in practical reasoning. While trying to accommodate conflict over the good, liberal theory misdescribes the nature of social conflict and deprives itself of the resources necessary to understand and work through political differences. History in liberalism becomes a necessary shared, unconflicted background, not the site of conflict, resources, and self-interrogation.

Rather than continuing with my critique of liberalism, I focus on Jürgen Habermas, whose thought engages the wide-ranging issues involved in the transition to modernity and not just the "morals of modernity." Although Habermas and liberals have now split on the question of whether a theory of democratic reason should be formal and comprehensive or part of a substantive, historical tradition, their means of hiding from history are often similar.[30] Habermas is forthright in his rejection of the historical philosophizing that characterized his early work on the public sphere, saying that he came to realize that "the normative foundations of a critical theory of society" had to be placed "at a deeper level" than historical interpretation in the universal presuppositions of dialogue (1992a, 442).[31] Habermas hides from history through two moves: first, he joins Kant in making the meanings of his norms immune from historical change and the shape of particular forms of life; second, he blocks out history by his theories of language and communicative action, theories that unify and put out of play the public imagination of political communities prior to political debate. Habermas, like Larmore and Rawls, presupposes a fantastic collective learning experience that accompanies the transition to democracy, a transition that reconciles conflicted meanings and puts the problems of history and public imagination behind it once and for all.

I drive home these points by examining his interventions in the politics of history, the well-known "Historians' Debate" during the 1980s and the arguments surrounding Daniel Goldhagen's *Hitler's Willing Executioners* at the end of the 1990s. These debates bring to the surface how the specialized arguments of the historian and the philosopher intersect with the practical judgment of the citizen.

In the second chapter, I look at a group of thinkers who openly explore the constitutive power of public imagination elided by Habermas and liberals—the structuralists/poststucturalists, who show how modern thought has misformulated its conceptions of the democratic subject and the scientific object. These thinkers formulate their critique by taking the inherited meanings of public imagination and showing that meanings cannot be partitioned into the reasons for the action of the moral subject and the causes of phenomena for the scientific investigator. By presupposing its ability to isolate an object of research and a subject of action, modern thought has constricted our social and political shapes in ways that it does not acknowledge. These shapes become visible when the researcher steps back from both the moral and the scientific projects and displays the mechanisms that constitute them.

If Habermas and liberals obscure the social imaginary, structuralists/poststructuralists elide the subject of judgment. I begin with structuralism and the best known structuralist historian, Hayden White. In mapping the operations of the historical imagination, White makes historical writing, and narrative in particular, an ideological lure that should be the object, and not the resource, of critical judgment. Divorced from historical imagination, the citizen's reasoning becomes arbitrary personal preference.[32] I then look at Paul Ricoeur's conception of language and imagination, which has been so influential as the great mediator of philosophical disputes. Although Ricoeur is usually classified as a hermeneutic phenomenologist, the heart of his conception of imagination depends on structuralism and Husserlian formalism, both of which give a reductive portrait of the subject's relationship to institutions of meaning. I reveal these weaknesses through an examination of his analysis of language and literature.

The poststructuralist thinkers I discuss fall into two categories: those who follow in the wake of Derrida—my examples are the philosopher Judith Butler and the historian Joan Scott—and those who follow in the wake of Foucault. What distinguishes Derrideans is that they, like Habermas, rely on a transcendental argument for their conception of language and history.[33] While Habermas maintains that language oriented toward understanding is the originary dimension of language on which all other uses depend, Butler and Scott argue that the public imagination through which we understand ourselves results from a demiurgic originary force so overwhelming that we can think of ourselves only as the historical effects of unimaginable traumas inscribed within regimes of power. Trauma is not a historical event but transhistorical or structural.

Foucauldians, by contrast, reject transcendental arguments, whether by Habermas, Derrida, or hermeneutic thinkers. For Foucault, such arguments homogenize the diversity and discontinuity of historical change.

When he asks questions about the conditions of possibility, he is referring not to transhistorical conditions but to specific discursive rules and practices that make institutions possible at a particular time.[34] Indeed, Foucault puts the historical and the transcendental at odds with each other.[35] He probes the discursive transitions in history either by interrogating the shifts in the constituting discursive rules of society's institutions or by genealogical rewriting of existing narratives. Foucault takes critical aim at the historical interpretations, particularly about the Western transition to modernity, that underwrite contemporary self-understandings. These often productive challenges nonetheless leave out the site of reasoning that orchestrates historical revision. My point is not the familiar Habermasian charge that Foucauldians do not acknowledge the norms that inform their critique. Rather, my point is that one cannot throw into darkness all the self-understandings of the past, all the discursive space of reasoning, and then claim to stand above it, for in doing so one has ignored the institutions of meaning, the space of reasons, that underwrite this way of arguing. This is not to say that the third-person perspective of discourse dear to Foucauldians is not crucial for articulating public imagination; rather, I merely insist that such approaches depend on a philosophy of reasoning or judgment for their employment rather than on a knockdown third-person epistemological or ontological claim about the illusion of the dialogical subject.

Thus, there is no theoretical answer to the question of whether we should discuss the events of September 11, 2001, through the angle of shifts in discursive formations, from the point of view of the systems of global capitalism, or from the perspective of actions and events. There is no theoretical answer to how we should periodize history or whether we should use a microscope or a telescope to sift through the archives. There is only a practical, historicized one in which it behooves us to justify our decisions about the employment of interpretive, explanatory, and genealogical apparatus. Such a conception of judgment is excluded by the third-person perspective.[36]

The philosophical burden of the first two chapters is that the figures in question misdescribe the relationship of citizens to public imagination and ignore the inescapable role of historical argument in practical deliberation. My point of entry for responding to these challenges will be the work of Charles Taylor, whose problematic is directed explicitly at the relationship between the transcendental and the historical in practical reason. Taylor has been largely misunderstood, both in political theory and in literary/cultural study, for he is most often seen as a "communitarian"; he is not arguing for community, however, but articulating the inescapable commitments of historical, linguistic beings, commitments that are blocked out by disengaged understandings of reason that dominate Western modernity.

In *Sources of the Self,* Taylor gives us an ontological portrait of public imagination that makes possible his historical readings of modernity's achievements and losses. I use the word "ontological" to emphasize his break with all forms of modern reasoning that try to evaporate the reality of meanings in the world.[37] The transcendental and the historical are linked through the idea of transitional arguments, in which the historical shifts of different strains of modern culture are assessed not just in terms of their worth but also in terms of their philosophical priority and the historical conditions of their emergence. Transitional arguments appear in the everyday deliberations of individual or collective actors who are trying to account for change—for instance, individuals or nations in midlife crises. In philosophy, we find transitional arguments as the common thread shared by hermeneutic thinkers, such as Taylor, and genealogical thinkers, such as Nietzsche and Foucault, but which liberalism treats reductively as simple adoption of the moral minimum that respects disagreement. Hermeneutic and genealogical thinkers interrogate and assess the changes in the shapes of inherited meanings so that the losses and gains of historical changes can appear. Moral and political reasoning is intimately bound with historical thinking, for it is only through comparative examination of past and present that the ideals and shapes of the present are justified. This understanding of transitional arguments enables us to think of narrative and genealogy not as mutually exclusive alternatives, but as complementary modes of historical argument. We narrativize aspects of the past that we wish to retrieve and give genealogical accounts of those aspects that we wish to repudiate.

Such reasoning does not ignore or repudiate the empirical and causal work of historians, but instead provides an interpretive framework that permits historical research to engage the normative and evaluative concerns of the present.[38] Taylor is only a point of departure, however, for his work must answer to legitimate criticism that he abstracts from the historical horrors of modernity, from the explanatory analyses of historians, and from the genealogical analyses of cultural/literary theorists.[39] What emerges in this chapter is an account of the institutions of meaning that reveals the inescapable political ambiguity of public imagination. Public imagination is neither a refuge nor a horror; we cannot isolate it as an object or reduce it to a subject. It is inside and outside us, the very condition of our reasoning. This political ambiguity is nicely captured by works of literature, works that incarnate and articulate the damage and achievements of political communities.

Chapter 4 takes the conclusions of the previous chapters and brings them to bear on the argument between Hannah Arendt and Ralph Ellison over the desegregation of schools in Little Rock, Arkansas. The political differences between Arendt and Ellison turn on their different understandings of language (public imagination) in political judgment. Here I show the weaknesses in Arendt's understanding of language, storytelling, and judgment, which she develops through Kant's *Critique of Judgment*. I then contrast her view with Ellison's ontological conception of public imagination as the politically ambiguous but inescapable medium through which political debate is conducted. Ellison's novel *Invisible Man*, like *Sources of the Self*, offers a structural parallel to Hegel's *Phenomenology of Spirit*. Ellison begins by problematizing the packages of beliefs that readers bring to the text and offers a transcendental argument for a new way of reading the threads of historical meaning. He then shows the historical changes that made this transcendental argument possible. Ellison's *Invisible Man* brings to the surface and dramatizes the relationship of citizens to public imagination in a way that establishes the links among a philosophy of practical reason, literature, and everyday life that I could only sketch in chapter 3. My discussion of Arendt and Ellison as storytellers, philosophers, and cultural critics reveals the ways that public imagination informs debates across the humanities and social sciences.

In chapter 5, I continue the development of the relationship of public imagination and practical reason from a global perspective. I begin with the debate surrounding the work of Edward Said, whose research has drawn the attention of various disciplines. While Said clearly shows how the cultures of the West and the Middle East have been morally compromised by the imperial project, he does so only by making an epistemological and moral abstraction. Said combines a constructivist political interest in the disciplinary power of culture with a Kantian cosmopolitan ethics. The result is that the cultural texts under analysis are isolated as facts for moral judgment, detached from their social and political histories and the explanations of social science. Moreover, the values he esteems drop from a noumenal realm rather than emerging from historical institutions of meaning. He thus combines two modes of hiding from history that we have outlined. Hence, when he confronts Samuel Huntington's claim that global politics will be driven by civilizational identities that cannot be negotiated, Said can only offer a familiar, empirical critique—for example, civilizations are more heterogeneous than Huntington says.

The real challenge of Huntington's claim is to show how we can reason through culture. I develop my response to this challenge in two steps. First, I look at Amartya Sen's critique of Huntington, for Sen opens up the cross-cultural political histories of cultures to show how important political concepts, such as freedom and tolerance, are not the unique possession of recent Western democracies. In the second part, I examine how Sen nonetheless pulls back from putting public imagination at the heart of his idea of reason. The limits of Sen's conception are made clear by looking at how he retreats from the claims of public imagination in his debate with Ashis Nandy over secularism and modernity.

Thus by introducing the conception of public imagination, I show that political ideals and principles do not have to hide from history in order for political philosophy to maintain a grip on rationality. Once a polity's complex historical meanings are given this new place, then defending a claim cannot be limited to abstract moral norms. When political dialogue engages the full social imaginaries of citizens, then practical reasoning will require a new interpretive agility that can address hermeneutic, genealogical, and causal claims. Such an expanded conception of the rationality of political dialogue does not stand or fall on the separation of principles from history as philosophers of practical reason and their critics, such as Stanley Fish, maintain.[40] Only if one stands with the languages one cares about and makes them vulnerable to the complex political and historical claims of others in a space of mutual recognition can the losses, traumas, and challenges of global dialogue emerge and be witnessed.

We have an intuitive knowledge of the intricate
relations among past, present, and future where
the individual is concerned; but it is far from obvious
how to apply that knowledge to a collective actor
like a nation.—Jürgen Habermas[1]

Eliding Public Imagination

HABERMAS'S ISOLATION OF
PRINCIPLES FROM HISTORY

If there has been one political philosopher of the last generation who has engaged the historical questions of his time, it is surely
Habermas.[2] From the student movements of the 1960s to contemporary
debates on globalization, he has always intervened in important ways.
Despite his attention to changes in historical circumstance, however, he
never incorporates historical public imagination into his political philosophy. This contrast is well illustrated nicely in his contribution to the disputes over German history, for they show how important the past is to his
politics at the same time that they dramatize the limits of his approach.

Both Habermas and liberals stand in the social contract tradition of
political philosophy, which abstracts from the historical particulars of a
community's public imagination in order to base the principle of political
organization and deliberation on formal concerns: universal rights and the
rules and procedures for political dialogue. Typically, this strain of Enlightenment universalist argument is placed against Romantic nationalism
based on a substantive shared history of a people, and Habermas relies on
this opposition in his intervention in the *Historikerstreit*.[3] What is obscured
by this opposition is that the universalist strain of modernity is not just
opposed to Romantic nationalism but always finds itself in tension with
modernity's new forms—collective temporal and cultural forms of imagination, as noted by Anderson, Taylor, and others. Habermas not only
resists incorporating these forms into his model of reasoning, he also
gives no philosophical place in his model of practical reason to historical
forms of life and their modes of subjectivation as they move through time.
Since he assumes that we cannot reason through the historical social

imaginary, he relies on grand theories of modernity coming from Kant and Weber that reduce historical forms of self-constitution to abstract conceptions of rationalization.[4]

My claim is that Habermas misdescribes the subject's relationship to inherited historical meanings or what I am calling "public imagination," the medium of public reasoning. While I share Habermas's interest in putting language and intersubjectivity in place of a philosophy of consciousness, I disagree with how he characterizes this medium. To give a proper characterization will require a transcendental argument about language and the social imaginary so that the citizen can move between first- and third-person perspectives.[5] While I will not spell out such an argument until chapter 3, the dynamics of my approach to meaning and subjectivity and its differences from Habermas will become clear during the course of the chapter.

Here I trace Habermas's elision of public imagination in four steps. First, I quickly examine the ways that he isolates history from the tasks of reason. Second, I show how his philosophy of language and of the lifeworld blocks out historical shapes of meaning and modes of reasoning as well as the historicity of practical reason itself. My point is not to collapse Habermas's moral universalism into his ethical-hermeneutical domain (where the question of historical interpretation is addressed) but to criticize from the ground up the way he understands the task of philosophy, history, and literature in public reasoning. For Habermas, it is not the familiar scientific positivism that drives out public imagination; instead, it is a particular kind of holistic understanding of society and language that frames and renders insignificant the multiple argumentative spaces that citizens inhabit and the dynamics of public reason. To open up this space, I explore philosophy's role in speculative and historical issues, which Habermas occludes. Third, I bring my critique of language and public imagination to Habermas's idea of "constitutional patriotism," the notion by which he tries to show how dialogical universalism accommodates particular histories. In the last section, I look at Habermas's interventions in two important historiographical disputes—the famous *Historikerstreit* in the 1980s and, more recently, the controversy surrounding Daniel Goldhagen's *Hitler's Willing Excecutioners.*

DIVIDING THE TASKS OF REASON

Habermas's political philosophy emerges from his reading of the transition to modernity as a transition from a philosophy of metaphysical substance to a philosophy of procedures: "Both modern empirical science and autonomous morality place their confidence in the rationality of their own approaches and procedures—namely, in the method of scientific knowledge or in the abstract point of view under which moral insights are possible" so that "the rationality of content evaporates into the validity of results" (1992b, 35). Habermas accepts Kant's and Weber's vision of the division of labor for the social sciences, philosophy, and aesthetics. In the disenchanted world, knowledge becomes the province of the social and natural sciences. Philosophy is concerned primarily with two projects: moral universalism and the reconstruction of the rules of pretheoretical competence of speaking and acting subjects.[6] Aesthetics addresses the expressive concerns of individuals. The fourth domain of reason is what Habermas calls the ethical/hermeneutic domain, which is where we find his truncated conception of the hermeneutic practical reason of everyday life with its concern for the good and the relationship of past and present. The reason that "politics may be not be assimilated to a hermeneutic process of self-explication of a shared form of life or collective identity" is that democratic values must be immunized from the historical and interpretive processes in which other meanings operate (1996c, 23–24). Habermas's divisions are not mere descriptions of the modern world. Rather, he ties these divisions to his philosophy of language, in which the boundaries of the various validity claims are established and public imagination is driven out.[7]

This division of labor explains why Habermas has moved increasingly away from the historical analysis characteristic of his work on the public sphere (1989b). When the public sphere appears in his work, it is usually in the context of law rather than that of the history of other institutions of meaning that shape public imagination.[8] What pushed him away from history was the recognition that his early work was "propped up, at least, implicitly by background assumptions belonging to a philosophy of history that has been refuted by the civilized barbarisms of the twentieth century" (1992a, 442). However, rather than trying to change his understanding of history so as to bear witness to these "civilized barbarisms," he elects to abandon history altogether so as to place "the normative foundations of a critical theory of society [. . .] at a deeper level" than any particular epoch (442). In his view, no forms of historiographical writing can provide modes of political critique.[9]

This move against history can be found most openly in his essay "History and Evolution" and in *The Theory of Communicative Action*. In these works, he explicitly sets up his critical theory against Marxist philosophy of history. In attempting "to free historical materialism from its philosophical ballast" (1983, II, 383), Habermas abstracts moral development from historical events and cultural specificity.[10] Thus, "social evolution reaches right through history, it makes history an epiphenomenon" (1979a, 23). In these and subsequent works of the period, he joins social science and philosophy of language. The cognitive theory of moral evolution is linked to the psychological theories of Jean Piaget and Lawrence Kohlberg, while his philosophy of language invokes timeless Kantian presuppositions for every speech act in history.[11]

But how does the historical life of political communities figure in this theory? History counts only insofar as it charts the emergence of the awareness of his pragmatic formalism. In *The Philosophical Discourse of Modernity*, he maps the ways his predecessors anticipated but failed to arrive at his problematic. He begins with Hegel's famous "wrong turn" to a supersubject (1987, 27–30, 37–40) and then examines previous problematics for language and subjectivity and how these problematics failed to see how democratic ideals were the necessary presuppositions of interactive rationality—Marx (62–65), Heidegger (136–137), Derrida and Husserl (168–172). The only history we find here is reference to the familiar Hegelian reading of the rise of the modern subject: "The key historical events in establishing the principle of subjectivity are the Reformation, the Enlightenment, and the French Revolution" (17). In his more recent work, this philosophical history is given a sociological complement so that constructed nationalist consciousness becomes the necessary political precondition to the realization of a constitutional state.[12]

However, the history that underwrites this achievement stands apart from any particular forms of life and traditions. The "dependence" of the universal on a form of life here is about implementation more than it is about knowing the universal, for Habermas has to keep universality separate from any particular tradition so that those in damaged traditions still have access to the universal: "Everyone, even those not among Jefferson's fortunate heirs, should be able to recapitulate this impartial judgment. The presuppositions under which these parties make their agreements elucidate a moral point of view that goes deeper, in fact is ultimately anchored in the symmetries of the mutual recognition of communicatively acting subjects in general" (1996a, 62). Hence, there are many routes to the recognition of these idealizations, and we need to be concerned with giving an account not of the diverse linguistic self-understandings of the historical actors but only of the formal properties of the normative problematic. Habermas's treatment of the historical imagination is like Kant's in "The Idea for a Universal History with a Cosmopolitan Intent." What is important for a political community is that it get knocked around in enough ways so as to activate and make accessible the Kantian formal architecture.[13] The historical transitions of a political community's movement to this understanding do not figure in public debate. Political reasoning does not have to give an account of how its key ideals and institutions have been bound up with meanings and institutions that it now wants to move beyond. Ideals do not need to be reworked as part of a historical argument about political actions, past and present, but deduced as rational necessities. Public reason relegates history to the status of an object and does not address the historicity of language.

The ideals of democracy must not simply trump other moral goods in public conversations; they must also stand outside the historical institutions of meaning in order to have a permanent critical force. Habermas states this split explicitly: "Participants in processes of self-clarification cannot distance themselves from the life-histories and forms of life in which they actually find themselves. Moral-practical discourse, by contrast, requires a break with all of the unquestioned truths of an established concrete ethical life" (1993, 12). "Distance," of course, means invoking an idealizing counterfactual norm, as if the only way to make a legitimate critique is to invoke a thought experiment that claims to transcend the language of one's epoch.

Since I examine his philosophy of language in detail momentarily, first I want to look briefly at his treatment of religion in his theory of modernity, for it is here that his occlusion of public languages of historical communities is perhaps most egregious. "The disenchantment and disempowerment of the domain of the sacred takes place by way of a linguistification of the ritually secured, basic normative agreement [. . .]. The aura of rapture and terror that emanates from the sacred, the spellbinding power of the holy, is sublimated into the bind/bonding force of criticizable validity claims and at the same time turned into an everyday occurrence" (1983, II, 77). There are two related features here that are important for my purposes. First, the languages and meanings of this religious inheritance disappear as an object of social and political inquiry once the normative transformation to dialogical reason takes place. The only important aspect of the transition to modernity is that the sacred is transformed into modern norms. The ways that religion continues to inform the languages of public imagination are not important. Second, this reading of secularization blocks out an interrogation of whether this "sublimation" account is the best way to show how we want norms to guide public reason.[14] My point on both of these issues is not to criticize the norms per se but to criticize a way of reasoning that hides rather than airs transitions in public historical meanings so that they can be subjected to continuous re-examination. These buried transitions are the background of differences that continue to shape the contested subject positions in contemporary debate. The need for such an opening of historical meanings becomes even more acute when the conversation is between communities with different religious inheritances, where the opportunities for conflict and mutual enrichment are greater.

Thus, Habermas's version of Critical Theory rejects Marxist attempts to ground politics on the truth of history or human nature. Having abandoned the psychoanalytic model of critique in his early work, he now joins liberals in not seeking an epistemological unmasking of everyday practices, preferring the more limited emancipatory ideal of Kantian autonomy—that is, formal self-determination through rules. However, there is an important difference between grounding a politics in history in the Hegelian or Marxist sense, and having an interpretive historical account of how a society's history informs practical reason. Habermas does not make this distinction, and he shows little interest in recent historiography and the concrete histories informed by these considerations. Instead, he points toward three unacceptable views: Marxism, hermeneutics, and poststructuralism. Hermeneutics, for Habermas, ignores the discontinuities of history and the political failures of traditions: "Philosophers of history and hermeneuticians" share a premise in their reading of history, "namely, that we learn from history only if it tells us something positive, something worth imitating. [. . .] [However,] we learn historically chiefly from the way historical events challenge us, showing us that traditions fail" (1997a, 44). In the 1970s in his well-known debate with Gadamer, Habermas argued that the hermeneutic view of language and history gives "ontological priority of tradition over all possible critique" and ignores how language is a medium not just of mutual understanding but "of domination and social power" so that "it serves to legitimate relations of organized force."[15] While he was certainly right to point out Gadamer's neglect of power and symbolic violence, Habermas never develops a philosophy of language that is sensitive to the historicity and diversity of language.[16]

Poststructuralists, according to Habermas's reading, explode all standards for judging history, giving only genealogies of power (Foucault) or world-disclosing philosophies (Derrida) that have no political norms or continuity. Habermas's response to these views of history is not to come up with a subtler account of history that could include both continuities and discontinuities and alternative styles of writing that include narratives, causes, events, and genealogies. Instead, he separates his normative ideals from any historical account of changes in the social imaginary.

This is not to say that he has not moved away from an emphasis on determinant judgment toward a more contextual, reflective judgment.[17] However, the addition of reflective judgment only moves judgment away from formalist rules without addressing the issues thematized by my ontological conception of public imagination.[18] In order to clarify my position as well as Habermas's, we need to look at his philosophy of language.

LANGUAGE AND PUBLIC REASON: STARTING POINTS

My differences from Habermas over language, history, and public reasoning emerge from our very different transcendental arguments about where to begin. As is well known, Habermas moves to a "deeper level" than history by making a transcendental argument that "the use of language with an orientation to reaching understanding is the original mode of language use, upon which indirect understanding, giving something to understand or letting something be understood, and instrumental use of language in general, are parasitic" (1983, I, 288). The priority of the communicative use of language is the key to Habermas's philosophical project because it enables him to claim that communicative discourse is fundamental and liberating. He can thus avoid the normative or utopian claim that it should be given priority. Language as such brings speakers into a moral space of autonomy and responsibility.[19] Communicative reason does not "tell actors what they ought to do" (1996a, 4) but what presuppositions must inform their dialogues. Habermas appeals to the universal presuppositions of communication that one cannot help but invoke, and his conception of presupposition is not historical—that is, how speakers at different historical moments might understand their presuppositions—but Kantian: "The theory of communicative action detranscendentalizes the noumenal realm only to have the idealizing force of context-transcending anticipations settle in the unavoidable pragmatic presuppositions of speech acts, and hence in the heart of everyday communicative practice" (1996a, 19).[20]

Because these presuppositions are inevitable, they are ideals not imposed from the outside but discovered "already operating in everyday communicative practice. True, claims to propositional truth, normative rightness and subjective truthfulness intersect here within a concrete linguistically disclosed horizon; yet as criticizable claims that also transcend the various contexts in which they are formulated and gain acceptance" (1992b, 50). These ideals are then turned into dialogical procedures, which serve as tests for the outcome of the rational and legitimate exchange.[21] The idealizing presuppositions of formal pragmatics try to put a ring around the content of a cultural or political community so that the basic terms of dialogical validity—speaker, truth, claim—can be defined independently of the practices of a political community. What are the steps by which Habermas arrives at his conclusions?

Although I can hardly reconstruct Habermas's elaborate arguments with philosophers of language—as other commentators have done[22]—the issue in question boils down to the coordination of his concept of background with his theory of discursive argument. Habermas maintains that there are two different kinds of linguistic idealization relevant to public reasoning, one at the level of semantics (theory of meaning) and the other at the level of pragmatics (theory of use). The theory of meaning that subtends this theory of action combines the semantic approach with the pragmatics of speech-act theory. Habermas draws on semantic approaches to meaning in order to prevent validity claims from being circumscribed within the conventional validity of particular forms of life. "The ideal character of semantic generality shapes communicative action inasmuch as the participants could not even intend to reach an understanding with one another about something in the world if they did not presuppose, on the basis of a common (or translatable) language, that they conferred identical meanings on the expressions they employed. Only if this condition is satisfied can misunderstandings prove to be such" (1996a, 19). The apparently innocuous idealizing presupposition about identical meaning comes from a very particular school of philosophy of language that focuses on the semantics of the proposition, on the validity claim of the isolated assertoric sentence about the natural world.[23] He argues for the superiority of this conception against a philosophy of consciousness, but the relevant argument is with an alternative philosophy of language that does not isolate propositions and utterances from the ideological, interpretive contexts and their backgrounds, or from the dialogical dynamics of a living, historical language.[24]

The requirement of some common conceptual meaning cannot sever sentences from their background preunderstandings, from their connection to public imagination. When Habermas says that "we understand an utterance when we know what makes it acceptable" (1992b, 77), he ignores, as Christina Lafont points out, that "the conditions of acceptability are dependent on background knowledge, on particular and contingent linguistic world-disclosure that is constitutive of the processes of understanding. Given this, the universality claim of the theory of communicative action definitely appears to be indefensible" (213–214).[25]

The next level of idealization is in the pragmatics of use, for the propositional content of the sentence does not tell us whether an utterance is true: "The affirmation of a thought or the assertoric sense of a statement brings into play a further moment of ideality, one connected with the validity of the judgment or sentence" (1996a, 12). We have now moved from formal semantics to the intersubjective relations of speakers. The idealization condition here is that the speaker who raises a validity claim implicitly agrees "to vindicate the claim with the right reason" (18), not just to a particular interpretive community but to "the ideally expanded audience of the unlimited interpretation community" (19). While I would agree that "participants must consider themselves mutually accountable" (20), I would expand what giving an account means so as to include the kind of historical vindication of the languages of debate.

In order to clarify what such a historical vindication means, we need to examine the most important idea in Habermas's elision of public imagination, his understanding of the background and action coordination. In the theory of communicative action, speech acts as well as other social actions move within a background understanding of the lifeworld: "Insofar as speakers and hearers straightforwardly achieve a mutual understanding about something in the world, they move within the horizon of their common lifeworld; this remains in the background of the participants—as intuitively known, unproblematic, unanalyzable holistic background" (1987, 298).[26] The idea of "background" plunges speakers in a deep consensus of usage, for it "serves as a source of situation definition" (1983, I, 70) at the same time that it is beyond the articulatory reach of speakers. Even the critical theorist can go only so far as to reconstruct the rules of competence that unify a political community—that is, to disclose "the pretheoretical grasp of rules on the part of competently speaking, acting, knowing subjects" (1987, 298).[27]

Because background is at once shared and unanalyzable, we cannot engage the historical languages and practices. Habermas's lifeworld can thus simply internalize modernity's achievements without historical consciousness. On the one hand, "The lifeworld constitutes an equivalent for what philosophy of the subject had ascribed to consciousness in general as synthetic accomplishments [. . .]. [C]oncrete forms of life replace transcendental consciousness in its function of creating unity" (1987, 326). But what counts are not the shapes and self-understandings of these institutions but that the "particular forms of life [. . .] exhibit structures common to lifeworlds in general" (326). To be sure, Habermas is careful not to divorce these normative presuppositions completely from the everyday lifeworlds of particular cultures so that the ideals become external impositions. "As soon as the normative substance goes up in smoke—as soon as people feel they no longer have a chance of getting justice from the courts [. . .] the law has to be transformed into an instrument of behavior control" (1997a, 132–133). Indeed, he acknowledges that democratic institutions and ideals are historical products, that "moral universalism is a historical result," that "any universalistic morality is dependent upon a form of life that meets it halfway" (1990b, 208, 209). Habermas tries to steer between "pure transcendentalism," on the one hand, and "pure historicism" on the other (1986b, 193), by having transcendental counterfactuals check out historical particulars. However, the history and historicity of public culture never inform the subject of moral reasoning; rather, they are only an object judgment.

By pushing background outside of the space of reasons, Habermas can ignore the internal historical reasoning of the institutions of meaning of different societies as they make or do not make their transitions to modernity—for example, the debates over the gains and losses, the appeals to retrieval or transformation, the competing theories of modernity. In his view, such concern is unnecessary since all we need to know is the formal destiny of political communities. Moreover, the quasi-noumenal status of the norms exempts them from the process of working through the damage to the languages of democracy in the course of modernity—that is, the way democratic language has been imbricated with imperialism, sexism, and so forth.[28] (This is particularly troublesome since Habermas leans not just on democratic ideals but also on "the West," particularly the United States, as an example of where these ideals have reached unproblematic fulfillment.) Instead, meeting "halfway" simply means the mere presence of democratic features in historical institutions so that Kantian presuppositions are not completely detached from the lifeworld. Since practical reason does not need cultural or historical resources, there is no need to explore the phenomenology of lifeworld(s). The presence of some features of modernity, however inchoately formulated, assures that the project is not imposed from the outside and justifies the invocation of the grid of discursive rationality. In his largely acultural account of modernity, we find that the only criteria for assessing lifeworlds is the distinction between instrumental and communicative rationality.[29]

Thus, Habermas's world is not something that a political community can lose, gain, enrich, or impoverish, as we find in Hannah Arendt's analysis;[30] rather, it is an abstract theoretical posit that accompanies speaking as such. The lifeworld forms an empty, synchronic frame of common space that serves the crucial purpose of rendering language and reference unproblematic. The theoretical supposition of an unproblematic lifeworld joins the moral supposition of taking the perspective of others since both assume a communicative transparency: "The idealizing supposition of a universalistic form of life, in which everyone can take up the perspective of everyone else and can count on reciprocal recognition by everybody, makes it possible for individuated beings to exist with a community—individualism as the flipside of universalism" (1992b, 186).

Through these three theoretical steps—semantics, pragmatics, background—Habermas develops his own version of the widely accepted view that shared meaning is necessary for the coordination of behavior, and leverages it into the view that there is a common ground on which all differences in the social imagination rest. The fact that shared meaning is required for conversation to get off the ground does not mean that we need to construe "shared" in the way that Habermas does. A transcendental argument for common assumptions can be made that does not trivialize the social imaginaries of citizens.

Habermas moves from "success in action coordination" to the assumption that actors have fully shared social imaginaries. However, the fact that sexists and feminists can both buy coffee at a café, negotiate a loan from a bank officer, or engage a defense lawyer is not grounds for saying that they share significant evaluative and political vocabularies. The fact that Pat Robertson and I can both coordinate our action and accept common meanings well enough to meet at a lecture does not provide a ground for our political debate. The political is precisely the space where the differences we ignore in everyday life come into play. The political imagination of citizens does not limit itself to the self-understandings of the institutions that coordinate actions. My point is not simply that we have different comprehensive philosophical views but that these views constitute public space and that they cannot be disentangled from public history. Habermas assumes that the different understandings of practices and meanings in a political community do not depend on deciding between the competing historical narratives and genealogies that constitute the identities of speakers and institutions. Backgrounds do not simply sustain the reproduction of the lifeworld in an unproblematic way; backgrounds are contradictory and complex, and they are not equally available to political subjects. The background of the lifeworld, like the notion of competence, is a politically and philosophically contested concept.[31]

Although the background can never be completely thematized, we can reason through it, nonetheless. Background is not the merely the medium that serves "as intuitively known, unproblematic, [and] unanalyzable"; rather, it is space to interrogate, in which we seek, in Taylor's words, "to transfer what has sunk to the level of an organizing principle for present practices and hence beyond examination into a view for which there can be reasons either for or against" (1984b, 28).[32]

In order to see how background social imaginary can be articulated and argued through, we need to look at the beginnings of some well-known texts that challenge their readers' assumptions about their shared linguistic world and historical narratives. These authors cannot make their validity claims in an isolated sentence; instead, they need to unpack the historical assumptions, practices, and meanings that underwrite dialogue in order to change the framework of questioning. A new semantic space must be created out of the conflicted historical resources of the background so that the individual utterance may be properly understood. The opening of Alasdair MacIntyre's *After Virtue* asks us to imagine a world after the destruction of most of the documents of moral history, only to flip the thought experiment around so that we are asked to understand our current lifeworld on these terms; the beginning of Proust's *A la recherche du temps perdu* deprives the reader of his or her presuppositions of the realist novel in order to ask for wholesale revisions in the reader's philosophy and languages of self-understanding; Proust is offering not a "perspective on reality," but an argument from the ground up about how we are in the world. Ralph Ellison's *Invisible Man* problematizes the racial vocabularies and discursive strategies that infect America's institutions of meaning, from literature and media to the public school. Foucault's historical analyses force readers to think of time and meaning in the blocks of the episteme in *The Archaeology of Knowledge* and then in fragments in his genealogies.[33] *Gulliver's Travels* argues in a comprehensive but indirect, satiric way with the emergent modes of modern reason—with the science of the Royal Society, with state-of-nature political reasoning, with the conception of modern citizen as cosmopolitan traveler, and so on. Taylor's *Sources of the Self* begins with a transcendental redescription that challenges contemporary self-understandings and opens the space for his historical reading of the different strains of modernity.

My point in these different examples from philosophy, literature, and history is not to endorse any particular one, but to make clear the inescapability of the speculative and historical dimension of everyday speech and its potential for public reason. These texts are asking for revision at the level of the concept and the level of conception, without proposing that the concepts and conceptions they are discrediting are unintelligible.[34] On the contrary, their arguments are premised on deep familiarity. They are seeking to discredit certain packages of beliefs and to provide a transitional argument to a superior package of beliefs or languages. The texts thus answer Habermas's demand that "world-disclosive languages" prove their worth against "everyday communicative practice."[35] These critiques are made not by recourse to the formalism of a performative contradiction but by rich recontextualizations of the shapes of public imagination.

What I mean by "context" is not what Habermas means when he opposes discrete empirical particulars to universals. In my understanding, "context" refers to semantic packages of beliefs and meanings as well as to practices in public imagination. These packages are not universal, but they are historically generalizable. In some ways, my idea here is close to Richard Rorty's idea in "Inquiry as Recontextualization." Rorty makes a transcendental argument against Habermas's assumption that there is a "way to divide things [or norms] up into those which are what they are independent of context and those which are context-dependent" (1991b, 98). What follows from this argument is that political, moral, social, and aesthetic arguments cannot be isolated into semantic propositions or singular utterances. Therefore, "the unit of persuasion is vocabulary, not the proposition," for only a wide-ranging argument about presuppositions can flush the imaginative context of argument (1989, 78). Hence, great works of philosophy, history, and literature make their cases, as I said in the introduction, by "recontextualiz[ing] much of what you previously thought you knew" (1998a, 133), not by local, empirical claims.[36] The institutions of the social imaginary are to be explored not only by the theoretical constructions of the rules of discourse or by sociological explanations of historical processes, but also by the speculative dimension of language that is in the potential of all speech.

Habermas uses the term "world-disclosing" to characterize such supposedly nonstandard ways of speaking or writing, and the above examples show why he throws the term loosely at hermeneutic philosophers and literary writers, not just at Derrida. The unifying feature of all these groups is that they thematize the speculative dimension of language in which claims about entire packages of belief are made. Habermas tries to separate such speculation from argument, but, as my examples above show, this claim will not hold. Arguments against prevailing assumptions of meaning and usage are thus not just the province of poststructuralists but a well-known common argument strategy in everyday life, literature, and philosophy.

Habermas's sequestering of the "poetic world-disclosing function" of language (1987, 204) has the same goal as his elimination of history—that is, the desire to create a world of meaning that will keep the issues of content and identity off the table and permit his formal operations to work. Habermas's version of holism keeps innovative speech and the conflicted character of contemporary debate from appearing. From the point of view of my argument, the tactic of making art about "the extraordinary" is a way of covering up what the institutions of art are after: the thematization of the speculative character of everyday speech, the way in which every utterance is not just the instantiation of rules but, potentially, an engagement with the full social imagination on which it depends.[37] Critique is not limited to third-person theoretical reconstruction or formal checks; rather, it is also available in first-order conversation. The issue is not "misunderstanding," as Habermas says, but different conceptions of subjectivity and meaning that compete in the public imagination and that logically precede any discussion of external referents or moral norms.[38]

Hence, Habermas's very narrow reading of the speculative presuppositions that subtend everyday speech as counterfactual idealizations does not, as he claims, provide much of "a critical standard against which actual practices [...] could be evaluated" (1996a, 5). Inside the West, few interlocutors would refuse to acknowledge Habermas's abstract democratic normative ideals, so it is hard to see how much critique the performative contradiction offers. These interlocutors on the Left and the Right would acknowledge these norms in different ways by their own lights, so we would have to leave the plane of abstract ideals in order to get any argumentative traction. For interlocutors who are not signed on to Western modernity and who might object to the ideals even in abstract form, engaging in comparative historical thinking rather than arguments over normative presuppositions is even more important, as we'll see in chapter 5.[39] In order for public reasoning to get the resources it needs for rich political dialogue, it has to be able to interrogate and argue about the complex and conflicted social imaginaries in which these norms appear. We can engage the social imaginary with a variety of argumentative styles—from the discourses of the social sciences to the kinds of transcendental arguments, parodies, and other kinds of first-order speech, mentioned in the texts above.[40] By focusing his arguments on a thin universality, Habermas blocks out public reason's tasks of reworking the past and articulating new practices so that democratic politics is desirable rather than already presupposed. If we accept Habermas's second pragmatic idealization—that is, that speakers defend their claims to truth, rightness, and the like—we can say that such a defense involves a historical and philosophical defense of the very languages one uses to articulate the issues in question. We do not always engage in such wholesale critiques of our interlocutors' assumptions, but any defense of our isolated proposition depends on such larger account. Enriching the mode of justification in this way means that public reason depends on historical readings.

Public imagination is a constitutive historical force that cannot be held at arm's length by noumenal ideals or procedures, nor can different interpretations of the relationship of past and present be marginalized as ethical questions of the good. In Habermas's philosophy, a political community's historical inheritance of meanings becomes simply the temporally frozen, abstract condition of the possibility of speaking at all. But democratic subjects are not standing in a synchronic lifeworld together. Our inheritance does not simply stand in the background; it asks us questions, nourishes, and oppresses, and not in the same way for all members of a political community.

By ignoring competing forms of public imagination both historically and synchronically, Habermas's conception of shared meaning truncates the picture of what is on the table in public debate. He can give no place to the transformation and loss involved in daily life and political deliberation—as the initial quotation in this chapter says all too clearly—because he offers a subject of deliberation so separated from everyday life that loss makes no political sense.[41] Habermas's theory of meaning and his regulative ideal of a horizon of consensus misconstrues the dialogical processes of practical reason and the labor of what it means "to change one's mind" about an issue. The point of texts such as Taylor's, Ellison's, or MacIntyre's is that speakers in everyday life situate themselves in the history of public, social imagination implicitly or explicitly by their assumptions about subjectivity, narrative, and history. Such projects are interpretive and historical, not reconstructive, because the self-understandings and changes of the past cannot just be described and explained. Interpretive judgment must also simultaneously evaluate and make a historical argument against its predecessors. No, we do not have to rewrite Hegel's *Phenomenology* every time we speak, but our claims about the present or past depend upon an implied historical argument. Practical reason cannot be separated from the historicity of subjectivity and meaning, and hence any claim will depend on a historical argument.

NATIONALITY AND CONSTITUTIONAL PATRIOTISM

One of the principal reasons Habermas resists speculative historical reasoning is the role such thinking has played in modern nationalism. Here we find historical traditions and narratives of political identity invented and manipulated for genocidal, exclusionary, and imperialistic purposes. As Habermas rightly says, "The history of European imperialisms between 1871 and 1914, and the integral nationalism of the twentieth century [. . .] illustrate the sad fact the idea of the nation did not so much reinforce loyalty of the population to the constitutional state but more often served as the instrument to mobilize for political goals that can scarcely be reconciled with republican principles" (1998, 116).

Habermas comes to nationalism first as a sociologist who looks at the nation historically in terms of its integrative and legitimizing functions: "The achievement of the nation-state consisted in solving two problems at once: it made possible a new mode of legitimation based on a new, more abstract form of social integration" (1998, 112).[42] In order to avoid the disasters of nationalism, he proposes that we replace nationalism with constitutional patriotism so that social imaginaries become the object of normative and procedural judgment rather than part of the subject of judgment. Constitutionalism serves the double purpose of keeping moral legitimacy outside of historical institutions at the same time that it serves to stand outside alternative views of the good life. I will look first at his conception of constitutionalism and then at how this conception comports with the languages of nationality.

Habermas defines his idea of the constitution as follows: "In a pluralist society, the constitution expresses a formal consensus. The citizens want to regulate their living together according to principles that are in the equal interest of each and thus can meet with the justified assent of all" (1996a, 496). In this theory, the constitution is not considered as a historical text, either in its genesis or in its reinterpretation through time. Instead, constitutional history should be considered a progressive "learning process," in which "all the later generations have the task of actualizing the still-untapped normative substance of the system of rights laid down in the original document of the constitution" (2001, 774).[43] What is "learned" is the cognitive moral content that was there all along. Hence, constitutional history is progressive: "Once the interpretive battles have subsided, all parties recognize that the reforms are achievements, although they were at first sharply contested" (2001, 774). Can we say that the history of constitutional interpretation has been simply progressive, even on Habermas's terms? The recent decisions by the American Supreme Court, a frequent touchstone in his argument, seem to be "unlearning" the moral content Habermas discusses—for instance, the ways that recent decisions have equated affirmative action with the Plessy v. Ferguson decision.

Since Habermas wants to make moral principles come from their own logic rather than from rhetorical, political, or historical arguments, he puts Founders and contemporaries in "the same boat" (2001, 775). In other words, the Founders and the current interpreters think of themselves not as historical beings, but as otherworldly beings who are "able to recognize the project as the same throughout history and judge it from the same perspective" (775). This sameness can, of course, only be a noumenal abstract posit, not a historical interpretation. He thus abstracts from the historical circumstances and intentions of the time and from the historicity of language, rejecting interpretive reconstructions of law, such as Ronald Dworkin's, because the normative dimension of their readings depends too much on existing legal traditions. Norms cannot be held hostage to historical good fortune, to whether we are those such as "Jefferson's fortunate heirs."[44]

Nonetheless, Habermas wants to bring norms into contact with the historical particulars of political communities, so that principles "enter into a binding relationship with the motives and attitudes of the citizens themselves" (1996a, 499).[45] However, when he characterizes how the tension between universals and particulars can be overcome so they can work together, we find elusive metaphors such as the following: "The political culture of a country crystallizes around its constitution. Each national culture develops a distinctive interpretation of constitutional principles that are [. . .]" (1998, 118). Because he looks at the nation only from the outside, we are not given portraits of what the internal reasoning of institutions of meaning within and between nations looks like. Instead, Habermas resorts to elusive metaphors to characterize the relationship of universals to particulars, such as "crystallizes" in the above citation.[46] I will develop what is missing from this account by looking at an example in which language, history, and memory work together in practical deliberation.

Let's consider the typical American student confrontation with Gloria Anzuldúa's *Borderlands/La Frontera*, a text written in Spanish and English combining poetry, narrative, and expository prose. The student does not respond to a moral, factual, or aesthetic claim. Instead, she must respond to a more global and indefinite claim on the symbolic inheritance through which she understands herself and her world. Anzuldúa's text ventriloquizes historical voices, ruptures the seams of everyday linguistic practice, and demands a reunderstanding of the past. This is not just matter of understanding certain facts that the student may not have known about— for example, the treaty of Guadalupe Hidalgo (1848), which set the cultural and political terms by which much of what is now the western United States was transferred from Mexico, including the right to retain the Spanish language—but a reunderstanding of her personal and national identity and the interpretive institutions that sustain them, such as the school and the narratives in textbooks. The treatment of these historical facts and the democratic ideals that have been used to rationalize and justify them have inscribed violence into the public imagination and meanings in ways that cannot be thematized by Habermas's ideals. Is the best starting point for analyzing the alternative languages of the public spheres that have developed since the treaty a transcendental argument that maintains that this discursive conflict must be subtended by deep agreement if it is to be intelligible? What about the violence carried by the words of the past? Can we really assume, like Hegel, that "the wounds of the Spirit heal, and leave no scars behind"(407)?

To recognize the claim requires a change in identity and public imagination, a political thematization and interrogation of the languages of debate.[47] The claim cannot be divided into empirical facts that are assessed by normative ideals because of the way the language of norms is bound up with the language of facts. Linguistic usage is intertwined with an interpretation of the past. What is at stake is what falls "between facts and norms"—namely the interpretive domain of public imagination.

When Habermas discusses the "recognition" of marginalized cultures, he looks at them only in terms of rights rather than through the languages of the public imagination.[48] The case of Chicanos in America is a good example of his misphrasing of the issue simply in terms of the right to recognition and survival of certain cultural understandings. The "recognition of this other" should begin with an interrogation of the ways in which the terms of the treaty were ignored or denied in the public treatment of American history and literature. Recognition is not about "adding on" new perspectives to an existing world of meaning but reworking the differences and the damages in the institutions of meaning that inform the different communities involved.[49] Recognizing others' painful truths often means that some citizens will have to give up a self-understanding. This is why the American History Standards caused such a political storm, inciting then presidential candidate Bob Dole to call their supporters "worse than enemies."[50] Recognition can involve a transformation of the self-understandings of the dominant culture, a revision of national identity and history. These debates involve complex, comparative negotiation of these histories and the languages through which we have remembered and ought to remember them. Moreover, the arguments themselves have a temporality that is measured not just in individual time but in collective time. Political judgment does not merely shuttle between facts and norms; rather, the interpretive process inevitably engages who we are.[51] As Craig Calhoun says, "what is missing from such account is the role of public life in actually constituting social solidarity and creating culture" (2002, 283). We do not just bring inherited identities to the public sphere; we reimagine them there through conversation and other forms of engagement.[52] Constitutional principles are not isolated from history and cultural particularity; rather, the constitution is reimagined together with the national and international past, so that founding "is not simply about the imagining of counterfactual possibilities—for example, utopias [. . .] but about the ways of imagining social life that actually make it possible" (Calhoun 2002, 280).

Habermas's particular transcendental arguments about norms and holistic meaning split off the work of historical sociologists about a political community's inevitable historical struggle over language, history, and memory from public reason. Historians of nationalism from Gellner to Hobsbawm and Anderson have shown how democratic nations worked to try to forge and enforce an often fragile semblance of homogeneity from the multiple traditions and languages that compose them.[53] The commonality among these languages—if it is not imposed by force—can only be developed through public conversation and difficult transitions and losses, not whisked into place as an inevitable presupposition. For Habermas, these studies only point to the manufactured character of national consciousness—necessary for social and political integration—and to the morally compromised nature of all forms of cultural reasoning. He oscillates between a wholesale indictment of historical languages as a critical sociologist and letting these same languages off too easily as a philosopher of transcendental arguments.[54]

HABERMAS AND THE HISTORIANS

Habermas's interventions in the "Historians' Debate" and in the controversy surrounding the work of Daniel Goldhagen draw him into addressing the dependency of a democratic society on its historical beliefs, and they nicely show the limits of his theory. The Historians' Debate was provoked by Habermas's critique of the work of Andreas Hillgruber and Ernst Nolte. Hillgruber's *Two Sorts of Destruction: The Smashing of the German Reich and the End of European Jewry* puts together the history of genocide with the fate of the Wehrmacht on the eastern front, giving greater sympathy to the latter. Nolte, on the other hand, puts the Holocaust in the context of other forms of genocide in the twentieth century.[55] By maintaining that the Nazis feared the Bolsheviks and copied their genocidal practices, Nolte relativizes the Holocaust and diminishes its role in Germany's national self-understanding.

Habermas responds with two claims. First, he places these neoconservative searches for a national identity through a "functional understanding of the public use of history" in the context of nationalist discourses, whose full horror was realized by fascism: "It was the original nationalism embodied in such figures as Hitler and Mussolini that [. . .] released national egoism from its ties to the universalist origin of the democratic state" (1989a, 262, 255). Only constitutional patriotism is capable of confronting the "barbaric dark side of all cultural achievement of the present day" (257). These principles insist that "national traditions can no longer remain unexamined, but can only be critically and self-critically appropriated" (1992c, 99). Constitutional principles thus offer the "common horizon of interpretation" for dealing with "public debates about the citizen's political self-understanding" (1994a, 134).

Although Habermas concedes that universal ideals "have to be nourished by a heritage of traditions that is consonant with them" (1989a, 262), his objection here is to the appeal to history per se as much as it is to Hillgruber's and Nolte's versions of it.[56] Indeed, he explicitly drives a distinction between the moral perspective of judge and the historian's observational positions, warning that we will descend into a "politics of history" if these are not kept separate: "The moment that the analytic perspective of the observer blurs with the perspective assumed by participants in a discourse of collective understanding, historiographical science degenerates into the politics of history" (1997b, 4). There is, indeed, a legitimate distinction between the historian and the judge,[57] but once we limit political judgment that way, we need to ask how such constitutional patriotism helps us deliberate about the politics of narrative point of view (Hillgruber) or historical comparison (Nolte). Would not Saul Friedlander's histories of Germany during and after the war run afoul of Habermas's principle as well?[58] How educators should deliberate about the kind of history taught in school is a particularly crucial issue not just for postwar Germany, but for all countries.

In his second claim, Habermas makes a historical and moral assertion that is completely detached from "constitutional patriotism": "Our own life is linked to the life context in which Auschwitz was possible not by contingent circumstances but intrinsically" (1989a, 233). Hence, "there is the obligation incumbent upon us in Germany [. . .] to keep alive, without distortion and not only in an intellectual form, the memory of the sufferings of those who were murdered by German hands" (233). Isn't this an obligation for historian and citizen alike? How does this fit with merely procedural requirements? Is this a personal moral obligation? Don't all constitutional democracies have historical legacies that need to be confronted politically?

In order to give a place to these questions, Habermas has to give up his conception of the division of the tasks of reason. First, historians' concerns cannot be reduced to seeking explanations. We can get some clarity on this question by adopting Paul Ricoeur's recent analysis of the "historiographical operation" practiced by contemporary historians. It falls into three recursive steps—sifting the archives, constructing explanations, and organizing the results into the textual representations. The historian's interpretive judgment—a judgment that is not limited to what Habermas consigns to the "ethical/hermeneutic" but is also moral, as he himself admits when it comes to Auschwitz—intervenes in all of these. This judgment is informed both by the professional techniques of the institutions of history and by the lifeworlds historians share with citizens. What further connects historians and citizens is "the second-order reflection on the conditions of possibility of this [historiographical] discourse, . . . a reflection destined to occupy the play of a speculative philosophy" (Ricoeur 2000, 373). Both historian and citizen are always living out, speculating on, and working through the conflicted symbolic inheritance. The hard boundaries separating explanatory, ethical/hermeneutic, and moral reasoning need to be opened if history is to enter political deliberation. Habermas moves toward these positions in the Goldhagen debate but pulls back.

While the politics of the Historians' Debate divided neatly along the lines of Right and Left, the controversy surrounding Goldhagen's *Hitler's Willing Executioners* did not fall out this way. Goldhagen's thesis is that the principal cause of the Holocaust was the intentions of the historical actors, intentions that were released in the political turmoil of the Third Reich. "My explanation—which is new to the scholarly literature on the perpetrators—is that the perpetrators, 'ordinary Germans,' were animated by anti-semitism, by a particular type of antisemitism that led them to conclude that the Jews ought to die" (1996, 14). Goldhagen is not just saying that widespread anti-Semitism was an enabling condition of the Holocaust but that Germans made their "choices as members of an assenting genocidal community, in which the killing of Jews was normative and often celebrated" (1996, 406). He offers a dramatic phenomenology of perpetrators' minds during killings in order to assign them "responsibility" for their actions. Among historians, Goldhagen's monocausal thesis was widely challenged and even dismissed as simplistic. The general public, on the other hand, found it compelling. The book became a bestseller, and Goldhagen was invited to make many public appearances in Germany and in the United States.[59] When Goldhagen received the Democracy Prize from the *Blätter für deutsche und internationale Politik* (Journal for German and International Politics), Habermas gave the honorary address at the award ceremony, which was later published.

He begins the essay by saying that he wants to steer clear of the criticisms historians have made of Goldhagen's work (epistemological discourse) and focus on his effect on public consciousness (ethical/hermeneutic), thus apparently opening the interpretive horizon of citizenship beyond the constitutional imagination. He wants to consider Goldhagen's book as if it were a film or art exhibit, as part of "the public discourses of self-understanding."[60] Unlike the legal context, where the question is guilt or innocence, the public sphere is concerned with "trying to bring about some clarity concerning the cultural matrix of a burdened inheritance, to recognize what they themselves [citizens] are collectively liable for, and what is to be continued, what revised" (1997b, 5).

While Habermas seems to be suggesting precisely what the initial quotation in this chapter denies—that is, how "a collective actor like a nation" works through the past—he quickly boxes out such a reading. First, his attempt to isolate the controversy over Goldhagen's work in the public sphere from the historians' professional debates won't hold. The worth of Goldhagen's argument for the citizen needs to be assessed in terms of the long line of historiographical debate surrounding the question he raises— how should we understand the relationship of modernity to the Holocaust. For instance, Goldhagen criticizes Arendt's claim that the perpetrators had lost a world. "Contrary to Arendt's assertions," Goldhagen tells us, "the perpetrators were not such atomized, lonely beings. They decidedly belonged to their world and had plenty of opportunities, which they obviously used, to discuss and reflect upon their exploits" (1996, 581). The argument here between Arendt and Goldhagen is not just about the explanatory concerns of the professional historian. Arendt's analysis, which implicates the modern conception of freedom as emancipation from tradition in the arrival of totalitarianism, problematizes not only Goldhagen's explanation but his understanding of the relationship of past and present.

Arendt's line of reading has been developed by structural-functionalists, such as Zygmunt Bauman, Omer Bartov, and Christopher Browning, who take on the intentionalist position directly. For structural-functionalists, interpreting the Holocaust requires that we reexamine Western modernity and its social/economic institutions. As Bauman says, "I propose to treat the Holocaust as a rare, yet significant and reliable, test of the hidden possibilities of modern society" (1989, 1). Intentionalists, on the other hand, focus on the anti-Semitic ideologies of the perpetrators that were released by the turmoil of the Third Reich. The site of judgment for intentionalists is unproblematically in the democratic and economic institutions of the West as they are currently constituted. The implicit assumption is that the German story is so different from that of the rest of Europe and America that it can be narrated and evaluated from the outside without calling into question the cultures of the subject of historical judgment. It is this refusal to interrogate the site of judgment that troubles the structural-functionalist. Bartov's *Murder in Our Midst*, published in the same year as Goldhagen's book, 1996, proposes to counteract the simplistic story "in which antisemitism led to Nazism, Nazism practiced genocide, and both were destroyed in a spectacular 'happy end'" (1996a, 53).[61] Such an account "fails to recognize that this extreme instance of industrial killing was generated by a society, economic system, and civilization of which our contemporary society is a direct continuation" (8).

Goldhagen's book thus participates in a long-standing argument: to what extent can the historical forces that shaped these events can be localized in an ideology and worked on (Goldhagen's perspective) and to what extent are they the products of forces and self-understandings that continue to damage us today? These are not matters just for professional historians but for citizens trying to decide what politicians to vote for and what kinds of textbooks should be used. Goldhagen himself is not reticent on the connection between history and democracy: "The development of an appropriate general framework for understanding the past has been critical in the development of a responsible democratic political system" (1998, 277). Although Habermas may well agree with this statement, he has no way of incorporating this idea into his model of practical reason.

While he occasionally flirts with an interpretive problematic for political judgment,[62] what he means by "working through" is the elimination of anti-Semitism and cultural nationalism, the establishment of constitutional democracy, and the remembrance of those killed. What seems to underlie his praise of Goldhagen is the nature of the latter's political solution to Germany's historical baggage: Root out the long-standing strains of anti-Semitism in public life and install constitutional democratic institutions so that history and public imagination can disappear from the political horizon. Even the content that Habermas does give to public imagination—remembrance of those killed—shows how he wants to reduce memory to individuals and thereby to ignore, for instance, the claims of the Jewish traditions and literature on German public life and imagination. Remembrance is complex and culturally specific, demanding not just constitutional principles but the identities of those remembering and those remembered. Remembrance demands that citizens engage with who they are and not just with what principles they hold dear, as Habermas at times suggests.

The eruption of history in politics, such as we find in the disputes over the Confederate Flag and the Holocaust, is not a passing crisis that a universal theory of communicative action will be able to put behind it through public memorials. Instead, these debates offer us the opportunity to enrich our vision of political dialogue. Before developing how practical reason can address demands of history, we need to look at the radically different understandings of subjectivity and historicity that we find in the structuralist and poststructuralist theories.

Avoiding Judgment

STRUCTURALIST AND POSTSTRUCTURALIST

APPROACHES TO HISTORY

When we move from the philosophies of Habermas and liberalism to the poststructuralist theories that dominate literary and cultural theory, we find original theories of public meaning but little interest in connecting these theories of meaning to a conception of practical reason or interpretive judgment. This chapter will not replay the debate between Habermas and the poststructuralists, which has been the focus of so much analysis, because neither side has formulated the question of public imagination and interpretive judgment in a satisfactory way. Instead, I will look at selected figures in the structuralist/poststructuralist tradition and trace how their conceptions of meaning elide the subject.[1]

My analysis falls into four parts. I begin by looking at two poetics of the imagination that develop from structuralism, Hayden White's first critique Kantianism and Paul Ricoeur's mixture of structuralism with a third critique form of Kantianism and phenomenology. White's pathbreaking historiography brings out the constitutive dimension of public imagination common to historians, novelists, and everyday citizens; however, his rich explanation of the imagination's workings is severed from any conception of public reasoning or judgment. Ricoeur comes next not only because he responds directly to White's shortcomings but also because he draws on a structuralist theory of meaning. Although Ricoeur's work is usually categorized as a hermeneutic phenomenology, I will argue here that there is a Kantian core that works with Husserlian phenomenology and structuralism in order to block out the dynamics of public imagination and the subject of judgment. In the next section, I look at two different poststructuralist theories of meaning and historicity. I begin with the Derridean transcendental arguments of Judith Butler and Joan Scott and show how their approach to history dissolves judgment. I then examine Foucault's antitranscendental theories of history from two points of view. First, I look at his critique of transcendental argument and show why this critique does not preclude transcendental arguments per se but only specific ones. (I will thus be preparing the way for my discussion of Taylor in chapter 3.) Then I look at Foucault's investigation of "historical a prioris" and genealogical transitional arguments to show how they can work with the hermeneutic mode of argument I will be making later on.

HAYDEN WHITE: THE STRUCTURAL
IMAGINATION AND DECISIONIST JUDGMENT

Hayden White's work aptly illustrates the strengths and weaknesses of the structuralist approach. It highlights the way common modes of imagining inform history, literature, and everyday life. At the same time, his work dramatizes the structuralist crisis of interpretive judgment. Before examining the particulars of White's dilemma, however, we need to look briefly at how the structuralist explanatory project pushes out the subject of judgment.

Structuralism's two major theorists, Ferdinand de Saussure and Claude Lévi-Strauss, are too well known to require extensive discussion, yet they initiate two lines of research that are frequently conflated. Lévi-Strauss seeks the invariant ahistorical structures and rules of the collective mind— a transhistorical a priori—while Saussure's idea of the linguistic system includes historical change as part of its project—the system as historically variable a priori. The Saussurean line is consistent with the direction taken by Foucault and the New Historicists—though they are hardly Saussureans. White develops along the Lévi-Strauss line.[2]

Lévi-Strauss characterizes the relationship of history and anthropology as follows: "History organizes its data in relation to conscious expressions of social life, while anthropology proceeds by examining its unconscious expressions of social life" (1963, 18).[3] The unconscious here consists, of course, of the forms that "are fundamentally the same for all minds—ancient and modern" (21). History lays out the material from which anthropology seeks to abstract: "By showing institutions in the process of transformation, history alone makes it possible to abstract the structure which underlies the many manifestations and remains permanent throughout a succession of events" (21). Lévi-Strauss speaks of his project in Kantian terms: "In allowing myself to be guided by the search for the constructing structure of the mind, I am proceeding in the manner of Kantian philosophy" (cited in Dosse 1994, 87). By "Kantian" here, Lévi-Strauss is referring to Kant's epistemological project in the deduction of the categories and divorcing it from Kant's moral and overall philosophical project. In place of the deduction of the categories Lévi-Strauss puts his structuralist conception of language: "Language, an unreflecting totalization, is human reason which has its reason and of which man knows nothing" (1966, 252).

In articulating his project, Lévi-Strauss has in his sights not only liberal individualist conceptions of meaning but Hegelian and Marxist holistic narrative accounts, such as those of Sartre. Sartre makes two mediations that structuralists reject: 1. a phenomenological account of the intentions of the historical individual actor and the collective meaning of the historical moment; 2. the theoretical subject and the practical subject.[4] Instead of trying to finesse the problem of third-person causal explanations and first-person understanding in the manner of Hegel, Marx, and Sartre, Lévi-Strauss insists on the truth of the structural explanation of the theoretical observer without a hermeneutic complement: "Marx and Freud [. . .] taught us that man has meaning only on the condition that he view himself as meaningful. So far I agree with Sartre. But it must be added that this meaning is never the right one: superstructures are faulty acts which have 'made it' socially. Hence it is vain to go to historical consciousness for the truest meaning" (1966, 253–254).[5] Interpretive judgment does not have to sort through explanations and self-understandings, causes and reasons, but instead can rely on the reconstruction of the rules of the symbolic system. But how does this agenda inform White's project?

First, he joins Lévi-Strauss and the Annales historians in their critique of the epistemological status of narrative, a critique aimed at those "who try to claim that the stories told in narrative histories inhere either in the events themselves [. . .] or in the facts derived from the critical study of evidence" (White 1992, 39). For White, narrative is an epistemologically suspect yet inevitable structure imposed on chaotic individual and collective existence. Narrative is a retrospective construction that does not inform the phenomenology of daily life, "No one and nothing lives a narrative" (1978, 111). Historians should distinguish "factual statements (singular existential propositions)" organized as a chronicle from the "poetic and rhetorical elements by which what would otherwise be a list of facts is transformed into a story" (1992, 38).

Interpretive conflicts, according to White, have "less to do with the facts of the matter in question than with the different story meanings with which the facts can be endowed by emplotment" (38).[6]

Because narrative is external to historical events, we should view its claims to truth with deep suspicion, for narrative order merely "arises out of a desire to have real events display the coherence, integrity, fullness, and closure of an image of life that is and can only be imaginary" (White 1988, 24). White says that structuralism and poststructuralism aim to show that "narrative was not only an instrument of ideology but the very paradigm of ideologizing discourse in general" (33).

The second part of his project is to provide an explanation for the various shapes the narratives assume by recourse to a theory of poetic language that will "characterize the deep structure of the historical imagination" (1973, 38). He seeks to map the constants of the imagination—for instance, the four tropological modes of metaphor, synecdoche, metonymy, and irony and their combinatory possibilities—in order to provide the rules that govern the production of narrative: "It is my view that the dominant tropological mode and its attendant linguistic protocols comprise the irreducibly 'metahistorical' basis of every historical work" (1973, xi).[7]

The third part of White's project is to make narrative a part of public imagination and give it a legitimate, if metaphorical, claim to truth rather than dismissing it as merely false. This goal is quite distinct from the second, a purely explanatory interest that makes no claim about the worth or validity of particular features of the public imagination. Thus, his attack on narrative for "noveliz[ing] historical processes" only shows that "the truths in which narrative history deals are of an order different from those of its social scientific counterpart" (1988, 44). Narrative should be understood as allegoresis that "figures the body of events that serves as its primary referent and transforms these events into intimations of patterns of meaning that any literal representation of them as facts could never produce" (45). White uses the standard of literal correspondence to the past as it was in order to consign all narrative to "metaphoric" treatment. By holding out the past as an unattainable ideal, the theorist unmasks naive realism. The task of the socially responsible historian is limited to the neo-Kantian detection of mistakes of those who still confound narrative and reality.[8]

There are a number of problems here. First, White has tried to stave off relativism by introducing an untenable distinction between form and content, in which the preinterpretive information of "singular propositions" stands outside all interpretive schemes. Are not the archives themselves often emplotted? Do we really want to ignore the shape of survivors' testimonies and their claims on us? Second, he relies on an outmoded correspondence theory of truth. As Noel Carroll says, "White seems to make us choose: historical narratives are copies [. . .] or they are fictional" (1998, 44). Moreover, the literal/figural distinction as a transhistorical claim about referential and fictional practices is difficult to fathom, and this ambiguity comes directly from his conception of public imagination. One wonders how such a positivistic reference is possible given that his theory of meaning is radically divorced from common sense.

White rightly takes public imagination as the common ground of history and fiction: "The affiliation of narrative historiography with literature and myth should not be a source of embarrassment because the systems of meaning production shared by all three are distillates of the historical experience of a people, a group, a culture. [. . .] In other words, just as the contents of myth are tested by fiction, so too, the forms of fiction are tested by (narrative) historiography" (1988, 35). Although he claims systems of meaning are the "distillates" of historical experience, the sorting processes of culture—what he calls "testing"—are never displayed, compared, and evaluated for their relative superiority—whether epistemological or ethical—because neither the historical actors nor the historian has any basis. How does the public imagination argue with itself and change through time? How do events have an impact on the plots and symbols of the social imaginary? Don't literary works themselves make arguments about historical and philosophical questions? He asserts that there is no way "to conclude on logical grounds that any real set of events is a farce. This is a judgment, not a conclusion. It is a judgment that can be justified only on the basis of a poetic troping of the 'facts.'" (47). Fair enough, but this is where an account of deliberation begins, not where it ends. White wants to defend the truth of the public imagination, but he never does so, contenting himself with saying that no one would want to deny "that literature and poetry have anything valid to teach us about reality" (44). Thus, all that can be assessed is the positivistic statements of chronicle, not any form of "imagination": "This is not to say that a historical discourse is not properly assessed in terms of the truth value of its factual (singular existential) statements taken individually and the logical conjunction of the whole set of such statements taken distributively. [. . .] Such assessment touches only that aspect of the historical discourse conventionally called its chronicle. It does not provide us with any way of assessing the content of the narrative itself" (45).[9]

Hence, when White gives us his famous one-liner—"There are no grounds to be found in the historical record itself for preferring one way of construing its meaning over another" (1988, 75)—he has not simply disconnected the past from any system of meaning, he has also dislodged the present from any. We are left with an unsituated theorist who juxtaposes a global fund of meanings, all of which are equally metaphoric, to some degree zero of reference as chronicle.[10] Therefore, I entirely agree with those who criticize White for leaving out the institution of history and public debate, such as Roger Chartier, who says, "History is indeed a discourse but a discourse whose determinations are to be sought not in the conventions perpetuated by a literary genre but in the practices determined by the technical institutions of a discipline, which differ according to time and place and are subject to various ways of separating truth from falsehood and to contrasting definitions of what constitutes historical proof" (1997, 42, cf. 38).[11] The institution of history is not just the site for empirical, theoretical, and transcendental arguments.[12] Instead, these arguments themselves can be characterized as historical and transitional for the superiority of the new account or for the genealogical displacement of the previous ones. (I will say more on such arguments in chapter 3.)

Why does White refuse to situate the subject of historical judgment in historical arguments? The answer is that he thinks that such a move would compromise his Kantian conception of the spontaneity of human freedom—that is, that human awareness and action are spontaneously self-determining—which is antecedent to all theoretical or empirical conditions: "On historical grounds alone I have no basis for preferring one conception of the science of history over the other. Such a judgment would merely reflect a logically prior preference, either for the linguistic mode in which Tocqueville or Marx prefigured the historical field or for their specific figurations of the historical field" (1973, 432).[13] The historian's judgment comes down to pure decisionism. Deliberation about the multiple interpretations and theories is reduced to personal, subjective preference, a falling "back to moral and aesthetic reasons for the choice of one vision over another as the more 'realistic.' The aged Kant was right, in short; we are free to conceive 'history' as we please, just as we are free to make of it what we will" (433).[14] The work of Paul Ricoeur tries to avoid White's shortcomings by incorporating structuralism into a formal phenomenology.

Ricoeur comes at this point in my exposition for several reasons. He develops a conception of public imagination common to history and fiction that goes beyond White's structuralist conception, by connecting narrative to epistemology, phenomenology, and the social sciences.[15] The argument of this section is that Ricoeur offers an inadequate model of public historical imagination and a political dialogue because he blocks out an ontological and dialogical conception of language, narrative, and rationality. Although he reads himself as grafting hermeneutics onto his formalist concerns—Husserlian phenomenology, structuralism, and Kantian schematism—the graft never touches his philosophical architecture.[16] I will not attempt to survey Ricoeur's vast corpus; instead I look at his comments on White as a way of entering his conceptions of triple mimesis, language, and literature.

Ricoeur criticizes White for refusing to place the work of historians and narrative inside the institution of history, or what he calls, borrowing a phrase from Michel de Certeau, the historiographical operation. This operation falls into three moments: the documentary phase, in which the archives are sifted for proof; the explanatory phase, in which the historian works through reasons and causes of actions and events; and the representation phase ("la mise en forme littéraire"), in which the historian must "emplot." These moments are not sequential but recursive: "No one consults an archive without an explanatory project, without a hypothesis of understanding; no one undertakes to explain a course of events without recourse to a literary form" (2000, 170). Ricoeur criticizes White for isolating emplotment (the third moment) from scientific procedures (328). Ricoeur affirms that it is "legitimate to treat the deep structures of the imaginary for the common creative matrices of novelistic plots and historical plots [. . .] but it is just as important to specify the referential moment that distinguishes function from history" (328). To understand how Ricoeur brings together imagination and reference, we need to examine his understanding of triple mimesis, which lies at the heart of all his work.

In *Time and Narrative*, Ricoeur divides mimesis into three moments. Mimesis 1 addresses the preunderstandings of "the world of action, its meaningful structures, its symbolic resources, and its temporal character" (M1) (1984–88, I, 54). Mimesis 2 examines the emplotment, which mediates preunderstandings and readings (M2), while Mimesis 3, the reading, addresses "the intersection of the world of the text and the world of the hearer or reader" (I, 71). The reader's response to the text, M3, folds back into M1 as part of the new preunderstandings in the lifeworld, thus completing the hermeneutic circle.

In Mimesis 1, Ricoeur drives a wedge between narrative and experience in the world at the same time that he freezes the historical and dialogical character of language and literature. He does not place the subject in language and narratives so that inchoate narratives already inform experience.[17] To be sure, he acknowledges that history and fiction "are preceded by the use of narrative in daily life" (II,156). However, "prefiguration" is a cognitive capacity that stands against the experience of time, which in itself is "confused, unformed, and, at the limit, mute" (I,14). Thus, Mimesis 1 is "a structure of human praxis prior to the work of configuration by the historical or the fictional narrative" (III, 310).

Mimesis 2, or emplotment, is not an interpretive act through which the subject dialogues with traditions, as it is in Taylor or Gadamer. Instead, Ricoeur develops his conception of the novel as emplotment by drawing on Aristotle's *Poetics* and on Kant's *Critique of Judgment*: "I cannot overemphasize the kinship between this 'grasping together' power to the configurational act and what Kant says about the operation of judging" (I, 66–68). Emplotment "extracts configuration from a succession" in the same that way that a reflective judgment "reflects upon the work of thinking at work in the aesthetic judgment of taste and the teleological judgment applied to organic wholes" (66). In a stroke, Ricoeur has reduced the author's engagement with worth and truth of the languages of traditions to a formal aestheticism.[18] Thus, when he says that emplotment is the "synthesis of the heterogeneous"—that is, "the diverse mediations performed by the plot: between the manifold of events and the temporal unity of the story recounted between the disparate components of the action" (1992, 141)— the substantive epistemological, ethical, and ontological issues that narratives engage become a merely reflexive ordering. By looking at narrative as the emplotment of the heterogeneous, Ricoeur blocks out the way in which emplotment is always a reemployment of the narrative and symbolic shapes the subject inevitably inhabits.

By turning narrative into a merely formal question, Ricoeur abstracts generic literary issues from the historical dialogue in which they were formed and makes them subjective schematic possibilities in a Kantian sense. As Kantian schematism connects the understanding and intuition, so emplotment "engenders a mixed intelligibility between what has been called the point, theme, or thought of a story, and the intuitive presentation of circumstances, characters, episodes and changes of fortune that make up the denouement" (1984–88, I, 68). Ricoeur historicizes schematization by making it proceed "from the sedimentation of a practice with a specific history [. . .] called 'traditionality.'" In Ricoeur's conception of tradition, the formal dimension of "traditionality" is separated from the material (the content of traditions), and the "apology for tradition" (legitimacy) (III, 221ff.), and these latter make no appearance in Mimesis 2. By isolating Mimesis 2, Ricoeur is able to speak not of a conflictual, dialogical tradition filled with wrenching negations but of a "self-structuring of tradition [that] is neither historical nor ahistorical but rather 'transhistorical,' in the sense that it runs through this history in a cumulative rather than an additive manner" (II, 14).

This transhistorical formalism emerges in his adoption of Northrup Frye's theory of genre—myth, romance, and the like—in *The Anatomy of Criticism*. Since literature's development is divorced from its substantive issues, tradition becomes a panoply of formal possibilities that are stripped of their ethical, political, and axiological importance. Ricoeur also excludes dialogue from his conception of historical change by employing the Husserlian vocabulary of "sedimentation" and "innovation," in which the subject's arguments with historical inheritance are given no place: "This schematism, in turn, is constituted within a history that has the characteristics of a tradition [. . .]. A tradition is constituted by the interplay of innovation and sedimentation. To sedimentation must be referred the paradigms that constitute the typology of emplotment" (I, 68). Ricoeur treats the subject's background as sediment rather than as presuppositions that call for articulation, which is Taylor's approach. Moreover, by speaking of sediment, innovation, and formalized traditionality rather than reemplotment, he blocks out the role of narrative "transitional arguments," whether individual or collective, in which alternative languages are assessed.[19]

Ricoeur rejects narrative self-understandings of a culture as part of a historical argument, in which one narrative engages the claims of previous ones; instead, he sees narrative changes as marked out with a neutral descriptive language concerned only with the question of innovation rather than negation, refutation, and retrieval. Ricoeur says, "Rule-governed deformation constitutes the axis around which the various changes of paradigm through application are changed. It is this variety of application that confers a history on the productive imagination and that in counterpoint to sedimentation, makes a narrative tradition possible" (I, 70). Traditions are not "cumulative" sediment unless the subject's historicity and being in language are put out of play in favor of a disengaged transcendental imagination.

Ricoeur's discussion of schemas is also a clue as to why he wants to make narratives always innovative—to flatter them out of existence. In narrative, just as in metaphor, "semantic innovation can be carried back to the productive imagination and, more precisely, to the schematism of its signifying matrix" (I, ix). Anyone who has been to a high school reunion or watched sitcoms knows that not all narratives are innovative, so why does Ricoeur insist on this? He needs the innovative dimension in order to make narrative an aesthetic judgment rather than a determinative judgment about truth and to keep narrative from being a constituent of our being in the world.

Thus, Ricoeur's discussion of the novel in *Time and Narrative* and *Oneself as Another* is remarkably ahistorical. Despite the fact that the rise of the novel is embedded in issues of modernity itself, such as individualism, liberty, and language, Ricoeur ignores all of them in his discussions of literature. For Ricoeur, novels are just examples of how the aporias of cosmic and experienced time are mediated by plot, or they are "thought experiments" in the Husserlian mold of imaginative variation: "Literature proves to consist in a vast laboratory for thought experiments in which the sources of variation encompassed by narrative identity are put to the test of narration" (1992, 148). This leveling transcendental eye stands far above and apart from the self-understandings of writers and readers, who are engaged with the substantive claims made by competing narratives.

Ricoeur wants to keep novelists out of the argument business, however, limiting them only to emplotment. "Historians are not simply narrators: they give reasons [. . .]. Poets also create plots that are held together by causal skeletons. But these [. . .] are not the subject of a process of argumentation. Poets restrict themselves to producing the story and explaining by narrating [. . .]. [Poets] produce, [historians] argue" (1984–88, I, 186). Not only does this exclude the commentary about the proper understanding of their novelistic worlds offered by such well-known narrators as those of Balzac and Proust, but it ignores the argumentative dimension of narratives that are devoted primarily to "showing" rather than "telling." When an advocate of showing, such as Henry James, emplots, he is not just ordering the heterogeneous in a form, he is arguing with the narrow epistemology and moral ontology of the realistic novel, as we find in the works of Flaubert or the Goncourts. How can we separate out the formal features of Kate Chopin's *Awakening*—such as her use of chapters, summaries, and narrative voice—without understanding how her formal critique of the *Bildungsroman* is tied to issues of feminism and subjectivity, to women's oppression in cultural plots and language—that is, to questions of "material" and "legitimacy"—and to the conflicts of traditions? This same formalism undermines Ricoeur's concept of narrative identity since identity becomes the ordering of components and not an argument with other self-conceptions, which is how I will develop it in the next chapter.

Because Ricoeur follows Kant in considering a narrative text as an isolated aesthetic object, his discussion of reception, Mimesis 3 (III, chap. 7), gives center stage to Wolfgang Iser's and Roman Ingarden's phenomenologies of the textual object, and they are presented as if they were merely complementing rather than truncating a dialogical hermeneutics of tradition (Hans-Robert Jauss). Ricoeur wants to preserve the "ideality of meaning," what he calls Husserl's "'logiscist' rejoinder" to historicism (1976, 90): "The text—objectified and dehistoricized—becomes the necessary mediation between writer and reader" (91).[20]

Despite his appropriations of Gadamer, Ricoeur remains a methodological individualist who rejects giving ontological weight to the institutions of meaning. We see this is not only in the chapter devoted to Hegel in *Time and Narrative*, volume 3, in which the question is whether to renounce Hegel—the answer is yes—but also in the revealing essay "Hegel and Husserl on Intersubjectivity," in *From Text to Action*. Ricoeur objects to all holistic conceptions, which include not only Hegel's *Geist* but also finite versions of the Hegelian idea of institutions of meaning: "The decisive advantage of Husserl over Hegel appears to me to lie in his uncompromising refusal to hypostatize collective entities and his tenacious will to reduce them in every instance to a network of interactions" (Ricoeur 1991, 244). To avoid such hypostatization, we must rely on "the analogy of the ego [as] the transcendental principle of all intersubjective relations" (245). The result of this methodology is that he seeks to mediate opposing positions that need to be abandoned as false starting points—for example, the Cartesian Cogito, the ideal of unmediated empathy.[21] Instead, we need a different transcendental argument, one that engages the institutions of meaning through and against which the subject is articulated.

Husserl's methodological individualism is not the only key to how Ricoeur reduces narrative to poetics in Mimesis 2, for he also appropriates structuralism to supplement his phenomenology. Working at a deeper level than schematism, structuralism can search for ahistorical "structures whose manifestation would be concrete narrative configurations on the surface of narrative" (1984–88, II, 29), or, it can focus on the individual aesthetic object in order "to reconstruct the internal dynamic of the text" (1976, 18). Structuralism's aim is purely explanatory rather than interpretive/evaluative; it provides the rules governing a linguistic, or in this case, generic system.

Ricoeur is comfortable with structuralism precisely because its conception of language as a homogenous linguistic system offers a version of the linguistic turn that can be made to fit with a Husserlian notion of the ideality of meaning, "the conquest of the empire of sense" (Ricoeur 1983, 188). For Husserl and for structuralists, meaning is clarified by procedures outside the world rather than through dialogues in the world. Structuralism's characterization of historical change speaks of new manifestations of a deep structure or, in the Saussurean version, of arbitrary shifts to a new system. Thus, structuralism joins a conception of tradition as sedimentation and innovation in driving out narrative as argument from one self-understanding to another. Structuralism formalizes the content, while transcendental phenomenology formalizes time into lived and cosmic.

Not only does Ricoeur's formalism drive out the historical shapes of the self; it also blocks a dialogical conception of narrative. Ricoeur acknowledges the threat of such a conception to his idea of emplotment when he considers the modern novel and the modern subject: "By sliding from the mimesis of action to the mimesis of characters, then to that of their thoughts, feelings, and language, and by crossing that final threshold, that from monologue to dialogue, on the plane of the narrator's as much as the characters' discourse, have we not surreptitiously substituted for emplotment a radically different structuring principle, which is dialogue itself?" (1984–88, II, 96–97). However, dialogism is not only a feature of the modern novel but a problematic for understanding our being in language. Emplotment itself is dialogical, for the novelist, or the selves of everyday life, are not just configuring a manifold but engaging the many languages of literary traditions and society. Dialogism moves us from an understanding of mimesis as the imitation of action to an understanding of language as the medium of subject and object. Hence, literature, for Mikhail Bakhtin (and Taylor) is a mode of reflection that "reveals not only the reality of a given language but also, as it were, its potential, its ideal limits and its total meaning conceived as a whole, its truth together with its limitations" (Bakhtin 1981, 356).[22] Dialogism is not just about multiple voices but also about the multiplicity of languages, as Bakhtin shows in *The Dialogic Imagination*. (Parodies of public discourse or other literary works are perhaps the most obvious example.) Ricoeur's presentation would have had to be quite different if he had started with Bakhtin's definition of the novel as "a diversity of social speech types (sometimes even diversity of languages) and diversity of individual voices, artistically organized" (1981, 262) rather than with Augustine on lived time and Aristotle and Kant on plot.

Ricoeur's formalism never lets the ontological aspects of our being in language appear as problems of interpretive judgment or practical reason. I do not wish to deny the great achievement of his work on narrative but to expose the costs of his particular transcendental approach woven from Kant and Husserl, costs that his generous and tireless efforts at mediation often hide. Although few other philosophers have devoted themselves to reconciling disputes, as has Ricoeur, his marriages are always performed in the courthouse of Husserlian phenomenology, in which language and literature make their entrance down the aisles of transcendental subjectivity.

BUTLER AND SCOTT: FREEDOM AS EFFECTS WITHOUT SUBJECTS

Unlike White and Ricoeur, Judith Butler and Joan Scott have fully embraced the ontological turn initiated by Heidegger and developed by Foucault and Derrida to criticize not only liberal political philosophy but also the work of feminists and advocates of cultural difference. In their recent works—Butler's *Excitable Speech: A Politics of the Performative* (1997) and *The Psychic Life of Power* (1997) and Scott's *Only Paradoxes to Offer* (1996)—both aim to show that their philosophies do not deny agency, freedom, and equality, as detractors such as Seyla Benhabib maintain, but in fact give a more perspicuous account of these ideas once we understand ourselves as linguistically vulnerable beings.[23]

Scott's and Butler's postmodernism criticizes the way that liberalism and deliberative democracy accept a political community's linguistic inheritance and ignore the dynamics by which subjects are produced. In Butler's and Scott's views, the only way to make available the workings of oppression and to give a space to difference and liberty is to think through the originary moments by which a community constitutes its meanings through excluding others. These originary exclusions are so deep that they are largely inaccessible to historical actors, and so the philosopher needs to avoid the subjectivist trap of reading hermeneutically and narratively. Instead, she tracks the movements of history by reading the self-under-standings of a society as the repetitive effects generated by these originary moments.

While they will join me in pointing out that Habermas does not give a space for interrogating the linguistic/political form of life, Butler and Scott formulate this point in a totalizing way that does not account for the achieve-ments that make their own judgment possible. If Habermas omits the argu-mentative step in which one interrogates and ultimately signs off on a particular reading of certain aspects of a form of life, Butler and Scott omit the step in which one brings the problematic for interpreting history as an object to bear on the interpretive subject. Our historical inheritance has indeed been complex and oppressive in ways that are constitutive of exis-tence; however, the way to deliberate about this inheritance is not by creating a formal procedural subject or by flattening ethical/political histories and their languages into the effects produced by transcendental paradox. The question that guides my exposition is how to develop an interpretive philoso-phy that can let women's oppression *and* achievement appear.

Constructivist Power and the Failure of "Her-Story" Histories

From Foucault, Butler takes the concept of power, which is the "forma-tive and constitutive" medium in which subject and world are made. Power's particular manner of constitution tends to produce a shallow, defensive self-understanding that disguises the way that power really oper-ates: "The conditions of intelligibility are themselves formulated in and by power, and this normative exercise of power is rarely acknowledged as an operation of power at all" (Butler 1997a, 134). This dissimulation produces the two levels typical of the hermeneutics of suspicion, a surface level that characterizes the self-understanding of the culture and the deeper level that her analysis seeks to make available. Power "works through its illegibility: it escapes the terms of legibility that it occasions" (134). Our superficial understandings of the production of meaning lead us to misframe issues, such as censorship, in terms of individuals and the state. We should not make the humanist mistake of seeing this as a question of what one can say; rather, we need to make the deeper ontological cut and interrogate the "domain of the sayable within which I begin to speak at all" (132). Unlike the hermeneutics of suspicion, she does not place an explanation behind the self-understanding—that is, a truth beneath the appearance. Rather, the point is to make the illegible legible.

The failure to interrogate inherited meanings is the reason Butler, like Scott, rejects forms of feminist or queer theory that retrieve women's practices (e.g., Carol Gilligan) or write what Scott calls "her-story" style history.[24] Those who write "her-story" focus on female agency and the valuation of women's experiences, while overlooking the ways that power and patriarchy construct those experiences in damaging ways. The exclusions of history cannot simply be resurrected and valorized because the structure of women's lives and values are constituted by the damaged system of meanings that excluded them: "Feminist history then becomes not the recounting of great deeds performed by women but the exposure of the often silent and hidden operations of gender that are nonetheless present and defining forces in the organization of most societies. With this approach women's history critically confronts the politics of existing history and inevitably begins the rewriting of history" (Scott 1986, 27).[25] These kinds of critical projects remain hostage to the institutions of meaning they are criticizing. Feminist historians should not conceive of their project as merely additive, "as an enlargement of the picture, a correction to oversights resulting from inaccurate or incomplete vision" (Scott 1991, 776). Because individual experience is always mediated by discursive processes that are not available to the subject, we should not "reify agency as an inherent attribute of individuals," for this precludes "questions about the constructed nature of experience, about how subjects are constituted as different in the first place, about how one's vision is structured, about language (or discourse) and history" (777).

Originary Arguments

But the key to understanding both Butler and Scott is not the familiar reworking of Foucault but the way they use Derrida. I will focus on Butler and her appropriation of Derrida's reading of speech-act theory. The choice of speech-act theory is apt because it embodies the liberal assumptions about subjectivity and language that she wants to challenge, assumptions that underwrite not only the work of Habermas but also the contemporary debates over pornography and hate speech, which serve as the examples for her critique.

For Butler, liberalism falsely associates agency and autonomy with the control of meaning, and her phrasing sounds very much like the hermeneutic critique of the atomistic subject found in Gadamer and Taylor: "The linguistic domain over which the individual has no control becomes the condition of possibility for whatever domain of control is exercised by the speaking subject. Autonomy in speech is conditioned by dependency on language whose historicity exceeds in all directions the speaking subject" (1997a, 28). Indeed, hermeneutics could only agree with her critique of the liberal interpretation of hate speech, which ignores such speech's inherited character: "The subject who speaks hate speech is clearly responsible for such speech, but that subject is rarely the originator of that speech. Racist speech works through the invocation of convention" (34). Hate speech and pornography are "traditions," which cannot be located only at the level of speakers.

However, she differs from hermeneutics in that she wants to break with the unifying ideas of hermeneutics, such as narrative, tradition, and understanding. All these ideas cover over where the action of language really takes place. In order to discern the way meaning operates, we need to recognize that the entire speech system depends on a repressed other, "the constitutive outside": "This 'outside' is the defining limit or exteriority to a given symbolic universe, one which, were it imported into that universe, would destroy its integrity and coherence. In other words, what is set outside or repudiated from the symbolic universe in question is precisely what binds that universe together through its exclusion" (1997a, 180).[26] Because coherence is achieved through exclusion, Butler justifies reading against the grain of meanings and understandings for "effects" so that we are not trapped in the symbolic system.[27] She is careful never to put the site of her theory "outside" the system since opposition is "implicated in the very processes it opposes" (1997b, 17). Indeed, she criticizes such spatializing notions of subjectivity, which block out the temporality of repetition, what Derrida calls "iterability," the agent of change, as we will see momentarily. However, if Butler refuses to spatialize her relation to the languages and subjects she addresses, she nonetheless claims superiority for her language over the languages that she targets. Her language blends together the explanatory ambitions of the work of Freud and Lacan with the ambition of transcendental philosophy to think of the conditions of possibility of being (Derrida). Through Derrida, she explicitly distances herself from the determinism that she finds in psychoanalysis and Foucault (1997b, 130). For Derrida, language itself manifests a disseminatory dimension that is covered over by attention to conceptualization, a dimension that he discusses through his neologisms such as "iterability."

Hence, when Butler discusses the historicity of speech acts and language, she draws from Derrida's idea of iterability rather than a hermeneutic idea of tradition: Performative acts "engage actions or constitute themselves as a kind of action, [. . .] not because they reflect the power of an individual's will or intention, but because they draw upon and reengage conventions which have gained their power precisely through a sedimented iterability." (1995, 134). "Sedimented iterability" is a way of referring to cultural channeling without presupposing that there is understanding or "know-how" that accompanies such redundancy.[28] Butler reminds us that for Derrida the break with existing contexts is a "structurally necessary feature of every utterance and every codifiable written mark" (1997a, 150). The break is a transcendental condition of the utterance, a break that goes all the way down, and not a recontextualization of a core of meaning that would provide a continuity of understanding. What Butler is getting at here is the difference between the transcendental and the empirical levels of deconstruction. Perhaps the simplest way to characterize this distinction is through Derrida's well-known debate with John Searle over how to categorize fictional speech acts. At the empirical level, Derrida is challenging Searle's taxonomy, but at the transcendental level he is challenging the capacity of any taxonomy to contain the disseminatory dimension of language, because "iterability blurs a priori the dividing line that passes between [. . .] opposed terms" (Derrida 1977, 210).[29]

We should not lament this truth about the interrupting other of our language, about our inability to control meaning, because such logocentric mourning (and melancholia) ignores how this disseminatory movement of language—and not the wills of actors—opens space for new possibilities and for a nonsovereign idea of freedom: "The disjunction between utterance and meaning is the condition of possibility for revising the performative [. . .]. The citationality of the performance produces the possibility for agency and expropriation at the same time" (Butler 1997a, 87). Hence, "untethering the speech act from the sovereign subject founds an alternative notion of agency and ultimately of responsibility, one that more fully acknowledges the way in which the subject is constituted by language" (15). The disjunction of meaning is the condition of the possibility of resignification, of linguistic change that no individual or institution can contain. Thus, those who want to ban hate speech attribute to the speaker and his or her language a sovereign power that overlooks the way that those targeted by such languages have fought back, have come to respond to and reinscribe the language of oppression by various means. These responses are to be attributed not simply to the punctual agency of individuals but to the transcendental uncontainability of language that makes discrete acts of revolt possible.

However, there is a tension here between Butler's account of the agency of the oppressed and their own self-understandings. The liberty of the subject for Butler comes from the disseminating effects of meaning as they work through and against the received self-understandings, which deny or ignore this truth. Butler senses that she must negotiate her two levels of meaning, one for the received vocabularies of the subject and one for those who think through her third-person vocabularies of effects.[30]

Butler makes the category "disseminatory effects" stand at such right angles to all the ethical and axiological vocabularies of philosophy and everyday life that the hermeneutic circle is forever broken and practical judgments are paralyzed. This paralysis emerges from a problematic that casts all empirical, normative judgments into the same radical doubt so that we have no way of comparing and assessing historical changes and differences. The goals of her project are uncontroversial: "the development of forms of differentiation [that could] lead to fundamentally more capacious, generous, and 'unthreatened' bearings of the self in the midst of community" (1995, 140). However, we need to ask how we should understand and cultivate such virtues and the intersubjectivity on which they depend when we are always looking from the transcendental site of effects. Without an account of how these ideals emerge from the history of effects, they simply drop from the sky, as does the subjectivity of the critic who is not ensnared in the same way as her predecessors.[31] Does the critic's insight not build on any previous insight?

Seyla Benhabib mounts two criticisms of Butler's deconstructive position, one empirical and the other normative. To the first issue, she says, "Some form of human agency [. . .] is crucial to make empirical sense of processes of psycho-sexual development and maturation" (1995, 110). In other words, "Can the theory account for the capacities of agency and resignification it wants to attribute to individuals?" (111). Her normative critique asks for clarification of the site of judgment: "A certain ordering of normative priorities and a clarification of those principles in the name of which one speaks is unavoidable" (27). Benhabib brings these criticisms together when she says to Butler and Scott, "Women who negotiate and resist power do not exist; the only struggles in history are between competing paradigms of discourses, power/knowledge complexes" (114).[32] While she agrees that "mainstream liberal feminist theory treats the tradition's views of women as a series of unfortunate, sometimes embarrassing, but essentially corrigible, misconceptions" (1992, 242–243), she proposes an alternative to poststructuralist approaches that she calls "a 'feminist discourse of empowerment'" (243). Her third view follows a radical critique in "revealing the gender subtext of the ideals of reason and the Enlightenment," but, unlike the poststructuralists, Benhabib does not want to discard these ideals. There are two parts to fulfilling these ideals. On the one hand, she exposes the exclusion of women from political traditions such as social contract theory, where we find "boys [who] are men before they have been children; a world where neither mother, nor sister, nor wife exist" (157). On the other, she reads "against the grain, proceeding from certain footnotes and marginalia in the text [. . .] toward recovering the history of those the dialectic leaves behind" (245).[33]

For Benhabib, this is ultimately a moral question rather than a question about epistemology or ontology: "Should we approach history to retrieve from it the victims' memories, lost struggles, and unsuccessful resistances, or should we approach history to retrieve from it the monotonous succession of infinite 'power/knowledge' complexes that constitute selves?" (1995, 114).[34] Here we see how she conflates a historical question over the force of language and institutions with one of the morality of memory.

How we remember the lives of women is not determined by a historical reading of the causal efficacy of their actions. This stark opposition between agents and constructs blocks out a more perspicuous phrasing of the question of how to read history that both Benhabib and Butler avoid.[35] Should we read the languages that constituted the subjects in question as enabling or damaging forces (or both)? To what extent are our current languages continuous or discontinuous with these languages? We must make an interpretive judgment about whether we want to write a narrative of hermeneutical retrieval or a genealogy that helps us resist and escape. Both Benhabib and Butler/Scott stay away from a hermeneutic understanding of language—Benhabib for the sake of the formal dialogue of legitimacy and Butler/Scott for the sake of their epistemological commitment to the transcendental, sociological, and historical conditions of subjectivity.

This problem points to a larger issue in Butler's and Scott's projects. There is a limit to how far one can read one's predecessors and contemporaries as "dupes" of processes that they do not understand but that are available to the critic armed with a theory and a therapeutic interest. One has to be able to account for one's own ability to escape and for the values that drive this effort. This phrasing of the performative contradiction is historical, not Kantian, as Benhabib's and Habermas's are. Butler's problematic offers no way to discriminate among languages that empower and those that do damage, for this would require more guidance than reference to a transcendental generator of liberty through effects. This problem is nicely dramatized in the following statement by Butler: "If performativity is construed as that power of discourse to produce effects through reiteration, how are we to understand the limits of such production, the constraints under which such production occurs?" (1993, 20). "Effects" has the anti-hermeneutic dimension that characterizes language divested of its axiological character. This useful moment of distanciation must be appropriated by "we," and Butler puts this hermeneutic vocabulary in her sentence—"we" and "understand"; however, she never says how she makes the move from "performativity" and "production" to this "we."[36]

Moreover, this stance objectifies and silences the languages of the past. The ear for otherness is tone deaf toward the multiple achievements of social and literary texts. To be sure, deconstructiveness can open to otherness in a way that is left out by conceptual and humanistic categories such as voice and dialogue. But there is also a loss in trying to escape all humanist vestiges through a vocabulary of "effects," which divests these languages of their appeal and the dialogical relationship we can establish with them. Butler's recourse to a third-person transcendental perspective reproduces the reflective elevation of the philosophical observer out of dialogical perspective on experience by virtue of his or her access to a theoretical model. Of course, the holistic language of hermeneutics—"dialogue," "tradition," "self-understanding," "narrative"—can be broken down into alternative units of analysis that open and redescribe the phenomenological vocabularies of individual and collective actors. This was always the claim of social explanations against "subjectivism." However, to set up an absolute break with these understandings, even if through the auspices of a transcendental argument rather than a theoretical explanation, is a logical and ethical/political mistake.[37]

Butler confronts a similar problem when she speaks of Rosa Parks's agency only through the third-person language of "effects" (1997a, 147) and avoids discussing the resources of the traditions outlined by Beverly Guy-Sheftall's anthology of the history of African American feminist writings.[38] Moreover, Butler's philosophy of language does not help us understand the appeal of Rosa Parks's story, its claim on us. By refusing to move to a hermeneutic vocabulary in which subjects appropriate the "effects" of historicity, she cannot account for women's achievement and action or for the way in which texts move us to political change.[39] The deconstruction of identity and the unquestioned affirmation of difference per se both hide from the question of political judgment. As Nancy Fraser says, "There is no avoiding political judgments about better or worse identities and differences [. . .]. Which identity claims are rooted in the defense of social relations of inequality and domination? And which are rooted in a challenge to such relations?" (1997, 185–186).[40]

A similar problem of judgment arises in Butler's discussion of trauma. Trauma opens a dimension of historicity that is not available in hermeneutics. As Cathy Caruth explains, trauma is not an experience at all, but a skip in experience, in which the subject must check out in order to survive.[41] Traumatized persons, says Caruth, "become the symptom of history they cannot entirely possess" (1995, 5). However, Butler draws on this theory only to extend the distance between the violent construction of subjectivity and our self-understandings. "Social trauma takes the form, not of a structure that repeats mechanically but rather of an ongoing subjugation, the restaging of injury through signs that both occlude and reenact the scene" (1997a, 36). True enough, but now the task is to understand how the effects of trauma are to be ameliorated or "worked through" by witnessing, in which the intersubjective connection and the particulars of representation are crucial. Butler poses this question precisely: "The responsibility of the speaker does not consist of remaking language ex nihilo, but rather of negotiating the legacies of usage that constrain and enable that speaker's speech" (1997a, 27). However, she never addresses the question of how we make political judgments about historical inheritance, preferring to speak only of the "prior," transcendental condition of all languages through such phrases as "citationality."[42]

Although Butler's explorations of the limits of the sayable may expose the inconsistencies and inequalities of our linguistic inheritance, her work leaves us no way of choosing how to live through our languages instead of simply against them. Benhabib's moral certainties, on the other hand, cannot rise above their linguistic historicity. The dispute between Benhabib and Butler, between the separation of individual agency and language and the poststructuralist reading of linguistic agency without persons, comes from an overly grand and monolithic reading of the ambiguous ontological medium of women's being in language and history. An interpretive philosophy needs to be flexible enough to have a place for the complex history of women's internal and external oppression, for women's achievements, for the multiplicity of their languages, and for their revisions in light of causal accounts. The interpreter must make a move that Benhabib's Kantianism and Butler's transcendental linguistic generator prevent. Before developing how these transcendental and historical considerations can be brought together, we need to look at the arguments of the philosopher who argues most vigorously against any recourse to the transcendental, Michel Foucault.

FOUCAULT: HISTORIOGRAPHY AND INTERPRETIVE JUDGMENT

In this section, I do not attempt to survey the complex and diverse work of Foucault. Rather, I have the following goals: first, to show how Foucault's new forms of historical analysis configure the understanding of historical institutions of meaning in a way that the philosophies of thinkers previously discussed in this chapter do not, paying particular attention to his critique of transcendental arguments; second, to examine the ways his projects depend upon an account of institutions of meaning and the subject of judgment that he does not lay out. My point is neither to join Habermas's normative critique, nor to split the difference, as some have tried.[43] Rather, I aim to show how his legitimate critique of phenomenological attempts to link the subject and history does not justify his illegitimate attempt to escape from the problems left by this critique. That is, the subject of research cannot escape from evaluative judgment and the historical readings on which evaluation depends.

The Critique of Phenomenology and Hermeneutics

Although Foucault's work during the period of *The Order of Things* and *The Archaeology of Knowledge* was influenced by structuralism, this work does not search for invariant structures, as we find in both White and Ricoeur. If we want to put Foucault in relation to structuralism, it makes more sense to see him as following Saussure's investigation of *langue* as a historical system. Each system has an internal coherence for a certain slice of time and then is reconfigured in the next slice. This coherence is not available to historical actors, and the changes in the system are abrupt and not informed by the historical reasoning of those living through these changes. Instead, they are available to the investigator who takes a third-person stance toward the systems of meaning. Unlike Saussure, however,

Foucault is not merely interested in rules of language but in a wide range of historical practices and the relationship of these practices to the body. "It is not just in the play of symbols that the subject is constituted. It is constituted in real practices—historically analyzable practices. There is a technology of the constitution of the self which cuts across symbolic systems while using them" (1984, 369).

Unlike traditional historians, however, Foucault is not concerned with events, causes, actions, and facts. His analyses may be termed "interpretive" in the broad sense that they are neither factual nor explanatory. That is, whether in archaeological or genealogical form, Foucault investigated the rules, practices, and institutions that constitute the subjects of modernity. He accuses previous modes of thinking of "hiding from history," because their organizing concepts, such as "transcendental subjectivity," "text," "event," and "commentary" served to cover up, rather than display, the complexities of history and the problems of historiography. Foucault has transcendental subjectivity in his sights, whether in the dialectical historical line of Hegel, Marx, and Sartre, or in the line of Husserl and Heidegger: "Attempting to make historical analysis the discourse of the continuous and to make human consciousness the original subject of all knowledge and all practices are two aspects of the same system of thought. Time is conceived in terms of totalization, and revolution is never anything but reaching awareness" (1994, I, 720).[44]

We can see what Foucault is after if we look briefly at Husserl's treatment of the relationship between the lifeworld—the pregiven constellation of inherited meanings through which we live our everyday lives—and the critical transcendental subject. In Husserl's thought we arrive at objectivity by taking the meanings we inhabit in the natural attitude of daily life and carefully moving them to the object side. To bring this about, the philosopher does not move beyond the pregiven prejudices into a new world view, but instead reengages these pregiven prejudices through the purification of the epoche: "Through the epoche a new way of experiencing, of thinking, of theorizing, is opened to the philosopher; here, situated above his own natural being and above the natural world, he loses nothing at all of the spiritual acquisition of his world-life or those of the whole historical communal life; he simply forbids himself—as a philosopher" (1970, 151–152).[45]

For Foucault, such an approach through the intentionality of the subject keeps the diversity of historical practices from appearing and reduces their historical shifts to "the sediment of the tradition" (1970, 71). Getting clear about historical meanings cannot be done by purifying the intentional activities of empirical subjects but by examining the conditions that produced not only these particular discursive traces but also the practices that never appeared as such in the minds of historical actors.[46]

Foucault is also after Heideggerian analysis, which breaks with Husserl's attempt to work from a transcendental subject. Heidegger puts the subject, Dasein, in the world, in the inheritance of prejudice, rather than oscillating between an empirical and a transcendental subject.[47] For Heidegger, understanding is not just one kind of knowing—as opposed to explaining or making aesthetic judgments. Understanding is not something possessed by a subject but a constituent element of our being-in-the-world. Living in a hermeneutic circle means that we cannot get access to raw data or purified meanings.[48] Heidegger is nonetheless making a transcendental investigation in *Being and Time*—that is, he is laying out the fundamental structures of our being-in-the-world (such as, understanding, disposition) independently of the culture or time period to which we belong. These structures inform daily life but are hidden from it. The path from everyday understanding to a proper philosophical understanding is achieved not by the epoche but through a shift in philosophical problematics that makes authenticity possible. In authentic existence, we move from complacent acceptance of the everyday meanings and norms to the possibilities that emerge in the specific contexts in which we find ourselves. This shift does not deliver us forever from the realm of everyday speech in which we find ourselves; rather, we must always hearken to the call of authenticity, in developing our projects out of the heterogeneous public world of discourse, what Heidegger calls the "they."[49]

For Foucault, replacing Husserl's movement between the transcendental and empirical ego with Heidegger's movement within the hermeneutic circle still leaves us with an analysis that is entirely too narrow and historically vague. Heidegger's transcendental approach, according to Foucault, does not open a space to interrogate the diversity and complexity of history because it stays within the major pathways of subjectivity laid out by different strands of modernist, Christian culture.[50] The subject of research needs to break with inherited meanings and practices in a radical way, and to do so means "to free history from the grip of phenomenology" (Foucault 1972, 203). History is not just an "inheritance," or a "sediment," for the phenomenological subject but a dense articulatory system whose importance for the present and past go unnoticed by these subject-centered conceptions of meaning of Husserl and Heidegger.[51]

Thus, Foucault is opposed to a hermeneutics of trust as well as a hermeneutics of suspicion. I use Ricoeur's well-known distinction as it has been developed by Hubert Dreyfus and Paul Rabinow in their book about Foucault because that book has served to frame the debate between Foucault and hermeneutics.[52] In the hermeneutics of trust, which according to Dreyfus and Rabinow we find in Division I of Heidegger's *Being and Time* as well as in Charles Taylor and Clifford Geertz, the interpreter brings out aspects of the interpretive situation that historical actors may miss but that "they would recognize if it were pointed out to them" (1982, xxi). There is therefore a certain "continuity between everyday intelligibility and the deeper kind of intelligibility which the everyday view works to cover up" (Dreyfus and Rabinow 1982, 123). In a hermeneutics of suspicion, by contrast, such as we find in Freud and Marx as well as in Division II of *Being and Time,* the interpreter points out a motivated cover-up in the historical actor's self-understanding.[53] For Dreyfus and Rabinow, "Foucault captures all such positions" (xxiii) in his definition of commentary: "the reapprehension through the manifest meaning of discourse of another meaning at once secondary and primary, that is, more hidden but also more fundamental" (Foucault 1970, 373, cited in Dreyfus and Rabinow 1982, xxiii). For Foucault, a hermeneutics of trust and one of suspicion both posit a meaning that is not there and a search procedure that is too narrow.

Archaeology

Foucault's alternative to hermeneutics and structuralism in *The Order of Things* and the *Archaeology of Knowledge* is to pursue the historical a priori that governs the discursive production of a period. Foucault is looking for a new point of entry into what I am calling institutions of meaning, and he comes up with the archive. He begins by contrasting an archival analysis with previous "third terms" that mediate subject and object—*langue,* tradition, library (1972, 128–130). Unlike these modes of investigation, the archive is "the law of what can be said, the system that governs the appearance of statements as unique events" (129).[54] The way to investigate the archive is not through an ahistorical formalism or hermeneutics but through the search for the "historical a priori": "what I mean by this term is an a priori that is not a condition of validity for judgments, but a condition of reality for statements. It is not a question of rediscovering what might legitimize an assertion, but of freeing the conditions of emergence of statements" (127). With a priori, Foucault is looking not for transhistorical Kantian categories that would bind both the archaeologist and the historical periods in question, but for the historically specific discursive conditions to which utterances must conform if they are to be candidates for validity. Thus, when Foucault says that he tries "to historicize to the utmost in order to leave as little space as possible to the transcendental," he is not claiming to write empirical history (1989,79).[55]

The archaeologist's task is the reconstruction of these rules without any imposition from the outside that tries to say what is "really" going on or what is "really" true.[56] In other words, Foucault is trying to get around the inside versus the outside problem of hermeneutics, in which interpretation must either recover the subject's meaning from the inside or else impose an interpretation from the outside by recourse to alternative vocabulary, such as the causal forces of economics.

He uses the term "positivities" in the following citation to indicate that he has adopted an uncompromising third-person stance such that his claims are purged of any relationship to the subject: "The positivities that I have tried to establish must not be understood as a set of determinations imposed from the outside on the thought of individuals or inhabiting it from the inside, in advance as it were; they constitute rather the set of conditions in accordance with which a practice is exercised" (1972, 208). What is important is the self-constitution of both subject and object of research for the period in question. As Pascal Michon says, "Scientific topics such as labour, language or life don't have any actual continuity and it is necessary, in order to understand the meaning of these terms, not to reduce them to the so called identity of their anthropological conditions of possibility but to replace them in the general epistemic system, present in the various disciplines, which constitutes the historical a priori" (2002, 167). In other words, archaeological analysis permits the researcher to cut through the surface understandings of the human sciences and to thematize the mode of questioning common to diverse areas of inquiry.

This method attempts to be purely immanent, blocking out the discursive regime through which the historian operates. Although archaeology aspires to a kind of pure description, unlike phenomenological description, it achieves clarification not by performing an epoche on what is pregiven but by a rewriting that achieves exteriority without imposing its own regime of truth.[57] The archaeologist seeks to reveal what has hitherto been hidden by explanatory, hermeneutic, or phenomenological methods: "The reason for using this rather barbarous term is that this a priori must take account [. . .] of the fact that discourse has not only a meaning or a truth, but a history, and a specific history that does not refer back to the laws of an alien development" (Foucault 1972, 127).

To get a sense of how Foucault's immanent critique works, let's look at the notion of the individual as proposed by the social contract of Hobbes and Locke and criticized by Marx. Foucault does not say that the individual is either true with Hobbes or an ideological cover-up of the true story of capitalism with Marx. Instead, he says, "The individual is no doubt the fictional atom of the 'ideological' representation of society; but he is already fabricated by this specific technology of power that I have called discipline [. . .]. Power [. . .] produces reality; it produces domains of objects and rituals of truth" (1977, 194). The idea and practices of "individuality" emerge from a particular discursive constellation and have very real historical consequences. This constellation is not grounded in a truth about the individual or about the historical process.

Hence, instead of the continuities of dialectical Marxist thought or phenomenological analyses, archaeology reveals history as a series of sudden discursive ruptures.[58] If Husserl tries to eliminate any anthropological or psychological residue from his notion of the transcendental subject, Foucault goes further and pushes out any site of meaning conferral: "My aim was to cleanse [history] of all transcendental narcissism" (1972, 203). Nowhere is this clearer than when we look at his treatment of what historians often make the "decisive" modern political event, the French Revolution.

While traditional readings look for the ways that ideology transforms an entire society, Foucault introduces complexities and different temporalities that prevent the Revolution from appearing as a singular event. Discursive practices do not run roughshod over all other practices. "The French Revolution—since up to now all archeological analyses have been centered on it—does not play the role of an event exterior to discourse, whose divisive effect one is under some kind of obligation to discover in all discourse; it functions as a complex, articulated, describable group of transformations that left a number of positivities intact, fixed for a number of others rules that are still with us, and also established positivities that have recently disappeared or are still disappearing before our eyes" (1972, 177).[59] Thus, Foucault permits us to see such particular features as the ways in which the monarchy, the target of ideological attack, was also the source for reform

(Chartier 1997, 60).[60] He also opens up multiple temporal threads of different lines of practices, such as we find in his analysis of incarceration in *Discipline and Punish*. Here he gives separate developmental, temporal lines to the penal policy of detention, to the reduction of torture, and to disciplinary techniques in military, medical, and educational institutions (63).

From the point of view of my argument, we can say at this point that while Foucault's archaeological approach unquestionably opens up important new modes of historical practice, it has left unanswered many questions about the subject of historical judgment and his or her relationship to institutions of meaning. In the next phase of his research, he changes his problematic but continues to avoid these central questions.

Genealogy

In genealogical analyses, Foucault is not concerned with a system of rules but with what he calls the "history of the present" (1977, 31). Unlike the archaeological approach—which does not refer to the historian's present—this kind of analysis departs from the present and examines the way particular practices become part of the technology of power, such as the panopticon or confessional practices. There is no claim to capturing the practices of an entire period. Foucault is still concerned with constitution, but he speaks now of the "*dispositif*" (translated as "construct" or "apparatus") that attaches itself to subjects and objects. Thus, in the *History of Sexuality*, he shows us how "sexuality" was produced: "Sexuality must not be thought of as a kind of natural given which power tries to hold in check, or as an obscure domain which knowledge tries gradually to uncover. It is the name that can be given to a historical construct [*dispositif*]: not a furtive reality that is difficult to grasp, but a great surface network in which the stimulation of bodies, the intensifications of pleasures, the incitement to discourses, the formation of special knowledge [. . .] are linked to one another, in accordance with a few major strategies of knowledge and power" (1978, 105–106).

The subject is constituted not by discursive rules but by an ontology of power that takes hold of the subject's being in history in a way that implodes two of the best-known candidates for the subject of historical judgment: Hegel's dialectical subject and Gadamer's dialogical subject: "We should not be deceived into thinking that this heritage is an acquisition, a possession that grows and solidifies; rather, it is an unstable assemblage of faults, fissures, and heterogeneous layers that threaten the fragile inheritance from within or form underneath" (1984, 82). Foucault aims right for Hegel's Spirit or Gadamer's tradition in which facts and forces are transmuted into society's wisdom. "Knowledge does not detach from its empirical roots, the initial needs from which it arose, to become pure speculation subject only to the demands of reason [. . .]; rather, it creates a progressive enslavement to its instinctual violence" (96). In Hegel's reading of history, "the wounds of the Spirit heal and leave no scars behind. The deed is imperishable; it is taken back by spirit itself, and the aspect of individuality present in it, whether as intentional or as an existent negativity and limitation, straightway vanishes" (Hegel 1977, 407). In Foucault, history carves scars into that body, scars that are passed on: "The body manifests the stigmata of past experience and also gives rise to desires, failings, and errors" (1984, 83).

Thus, traditional history looks in the wrong place to map historical change: "an event is not a decision, a treaty, a reign, or a battle, but the reversal of a relationship of forces." Power and chance are the motors of history. History "operates on a field of entangled and confused parchments, on documents that have been scratched over and recopied many times" (1984, 76). If archaeology organizes into discursive blocks, genealogy fragments time.[61] If archaeology looks for the conditions of possibility of past discursive formations, genealogy looks for the conditions of possibility of change in the present or future. "The point, in brief, is to transform the critique conducted in the form of necessary limitation into a critique that takes the form of a possible transgression." This permits us to "separate out, from the contingency that made us what we are, do or think [. . .]. It [this kind of critique] is seeking to give a new impetus, as far and wide as possible to the undefined work of freedom" (45).

As in archaeological analysis, there is still an antihermeneutical thrust in the genealogical readings. But instead of splitting open the complicity of subject and object by looking for historical a priori as discursive rules, genealogy interprets by thinking through the metaphor of the palimpsest of power. "Whereas the interpreter is obliged to go to the depth of things, like an excavator, the moment of interpretation [genealogy] is like an overview, from higher and higher up, which allows the depth to be laid out in front of him in a more profound visibility; depth is resituated as an absolutely superficial secret" (cited in Dreyfus and Rabinow 1982, 106).

Practices of the Self in the Late Foucault

In his late works *The Uses of Pleasure* and *The Care of the Self,* Foucault changes his approach to subjectivity and history in order to bring into relief the contrast between Greek ethics and modern Christian morality. While the work we have discussed thus far cuts against the grain of modernity's self-understandings using the third-person points of view of archaeology and genealogy, these works explore ethical practices that are not part of the modern frame of reference, practices that moderns have repudiated, ignored, or forgotten. Foucault does not abandon the critique of modernity, but here the critique is offered not by a direct attack but by an articulation of diverse alternative subject formations from "periods when the effect of scientific knowledge and the complexity of normative systems were less" than in modern culture (1984, 339). Unlike "a history of systems of morality based, hypothetically, on interdictions," Foucault wants to write "a history of ethical problematization based on practices of the self" (1985, 13). In doing this history, he gives a place to the subject's agency: recognition and self-constitution, which do not appear in his previous work. For this project, he says, "it seemed appropriate to look for the forms and modalities of the relation to self by which the individual constitutes and recognizes himself qua subject" (1985, 6).[62]

Does his new emphasis on the recognition and agency of historical subjects contradict his earlier work? Béatrice Han puts this question sharply: "The Foucauldian analysis of subjectivity therefore appears to oscillate in a contradictory manner, between a definition of subjectivity as 'self creation,' on the one hand, and on the other hand, the need, in order to understand the games of truth through which recognition itself operates, to go back to the practices of power of which subjects are not masters and are usually not even aware" (Han, 172). This dispute raises important questions for my argument: 1. Are Foucault's archaeological and genealogical critiques of a hermeneutics of the subject historically specific objections to certain modern construals of the question, or are they transhistorical arguments against all such readings, as Han seems to think? 2. Is Foucault arguing against transcendental arguments per se or just the specific ones he cites? 3. How do plural historiographical approaches work together?

Foucault discusses the change in method in the beginning of *The Use of Pleasure*, but he does not criticize his previous modes of historicizing, either here or in interviews. He speaks of his long-standing concerns with subjectivity and truth and says the change in these works comes from a change in what is being investigated—that is, a change from theoretical (*The Order of Things*) and coercive practices (*Discipline and Punish*) to practices of the self.[63] In these earlier works, he wasn't attempting to explode self-constituting subjectivity per se but to criticize certain practices of subjectivation he saw in modernity. Second, he was not arguing for the necessary exclusivity of archaeology or genealogy by calling them a "method" or by making a transcendental argument on their behalf. Rather, they are historiographical strategies he deploys against particular narratives and assumptions, not inescapable truths.

Making genealogy a strategy rather than a necessity does not mean that any approach goes regardless of whether it contradicts other approaches. When Foucault examines practices of self-constitution in these late works, he is careful not to phrase his ideas on constitution in terms of the Husserlian or Heideggerian assumptions that he criticized earlier: "If now I am interested, in fact, in the way in which the subject constitutes himself in an active fashion, by practices of self, these practices are nevertheless something that the individual invents himself. They are patterns that he finds in his culture and which are proposed, suggested, and imposed on him by his culture, his society, and his social group" (1988, 11).[64] His concept of practice does show Heideggerian echoes, but this idea of practice is not tied to the Heideggerian anthropology of *Being and Time* or to the history of being of the late Heidegger. Foucault continues to reject phenomenologies of subjectivity that block out the historian's ability to let the specificity of historically diverse practices of subjectivation appear: "What I refused was precisely that you first of all set up a theory of the subject—as could be done in phenomenology and in existentialism—and that, beginning from the theory of the subject, you come to pose the question of knowing, for example, how such and such a form of knowledge was possible" (1988, 10).

Thus, Foucault's conception of self-constitution is thin, even though he cannot dispense with all transcendentals—for instance, a conception of subjectivity, practice, and historicity.[65] "Men have never ceased to construct themselves, i.e., to continually displace their subjectivity, to constitute themselves in a multiple and infinite series of different subjectivities, which will not end and will never place us in front of something which would be man" (1994, IV, 75). These transcendentals open a historically thick reality that can be examined either through a genealogical unmasking of self-understandings or through a sympathetic reconstruction. Practices of the subject do not deny agency; rather, they make it historically specific. We do not have a metaphysical division between historical determination and noumenal freedom. Whether to read the historical archives through the optic of archaeology, genealogy, or practice is a matter of the judgment and purposes of the historian.

What misleads critics—aside from their desire for a single answer to how we should read the history of subjectivity—is Foucault's reluctance to talk about the agency of the historian in the process of making choices or about the principles and purposes that inform his judgment. It seems that Foucault tells a genealogical tale about what he wants to criticize and a self-constituting story about what he wants to retrieve, although he never makes the politics of historiographical reasoning explicit.[66] This reticence is exacerbated by the fact that he employs the problematic of practices of the self with historically distant epochs, thus leaving open the question of what aspects of modernity he would read in this more sympathetic way.[67] Foucault would certainly acknowledge that he brings ethical and historiographical assumptions to the archives he studies, but he does not connect political judgment, historicity, and public imagination.

Critique of Foucault

My critique of Foucault begins with this refusal to elaborate a site of judgment. That is, his analyses depend upon historical institutions of meaning and a conception of judgment in a way that he refuses to acknowledge. (In this, he parallels Habermas, even though they give different views of the history of modernity.) In *Archaeology*, he admits, "For the moment, and as far ahead as I can see, my discourse, far from determining the locus in which it speaks, is avoiding the ground on which it could find support" (1972, 205). He also tries to defer the question by saying that it is not possible to describe our own archive "since it is from within these rules that we speak" (130). As many commentators have pointed out, this methodology is not coherent. Can the historian simply leap out of his discursive regime to reconstruct the past? Isn't this possibility blocked by Foucault's own understanding of history as radical rupture? Even when he is concerned with the "history of the present," his genealogies treat the present merely as an object—confessional practices—not as part of the site of judgment.

Thus, even though Foucault's later work gives new importance to the ethical self-constitution of ancient Greek subjectivities, it does not respond to my objection.[68] These premodern practices are simply the object of historical study, disconnected from the historical judgment of the modern interpreter. In his late work as in his early work, he fails to thematize the interpretive judgment of the subject of his own texts. The problematic of the late work does not "complement" the third-person problematics of the earlier work; rather, it leaves the same lacuna.

This is not to say that I endorse Habermas's well-known criticism that Foucault falls into a "performative contradiction" by presupposing normative criteria that he has theoretically excluded: "To the extent that it retreats into the reflectionless objectivity of a nonparticipatory, ascetic description of kaleidoscopically changing practices of power, genealogical historiography emerges from its cocoon as precisely the *presentistic, relativistic, crypto-normative* illusory science that it does not want to be" (Habermas 1987, 275–276, emphasis in the original). What Foucault has shown is that carving out a moral core from the "Enlightenment" through formal transcendental arguments about ahistorical shapes and norms and subjectivity is not only theoretically impossible but ethically and politically damaging. Habermas's argument excuses the philosopher from understanding the ways that political judgment is tied not simply to principles but to a reading of historical shapes of public imagination and the possibilities in the past and the future. We can't simply be for or against the Enlightenment ideals of equality and justice, as if they were a policy to be instituted or a presupposition that we could deduce. Rather, "the Enlightenment" released an avalanche of discourse and technology that shaped and continues to shape modern society. The apparatus of modernity flew under, around, and through the radar of the categorical imperative, and it continues to do so as the informational web spreads. Habermas's history from the normative skycam vindicates Foucault's suspicion here. We need to criticize Foucault's positions not from an ahistorical normative standpoint but with an account of political judgment that depends upon history.

Rather than using the word "normative," I will use the broader term "evaluative" to speak about what is missing from Foucault's accounts.[69] We find historical changes, whether in archaeological blocks or genealogical fragments, but never historical transitions, in which gains and losses of historical change are examined. Foucault claims his work enables us to "separate out, from the contingency that made us what we are, the possibility of no longer being, doing or thinking what we are, do or think" (1984, 45). But doing so requires that assessments and descriptions work together. When pressed on this issue, Foucault tries to dodge evaluation, saying, "My point is not that everything is bad but that everything is dangerous" (343). Dangerous for whom?[70] Are all things equally dangerous? Aren't things dangerous for different reasons? It's as if all changes must be greeted without evaluation because to speak of "transition" between discursive regimes might preserve a continuity that Foucault seeks to eliminate.

Moreover, by depriving the subject of research of a present and an evaluative language, he blocks all first-order challenges to discursive regimes in the past and present—by writers, political actors, and anyone else. This produces its own homogenization of the past. Can Romanticism, for instance, be folded back into discursive regimes that preceded it?[71] This need for evaluative language becomes even more heightened in Foucault's suggestions about the subject "who tries to invent himself" (1984, 42) or tries to turn her life into "a work of art" (350). Where does this freedom come from? How are we to understand its relationship to the past? It is one thing to say that "'we' must not be prior to the question" (385) so that we do not revolve within our own assumptions, and quite another to drive it out altogether. Yet in order to talk about these possibilities, Foucault needs an account of the first-order languages of everyday life and their historicity that takes up their constitutive, evaluative dimension from the inside as well as the outside.

Thus, Foucault's historiography offers resources for political judgment that are missing from the structuralist and Derridean modes of thinking of White, Butler, and Scott as well as the formalism of Ricoeur. To be sure, Foucault has not connected public imagination to practical reason in a satisfying way; however, he has shown that no theory of public reason can avoid engaging the diverse historical practices of culture. The task of the next chapter will be to connect the rich historical thinking made available by Foucault to a conception of public imagination and practical reason.

3 Reasoning through Public Imagination

Although philosophers have given considerable attention to the thought of Charles Taylor and his major work *Sources of the Self,* they have tended to misclassify him as simply a political communitarian or a hermeneutic philosopher in the same school as Ricoeur.[1] Literary theory over the past ten years has just ignored him. At first glance it may appear easy to see why. First, his readings of literature seem old fashioned, relying on critics from a generation ago, such as M. H. Abrams, Earl Wasserman, and Lionel Trilling; second, he appears to tell a grand metanarrative about modernity;[2] third, he has very limited engagement with the poststructuralist and neomarxist thinkers who dominate current literary theory. This neglect of Taylor is unfortunate because his misunderstood problematic can help overcome one of the central problems in philosophy and literary theory today: how to understand literature's role in connecting public imagination to practical reason and history. As we saw in chapter 2, literary theorists frame the question of meaning through third-person problematics that make culture and history only the objects of judgment without saying how they inform the site of judgment. In my reconstruction, I want to show how Taylor's problematic gives a space to the deep ontological critique dear to poststructuralists without abandoning the space of deliberation altogether. What is important for my purposes is not Taylor's reading of individual figures or his assessment of different features of modernity, which are obviously controversial, but the presentation of the connection between public imagination and practical reason.

One of the reasons that critics are misled into reading *Sources* as a metanarrative is that it bears a structural resemblance to Hegel's *Phenomenology of Spirit*. Both begin with a transcendental argument against an atomistic conception of the subject and then proceed to give a reconstruction of the historical background to this transcendental argument. Clarifying the nature of Taylor's transcendental argument, however, will dispel such misunderstandings.

Like other transcendental arguers, Taylor adopts this mode of reasoning because his challenge to modern self-understandings is global rather than local; he cannot address them head-on in the languages of the existing debates. What differentiates Taylor's position is how he understands the relationship of the subject to institutions of meaning, a relationship that emerges in the way he defines transcendental arguments. Such arguments "start from some feature of our experience which they claim to be indubitable and beyond cavil. They then move to a stronger conclusion, one concerning the nature of the subject or the subject's position in the world. They make this move by regressive arguments, to the effect that the stronger conclusion must be so if the indubitable fact about experience is possible" (Taylor 1995b, 20). Taylor's concern will be to leverage a certain phenomenological account of experience that can provide a perspicuous description of the strains of modernity that he wants to advocate as well as of those that he urges us to repudiate.

Taylor aims his argument at modernity's disengaged conceptions of reason, both theoretical and practical, and seeks to rule them out as impossible points of departure—for example, positivistic theoretical reasoning as well as Kantian and utilitarian practical reasoning. What these projects share is an effacement of the good and the proper ontological understanding of the subject's relationship to institutions of meaning. Unlike Kant's transcendental argument for the ahistorical necessity of the categories, Taylor's "transcendental argument was from the beginning situated in an historical context" (1998a, 37). Unlike Hegel's account, Taylor's posits no unified Spirit, no transsubjective, absolute narrator, and no dialectical progression. Instead of Butler's transcendental structural absence that replays itself through time, we have a transcendental argument that depends upon historical vindication.[3]

Nonetheless, the reader still might wonder why we should not take one of the Foucauldian stances, in which transcendental conditions are the objects under investigation rather than linked to both the subject and object of investigation. Don't transcendental arguments seem to make a danger-ously ethnocentric move in which one's own cultural assumptions are gen-eralized as the necessary assumptions of all cultures—including the cultures in one's own past? What about the simple anthropological point that Taylor's assumptions about such ideas as "the self" are Western and not universal?[4] Isn't this precisely the problem with Heidegger's transcen-dental anthropology of *Being and Time,* in which the diverse historical prac-tices of the West disappear behind the anguish of modernity that has lost touch with Being?

Taylor argues that transcendental investigation produces just the oppo-site effect—if we do it properly.[5] In seeking out the transcendental back-ground that subtends our first-order speech, Taylor does not aim to give rules of validity but to present the presuppositions and horizons of the pos-sible that cradle our sentences. If we enter a debate only with our position and those of others arrayed as individual positions, we miss points of simi-larity and difference that appear when we articulate backgrounds to our positions and the horizon of the possible that surrounds our individuated philosophical stances. When we see our present position as a possible out-come of a constellation of conditions that underpin it, then we have opened our own resources of debate: "Ethnocentrism [. . .] is also a consequence of collapsing the distinction between the transcendental conditions and the actual content of a culture" (Taylor 1989, 40).

In other words, there are no brute facts or values; nor are there singular statements of position. The articulation of a particular position on, say, the nature of autonomy, secularism, or negotiation in public life depends upon large-scale assumptions about language, subjectivity or historicity, and his-torical arguments.[6] Thus, transcendental conditions are not formal but descriptive and historical—how do you (individually and collectively) articu-late yourself as an historico-linguistic being? The history will involve not only developing the lines of argument that led to the current position but also making intelligible the discarded strands—for instance, positivism. Spelling these out will widen the argumentative space of discussion, though it will not necessarily lead to more agreement.

Yes, it would have been helpful if *Sources of the Self* had included a long section on the relationship of Western conceptions of subjectivity to some nonwestern conceptions and their histories.[7] However, to link his "a priori" to an idea of a formal subject per se across the globe is to miss Taylor's point. By opening with a transcendental argument, Taylor is providing a horizon of assessment and a horizon of the possible for the historical section—that is, so that he can, for instance, show the appeal of Romantic expressivism and positivism and why it is worth retrieving some of the former and discarding the assumptions of the latter. In his view, philosophy cannot abstract itself from its histories in the Kantian manner of Habermas or in the objectivist Foucauldian or constructivist manner. Taylor's appeal to transcendental argument also blocks any flat-footed appeal to history or identity as a ground. We saw this in Rawls's empirical appeal to the sedimented traditions of the American legal system in the introduction, and we'll see it in Rorty's appeal to "Western democracy" later in this chapter. Taylor is making a transcendental argument for transcendental arguments as the unavoidable, implicit horizon of possibility that surrounds one's particular claim in everyday life as well as in academic debates. No historical sociology of institutions of meaning, for instance, can get off the ground without implying such a philosophical argument. We are now ready to examine the substance of Taylor's philosophy.

EVALUATIVE FRAMEWORKS AND THE SUBJECT OF JUDGMENT

The understanding against which Taylor's transcendental argument is directed is the "pervasive bewitchment" that informs much of our moral and epistemological thinking—that we can live without evaluative frameworks: "Doing without frameworks is utterly impossible for us; otherwise put, [. . .]the horizons through which we live our lives and which make sense of them have to include strong qualitative discriminations" (1989, 27). We do not choose to commit to evaluative frameworks; rather, evaluative frameworks are logically prior to choice and reflection: "The point of view from which we might constate that all orders are equally arbitrary, in particular that moral views are equally so, is just not available to us humans. It is a form of self-delusion to think that we do not speak from a moral orientation which we take to be right. That's a condition of being a functioning self, not a metaphysical view we can put on or off" (99).[8] Two of the modern moral traditions that try to avoid such frameworks are naturalism and Kantianism. The naturalist tradition from Hobbes to Rorty links desire and the good in a purely instrumental and unmediated way.[9] Meaning in this view is understood as a projection by humans onto a morally neutral world (Taylor 1989, 53–62). Kantians, on the other hand, come up with a two-part self, a self-legislating part, the self of justice, and a utilitarian desiring part.[10] A third version of this disengaged subject appears early in Sartre's work and elsewhere, as the subject who stands over against his or her moral dilemmas, as if the moral dilemma had an objective intelligibility independently of evaluative frameworks.[11] A fourth version is the Foucauldian positivism that we saw in the last chapter, in which the evaluative frameworks of the subject of inquiry are bracketed.

Taylor brings this idea of evaluative frameworks to language through his conception of strong evaluations, that is, of second-order desires that evaluate our first-order wishes: "Whereas for the simple weigher what is at stake is the desirability of different consummations, those defined by de facto desires, for the strong evaluator reflection also examines the possibility of different modes of being of the agent" (1985b, 25). Strong evaluations "aren't just more desirable; they command our awe, respect, admiration" (1989, 19–20). Because we are inescapably embedded in these languages of strong evaluation, they partially constitute our experience rather than merely describing it. The languages of such interpretations cannot be disarticulated from who we are: "Our self-interpretations are partly constitutive of our experience [. . .], [which is] not to say that we alter our description and then as a result our experience of our predicament alters." Rather, it is that "certain modes of experience are not possible without certain self-descriptions" (1985b, 37).[12] That is, what is at stake here is not the phenomenology of an individual subject, but an argumentative space in the inherited discourse of a culture that is inhabited and affirmed by the speaker: "The meanings and norms implicit in [. . .] practices are not just in the minds of the actors but are out there in the practices themselves [. . .]. These must be the common property of the society before there can be any question of anyone entering a negotiation or not" (1985c, 36). This view is interested not just in the consensus or divergence of belief among individual subjects but in the institutions of meaning that make consensus and difference possible: "Intersubjective meanings are a condition of a certain kind of profound cleavage, such as was visible in the Reformation, or the American Civil War, or splits in left-wing parties, where the dispute is at a fever pitch just because each side can fully understand the other" (1985c, 36–37).[13]

It is here that Foucault's advocates would want to object that limiting ourselves to the surface meaning and its background boxes historiography into a search for how past actors and societies understood themselves. It is worth pursuing Dreyfus and Rabinow's Foucauldian critique of this very text in order to clarify Taylor's position. While acknowledging that Taylor's approach is superior to the positivistic one that he is criticizing in the essay, Dreyfus and Rabinow claim that such a hermeneutics is limited. Taking the example of Taylor's reading of the countercultural movement in America during the 1960s, Dreyfus and Rabinow claim that the social actors "were quite mistaken about their own significance, and so a hermeneutic which attempted to get inside and explicate their point of view would necessarily be equally mistaken" (1982, 164). These meanings "are themselves the products of long-range subjectifying trends in our culture" (164), and the ways in which the movement was coopted by the existing power structures only underline this fact. They conclude that his approach, therefore, should be abandoned for Foucault's.[14]

For the sake of argument, let's say that they are right about the counter-cultural movement's self-understandings. However, it hardly follows from this local point that Taylor's problematic is wrong. Taylor is telling us how to reconstruct the self-interpretations of social actors and insisting on their importance as one feature of our reading of events. He is not taking the absurd position that the only way to understand historical events is through the actors' self-understandings. He affirms that we can resort to explanatory or genealogical strategies for interpretation—rather than the actors' shared meanings—but that when and how we do depends on the historian's judgment and arguments, precisely the arguments that Foucault never puts on the table.

The researcher's judgment in particular cases is not determined by a methodology or cast into decisionism. Instead, judgment is informed by a space of reasoning described in the opening of *Sources,* a space that we will develop as the chapter progresses. Taylor's transcendental argument aims to block out, as starting points, approaches to institutions of meaning and their histories that claim to stand completely outside what they are treating—as Foucault does. This not only evaporates the workings of the researcher's judgment that need to be argued through; it also risks homogenizing history by eliminating, through a theoretical principle, the self-understandings of historical actors as the site of historical innovation.[15]

Holism as such, however, is not what makes Taylor's position distinctive; he sharply distinguishes himself from such holists as Richard Rorty, Stanley Fish, and Donald Davidson, as we'll see later. The key to his distinctiveness is his presentation of the subject's relationship to institutions of meaning. This conception of being in the world asks us to understand language not just as a tool of description—as in "my characterization of this table as brown" (1985b, 36)—but as a means of "articulation." Articulations are not "characterizations of a fully independent object" but "attempts to formulate what is initially inchoate, or confused, or badly formulated. But this kind of formulation or reformulation does not leave its object unchanged. To give a certain articulation is to shape our sense of what we hold important in a certain way" (1985b 36; cf. 1989, 28).

Taylor's ontological conception of meaning, of what I call public imagination, challenges modernity's separation of culture into spheres of inquiry, truth, morality, and art, which we find in theorists from Kant to Weber and Habermas, and the portrait of disengaged subjectivity that goes with it. The dominant conceptions of modernity fail to understand properly the subject's being in the world and its institutions, which is prior to any such divisions. (Taylor is not denying that there are different genres of discourse.) Because the disengaged account of subjectivity is so deeply ingrained in the modern self-understanding, Taylor is frequently misread as an idealizing holist or a "communitarian." He is not advocating community, nor is he making an empirical claim about moral agreement in contemporary society; instead, he is articulating the ontological commitments of historical, linguistic beings through transcendental argument.[16] His claim is that the disengaged conception of the subject, which came about in part to accommodate difference, in fact, has contributed to effacing it, a perspective developed in chapter 1.

Thus, we can think of transcendental argument as giving the conditions of reading the multiple shapes of public imagination either synchronically or diachronically. Taylor's problematic is unlike the abstract systems of culture constructed by Lévi-Strauss or Clifford Geertz not simply because of its hermeneutic construal of the subject of research but because it does not lock us into reading historical actors only through the abstract schemas of a linguistic system. These schemas have been rightly criticized by historians for overlooking contextual forces and the interpretive activity of historical actors.[17] We are now ready to look at how Taylor's embedded subject reasons, and the place to start is with his conception of "articulation."

ARTICULATION

"Articulation" means making explicit the tacit background of moral life, the background that permits us to define moral dilemmas to begin with, before the question of action is posed. What is being made explicit is the public imagination(s) through which societies constitute themselves. This background concerns not just language but the implicit and explicit practices that inform, but do not determine, social action.[18] Linking self-understandings and actions to practices shifts the locus of reasoning away from rules into local historical contexts; however, insisting that we attend to practices as ways of interpreting does not entail that we reproduce the language of the community, as critics of Wittgenstein and Heidegger often assert. Instead, the interpreter has a range of articulatory options from genealogy to Taylor's own version of hermeneutics.[19] Moreover, this public imagination or "social imaginary," to use Taylor's phrase, is not made up only of moral, legal, and political concepts, but also includes images and stories of art and culture.[20] I will divide articulation into three parts: (1) The contrast between the articulation of background and Kantian moral reasoning; (2) the historical dimension of articulation; (3) the speculative aspect of articulation common to art, philosophy, and everyday speech.

Moral Articulation

Articulation opens to scrutiny the resources and damage of what epistemological, social, and moral theories try to avoid or rationalize away—the historical shapes of culture. Arguing through articulation means rejecting the familiar oscillation between factual assertion and normative assessment since this move depends upon the absolute boundary between the object of judgment and the subject of evaluation that Taylor blocks.[21] Thus, a work of literature, such as Toni Morrison's *Beloved*, to take up our example from chapter 2, goes back to the slave narrative form and articulates an emotional and historical landscape that was not only inaccessible to Harriet Jacobs and Frederick Douglass but that subsequent writers and historians had failed to make available to public imagination. The narrator's voice, situated in an uncertain space of remembrance, opens a traumatic scar that has been historically closed off. Literature's engagement with the languages of public imagination shows that political dialogue is not confined to hair-splitting over the definitions of concepts; rather, literature argues with the ways that moral concepts, images, and situations are woven together in different sites of institutions of meaning. Attention to the embedded subject's languages and modes of articulation enables Taylor to give a historical finesse and particularity that is missing from the homogenizing holism often characteristic of the historiographical school associated with this kind of research, the history of mentalités, the study of the structures of the mental life of everyday people.[22] Taylor's holism must also be distinguished from Fish's pragmatist holism, in which history's contextual particularity dissolves political judgment. Fish gives an external third-person account of linguistic community that reduces historical change to jumps from one problematic to another divorced from an evaluative language or conception of rationality.[23]

Accessing Taylor's mode of argument means that the task of rationality cannot be divided, in Habermasian fashion, between the theoretical account of the rules of speaking, on the one hand, and the normative account of morality, on the other. Such an account simply evaporates public imagination into shared meaning. The philosophical project of reconstruction, which, by seeking to "explain the presumably universal bases of rational experience and judgment, as well as of action and linguistic communication" (Habermas 1990b, 16), drives out the shaping, constitutive dimension of language through the search for underlying rules. The truth of language is in front of it, in its disclosures and claims, not behind it in a generative matrix. Taylor's critique is not merely of discourse ethics but also of the pretensions of interpretive social science used to map reason more accurately than the dialogues of culture and literature. For Taylor, unlike Habermas, the key point of the dialogical conception of language is "not the presuppositions of communicative action, but rather the way in which human identity is formed through dialogue and recognition [. . .] of a crucial human good, and not simply on the pragmatic contradiction involved in the violation of certain norms" (Taylor 1991, 252–253).[24]

For Taylor, we should abandon the search for universalized moral rules that can swing free of life forms, that can stand "outside the perspectives in the dispute [. . .],[for] there cannot be such considerations" (1989, 73); instead, we reason by seeking "to articulate a framework [. . .], to try to spell out what is it that we presuppose when we make a judgment that a certain form of life is truly worthwhile, or place our dignity in a certain achievement" (26). In his view, Habermas, like Rawls, is surreptitiously appealing to the good and hence misdescribing his claims: "We have to draw on the sense of the good that we have in order to decide what are adequate principles of justice" since the good "gives the point of the rules which define the right" (89). It is "the background understanding surrounding any conviction that we ought not to act in this or that way that procedural theory cannot articulate" (87).[25] Since Taylor is making a transcendental claim, he argues that utilitarians, Kantians, and Foucauldians are strong evaluators who misdescribe themselves.[26] Thus, he is contesting not the priority of justice to other goods, but the way in which modern conceptions of justice exempt themselves from the ontological reach of institutions by generating an alternative self or ahistorical meanings.

Because the neo-Kantian self-understanding cannot attain the ahistorical, procedural, thin subject, the neutrality of its appeals to justice is "not a possible meeting ground for all cultures but is the political expression of one range of culture and quite incompatible with other ranges" (Taylor 1994a, 62). Because liberal and Habermasian projects rest on unexamined cultural and historical assumptions, they hide from view, rather than thematizing and making vulnerable to interlocutors, an individual's or collective subject's historical baggage. One does not reach common ground through procedural abstraction, for the deliberative process put in motion by liberal procedures drives out of play the hermeneutic work by which common ground is achieved. Since abstracting from moral intuitions makes one "incapable of understanding any moral argument at all," we have no choice but to engage the moral intuitions of our interlocutor (Taylor 1989, 73). This is not to say that procedural justice has never been effective or will not be in the future but that it depends upon unacknowledged commitments.

Instead of trying to make moral reasons stand outside all ethical frameworks in order to serve as an absolute check against different moral intuitions, we need to think in terms of "a qualitative distinction between ways of being, distinguishing a 'higher' or strongly valued way from its lower" (Taylor 1995a, 138). Since ethical/aesthetic goods are in touch with intuitions, not set against them, we argue our way in and out of identities and traditions. We are not claiming to catapult to an epistemologically and morally disengaged view in which all cultural histories are simply the objects of discourse that do not inform the site of interpretive judgment: "You will only convince me by changing my reading of moral experience, and in particular my reading of my life's story, of the transitions I have lived through—or perhaps have refused to live through" (Taylor 1989, 73). (I will return to transitions later in the chapter.)

Articulation and History

Moreover, the articulation of "background" also has a historical dimension that is completely missing from Habermas's conception of "background," a notion that designates the innocuous inarticulate medium that serves "as intuitively known, unproblematic, [and] unanalyzable" (Habermas 1987, 298). Taylor's articulations interrogate this space, seeking "to transfer what has sunk to the level of an organizing principle for present practices and hence beyond examination into a view for which there can be reasons either for or against" (Taylor 1984b, 28). Hence, Taylor wants to begin reasoning by reopening the assumptions of modernity and displaying the complex, conflicted historical inheritance that lies behind current usage. This means learning to reason historically about how we came to be who we are today by "undo[ing] forgetting" (28). Such a project is interpretive, not reconstructive, because the self-understandings and changes of the past cannot just be described and explained. Theory must also simultaneously evaluate. Such evaluations can take various forms, from "escaping from given social forms"—we could call this the Foucauldian response—to the recovery of lost practices—we could call this the hermeneutic dimension (39).[27]

Therefore, Taylor contests Habermas's Hegelian claims as much as he does the Kantian ones. Taylor does not see the self as a historical deposit dropped off by the cunning of history just prior to the advent of Kantian democracy. His point in retelling the story of modernity is to show that historical consciousness is about articulatory critique and retrieval in relationship to our predecessors, not an Hegelian *Errinerung*—that is, both remembrance and interiorization. Reasoning means digging into the wounds and the damaged languages that underwrite current practices and listening to the challenges of others against whom we have defined ourselves. In order to understand and defend a vision of the good, we must rely on "a certain reading of its genesis" (Taylor 1989, 73) and its historical reworkings. The Kantian in Habermas holds the formal moral truth that we already know outside of history, while the Hegelian side unifies the background through an account of achievements of modern rationality. For Taylor, history is not over in either of these senses: "The articulation of modern understandings of the good has to be a historical enterprise [. . .]. The very fact of this self-definition in relation to the past induces us to re-examine this past and the way it has been assimilated or repudiated" (103). Taylor's project of rationality seeks to ferret out and assess the background assumptions of the present lifeworld, not simply accept them as decided. Background for Taylor is the ambiguous historical/cultural medium through which we live but which we can never stand over or against, or take as given.[28]

Art as Speculative Argument

Such a conception of the social imaginary means the Habermasian understanding of the distinction between theory and practice needs to be revised. The institutions of the social imaginary are to be explored not only by the theoretical constructions about the rules of discourse or by causal historical processes, but by the speculative dimension of language that is in the potential of all speech, which literature and philosophy develop.[29]

Taylor's idea of public imagination explicitly rejects the subjectivization of aesthetics that we find in Habermas, like Kant and Weber, in which art becomes a matter of merely individual expression rather than an argument with the shape of public imagination.[30] Every utterance is an event of language that touches ontological, normative, and epistemological issues simultaneously. Philosophy's task is not to content itself with the insight that we are linguistic constructs or to seek truth and goodness beyond these "linguistic appearances" but to unfold the potential and the historicity of the medium that constitutes us. The speaker's relationship to public imagination is not just that of rule instantiator, as it is for Habermas and structuralists, nor is it the dupe of a symbolic order that only the poststructuralist theorist can decipher. Instead, speakers can interrogate the web of belief through first-order speech. This interrogation is neither theoretical nor observational; it emerges whenever we feel a tug on the threads of language. Hence, art, like philosophy, is one of the means for articulating the social imaginary through which we inhabit the lifeworld and make our backgrounds explicit.

Taylor boldly states this defiance of the methods of social science and the claims of philosophy and literature: "We delude ourselves if we think a philosophical or critical language is somehow more hard-edged and more free from personal index than that of poets or novelists" (1989, 510). This is not to say that I agree with Taylor's canon or with his emphasis on "epiphantic poetry" over prose. What I am emphasizing is the new space of deliberation that he opens up, not how he fills it in. Thus, the question for my argument is not, as Rorty says in his critique of Taylor, whether one "prefers Heideggerian and Rilkean gratitude [Taylor] rather than simply Deweyan or Whitmanian social hope" [Rorty] (1994, 200), but how one conceives of one's relationship to linguistic institutions.

Taylor rejects the idea that literature is only "a means of arranging the order of our internal lives by making an harmonious pattern of extremely complex attitudes, once thought to refer to an external order of metaphysics, but now seen to be a symbolic ordering of our inner selves" (1989, 490–491).[31] Literature, like other forms of discourse, discloses the world, makes claims for its superiority to rival configurations of the social imaginary. What is important for my project is that literature brings out what is already or potentially in everyday speech. Literature is not about mere imitation or the evocation of the ineffable.[32] As a way of developing the role of literature in Taylor's idea of practical reason, I will address some of the objections to his project since many of them are focused on his idea of literature as public imagination.

In his critique of Taylor, Gary Gutting, for instance, grants that literature has a certain objectivity, but then immediately falls back on subjective perspectivism—a position Taylor explicitly attacks—as a way of reconciling objectivity and plurality: "The objectivity of Proust's vision does not give it universal validity in the ordinary sense. It is a valid perspective on reality, but it is still Proust's perspective" (Gutting, 135).[33] But Proust is not casting his text into some vague aesthetic constellation; he is arguing with many of the received truths of the public imagination articulated by philosophers, social scientists, and literary writers. Proust is offering not "a perspective on reality" but a ground-up argument about how we are in the world. In Proust's case, as in many others, the novelist is making a kind of transcendental argument—that is, reworking common assumptions in order to leverage a large-scale revision in our vocabularies. Literary statements, just like everyday conversation, cannot be sequestered from the background and transcendental arguments implied through them. This is not to say that I agree with Proust's claim; writers can be wrong, just like anyone else, and the institutions of aesthetics should not insulate them from criticism any more than they should insulate the rest of the discursive universe from their claims. What literature shares with utterances in everyday life and in public political deliberations is that it is an argument with the languages of the social imaginary. What Taylor's account of subjectivity rules out is the picture of the disengaged subject who reads Proust's novel as one statement among a host of others displayed before her. In Taylor's view—and in some ways in Proust's as well—we are always already in the public imagination, committed to certain argumentative symbolic and narrative shapes. These shapes are not purely subjective desires, nor are they objective like the objects of the physical universe.

This is not to say that all literature necessarily has something to say about politics and public debate. However, it does mean that art should not simply be reduced to personal expression.[34] Whether a literary work—or any other public statement—has a purchase on public morality is not a question decided upfront; it must be argued out, just like any other claim.

Indeed, literature can be an important resource in exploring the domain of the political, the domain that normatively focused political theory misses precisely because literature, like philosophy, explores the constitution of social space (Lefort 1988, 11–12).

Literature can also help us answer another question posed by Taylor's critics: whether Taylor's embedded subjects are capable of open deliberation. Joel Anderson phrases this question tellingly: "It is hard to see why differences between individuals regarding the value they attach to certain projects, relationships, and ideals do not have to be viewed as evidence that one of them (at least) is mistaken [. . .]. [For example,] if my commitment to promoting humanistic education realizes an important good, then no one else can be justified in failing to share this commitment" (Anderson 1996, 25). In other words, if these goods are so deeply intertwined with my identity that they "play a role in individuating me as the individual I am" (27), how can I be open to reasoning about them? We can understand how objectivity and plurality of values can go together by thinking of conflicting arguments of literary traditions. For example, *Madame Bovary* objectifies values to which I am connected by virtue of a shared tradition, but the intelligibility and appeal of these values do not lock me into agreement. In fact, I, like Henry James, Kate Chopin, and Proust, profoundly disagree with Flaubert's portrayal of language, moral reality, and desire. This disagreement is articulated through other resources of the public imagination. My point is that being socialized into certain traditions so that their goods and narratives are intelligible in no way programs a particular outcome. Moreover, the objectivity of goods—that is, the fact that they are in the world, not that they are closer to truth—carries no particular relationship to generalizability (Anderson, 32). Some goods, such as equal respect, may claim wide generalizablity, while others, such as the relative worth of two alternative careers, may not.

What Taylor is working out is the subject's relationships to institutions of meaning in order to offer "a third possibility" between "an extra-human ontic foundation for the good on the one hand, and the pure subjectivism of arbitrarily conferred significance on the other" (1989, 342). This third possibility does not decide in advance our relationship to the medium of meanings and forces in which we find ourselves. Nonetheless, it does not make us relativistic; nor does it leave us caught between the "radical constructivism" of the linguistic turn and the "positivism" of documentary claims, such as we find in White, Butler, and others. Instead, Taylor insists that our languages or schemas can be ranked "and ranked because they permit us to grasp, or prevent us from grasping, features of reality, including causal features, which we recognize as independent of us" (1991, 220).[35] Taylor grounds the superiority of a particular language not by saying that it has finally latched on to the external world or to a final good but by appealing to "our best self-interpretation" (1989, 342). The idea of best self-interpretation includes transcendental arguments that emerge to address the particular historical dilemmas of the time; rather than serving as a deep structural feature of every historical moment, such an argument opens perspectives on the historical background. This account of meaning has consequences for how we understand change.

TRANSITIONAL ARGUMENTS AND HISTORY

We are now ready to address Taylor's understanding of change, whether this change is in the public imagination(s) of a particular culture or in the individual who deliberates about particular issues. The first part of this section is concerned with the philosophical/literary issues of practical reason and transition. The second section shows how this view is not relativist through a brief contrast with Rorty's "self-conscious ethnocentrism." The third addresses the explanatory concerns of historians and sociologists against Taylor's idealism.

Practical Reason and Transitional Arguments

Because we have not made Habermas's metatransition to Kantian procedures or Archimedian points that are outside the terms of debates in question, we must reason comparatively for the relative superiority of certain understandings vis-à-vis others: "The nerve of rational proof consists in showing that [a certain] transition is an error-reducing one. The argument turns on interpretations of possible transitions from A to B or B to A. This form of argument has its source in autobiographical narrative [. . .]. [For instance,] I see that I was confused about the relation of resentment and love [. . .]. Arguing here is contesting between interpretations of what I have been living" (Taylor 1989, 72). The idea of reasoning through comparison applies to historical, cross-cultural, and biographical examples—for example, a society that lives through a transition from hierarchical to egalitarian relationships, an anthropologist who enriches her understanding of the concept of family through living in another culture, or an individual who moves from a shallow to a deeper understanding of love and hate. In each case, the individual or collective subject makes an interpretive, comparative assessment of the transition in terms of gains and losses. In articulating such transitions, narrative and other forms of discourse take on both a temporal and an argumentative burden. This involves characterizing and narrating an understanding of the institutions of meaning prior to the change in light of the new understanding provided by the present.

An excellent example of how such articulation works in political dialogue can be found in Naeem Inayatullah's "Something There: Love, War, Basketball, and Afghanistan: An Antidotal Memoir" (2003). In this text, Inayatullah uses two personal stories to articulate the limits of liberal international relations theory and its method of argument. He begins with a story about his frustration with a discussion that he led on the film *Jung [War]: In the Land of the Mujaheddin,* in which heroic doctors create a hospital in war-torn Afghanistan. The conversation that followed the film showed how the audience's liberal assumptions can serve to insulate rather than open political cultures and therefore prepare the way for airdropping sympathy, aid, and bombs into the great lack. To counter these interpretive assumptions, Inayatullah does not engage in a straightforward normative debate on justice. Instead, he proceeds to tell a story about his roadtrip to Kabul as a basketball player for the International School of Islamabad, in which he describes his encounters with the mysteries, splendors, and peculiarities of Afghanistan. As he recounts his engagements with the individuals and cultures of Pakistan, Afghanistan, and America, he opens up the dynamics of cross-cultural understanding, the blind spots and insights that should inform international relations theory. He shows not only how normative conceptions cannot float free of the public imaginations of communities, but also how the languages of public imagination can be reasoned through.

Such transitional interpretive accounts cannot be understood only on the model of autobiography. Transitions can come about, for example, in the face of new statistical information about the period, problem, or person under study. They can also come about from new explanatory hypotheses, say, about how global capitalism works, or from large-scale readings of the historical connections, such as the relationship of religion and democracy.

But what makes such reasoning different from the transitional arguments we read about in history? For instance, E. P. Thompson's well-known *Making of the English Working Class* examines the transitions in discourses—and other causal forces—that helped bring about new class consciousness between 1790 and 1832. What is different in the examples I note above is that the articulation of the proper interpretive horizon in the present is in the foreground rather than the explanatory accounts of the events.

The politics of interpretive frameworks for history is nowhere more evident than when political regimes are working with a Truth and Reconciliation Committee to effect "transitional justice."[36] Such commissions are important, not just as transitions for former dictatorial military regimes, but also for long-standing democracies such as the United States; however, the dynamic interaction of past, present, and future in political reasoning cannot be reduced to acknowledging past abuses and finding a single symbolic memorial.[37] Acknowledgment of particular abuses must not lead political communities to forget the nature of the medium of deliberation and its articulation of loss, of forgotten social goods, and of new ways of remembering.[38] Political communities should also consider the political transitions that they did and did not make. What alternative forms of life and goods were abandoned, rejected, blocked, or never considered? This is the kind of historical, transitional thinking Hannah Arendt does in reconstructing democratic moments of the past—from Greece to the American Revolution—and in criticizing long-standing modes of political thought (homo faber), as we'll see in chapter 4. She is thematizing the losses in contemporary democratic politics and urging us to reconsider a transition that we now accept as given. The aim of transitional reasoning should be the negotiation of an improved language for discussing the issues in question, not the creation of a neutral, depoliticized linguistic medium in which conflicted linguistic embodiment disappears. This is the liberal and Habermasian dream of the final or "meta" transition.

What I want to emphasize at this point is that the importance of comparative thinking follows from the elimination of the objectifying, external theoretical or moral point of view of a society on itself, the point of view that tries, for instance, to isolate, for example, "elements" of modernity from their symbolic cultures. Although Taylor admits that "the ultimate result [of the process of comparison and contrast] is always tied to someone's point of view" (1995b, 10)—it is always an individual or group reading of the comparison—this does not mean that comparative reasoning does not represent a gain or an overcoming of ethnocentrism. "We should think about the conflicts between the requirements of incompatible cultures on analogy to the way we think about nonconjointly realizable goods in our lives. When we find we can't maximize both freedom and equality, for instance, we don't immediately conclude that one of these isn't a real good" (162). In other words, the presence of conflict does not mean that we have to fall back into incommensurability or relativism. Our understanding of political regimes is similarly comparative, a point developed by Lefort's reading of modern democracy against monarchical and totalitarian regimes.[39]

The idea of narrative that informs this comparative reasoning is not what Ricoeur describes as the configurational power of narrative, in which emplotting is an exercise of Kantian aesthetic judgment.[40] Such a purely formal notion blocks out the argumentative and substantive claims of first- and second-order narratives that we find in literary history, as our examples from Flaubert, James, and Proust illustrate. Transitional argument is not a Hegelian metanarrative in which the new self-understanding incorporates and transcends the perspective of the past or the other. Transitional arguments entail particular forms of remembrance, forgetting, and revaluation, as we'll see later on. The subjects of transitions are not necessarily individuals or groups; they can also be packages of beliefs or discursive practices. Transitions are never simply progressive, in the eyes of either the historical actors or the philosophical narrators. In Taylor's reading, the conflicted, heterogeneous positions of the contemporary public sphere are fed by multiple strains of modernity. These different strains are then reconstructed and assessed, in light of the opening transcendental argument.

Moreover, his conception of transition includes genealogical accounts of loss just as it does accounts of gain. Indeed, genealogy is simply one version of transitional argument. "Genealogy goes to the heart of practical reasoning" (Taylor 1989, 73) because it is one way of bringing out the hitherto unrecognized loss, and it works through a process of articulation rather than explanation. Thus, Taylor can say that Nietzschean attacks on the Kantian procedural ethic "resemble [Taylor's own] critique, because [they] both want to show that this modern philosophy has moral motives, instead of being uniquely determined by epistemic ones" (99). This vulnerability to counterclaim is also true for the stories of others that have been excluded. The Foucauldian genealogical project meets Taylor's project on the same philosophical, interpretive turf rather than as a causal, empirical claim. Genealogists do not seek to discredit a historical interpretation by pointing to causal forces that make the interpretive claim irrelevant; rather, they seek to discredit the evaluative ontological frameworks through which a particular historical account is rendered—for instance, Foucault's exposure of the losses in the transition from premodern to modern. Where Taylor parts company with Foucault is on the issue of whether genealogy has to spell out the values, institutions, and narratives to which it appeals. Hence, what bothers Taylor in Foucault's understanding of power is not his first-order critique of specific regimes, but the second-order claim that all truth is power, for this levels all transitions through history. From Taylor's point of view, Foucault's power thesis prevents us from being "in a position to affirm that one view was a gain over another . . . [for] transitions are between incommensurables" (1985a, 382).[41] The Foucauldian lessons about the correspondence theory of truth and the closing down of otherness are important, but they bring "us to the point at which the real debate ought to start, the fine-grained discernment of what has been gained, what lost, and what doors to otherness have closed, and how they can be opened" (383). What Foucault and Taylor share is an ontological account of being in the world against a correspondence epistemological account or the formalized Habermasian approach that posits a homogeneous lifeworld subtending the relationship of speakers. Taylor does not see the assessment of the subject as instituting a dialectical reading of history. There are losses that can never be retrieved as well as long-standing traditions in need of genealogical work. (To be sure, Taylor does not have much to say about this strand of his argument.) Unlike Foucault, Taylor requires that philosophical argument display the resources and justifications of one's own preferred strains.

By placing his commitments on the table, Taylor is better able to accommodate the shifts in levels between philosophical histories and literature than is Foucault. By "philosophical histories," I mean an account such as Foucault's archaeological examination of the historical conditions of possibility of a certain discursive formation or Taylor's discussion of the modes of the engaged or disengaged subject. Both thinkers are arguing at a level that is deeper than events and the fine-grained differences of the institutions of public imagination in a particular time and place, which is the level at which literature often operates. Because the literary examples we have looked at thus far have been philosophical ones, such as Proust's argument with realism, I will give some other examples developed by others that show literature's mode of engagement with questions of transition.

For instance, literature can dramatize complex psychological and social languages of ambivalence toward social change. Thus, a work such as *The Great Gatsby* can be read as Fitzgerald's uncertain engagement with the changing American public imagination of masculinity at a time when economic forces were deepening the gender split of male aggressive individualism and female receptivity. Terrified at either accepting or rejecting the new standards, Fitzgerald's text displays the forces and the difficulties of transitional arguments about the shape of modern gender identities.[42]

Literary texts can also help a political community congratulate itself for a transition that it has not fully made. In *Huckleberry Finn as Idol and Target*, Jonathan Arac lays out the novel's different appearances in America's public imagination. Although it was initially received as part of America's "literary narrative tradition" rather than as part of its "national narrative tradition," during the 1950s it was recategorized as a national narrative and put in the service of an argument that American public culture had overcome its racist past with the publication of this book. In recent years, it has been the focus of new racial concerns over its language, both in public schools and in scholarly journals.[43]

Yet another kind of transitional argument is provided by works such as *Beloved* or Art Spiegelman's *Maus*, texts that address the languages through which we understand the legacies of specific historical events (slavery and the Holocaust). Such texts do indeed argue for the superiority of their languages vis-à-vis their predecessors, but the languages are more specific than the candidates singled out by either Foucault or Taylor. These texts are concerned with historical witnessing to events and their intergenerational aftermaths.[44] *Maus* thematizes its own transitional argument in the protagonist's autobiography by including within it an excerpt from the writer's previous work (*Prisoner from the Lost Planet*).

Spiegelman's work, like Morrison's *Beloved*, is often discussed in terms of the psychoanalytic vocabulary of "working through," and this conception certainly includes the idea of transitional argument from one identity and mode of engagement with the world to another. The public working through of a trauma is not only therapeutic but political and philosophical as well. The kinds of political sites from which we witness become important. While *Maus* and *Beloved* both challenge existing languages of reference and self-understanding, insisting on their symbolic agency, their relationship to an understanding of the philosophical projects of practical reason and modernity are not explicit. I am mentioning them in connection with transition because I think their claims are consistent with Taylor's conception and because transition is precisely what is often left out of contemporary readings of these works. A short detour on studies of Holocaust literature will clarify my point.

In the field of trauma studies, Foucauldian questions about discursive regimes or genealogies are rarely at issue because the focus is on specific events rather than discursive regimes.[45] Instead, what emerges is a tension between the documentary desire and the unrepresentability of the events of the Holocaust. A good example of this line of thinking is Michael Rothberg's *Traumatic Realism,* which seeks to bridge the realist, documentary side, represented by historians, and the "antirealist" side represented by certain writers and philosophers who claim that "the Holocaust is not knowable or would be knowable only under radically new regimes of knowledge and that it cannot be captured in traditional representational schemata" (2000, 4). Antirealists include Elie Wiesel and Claude Lanzmann as well as philosophers such as Lyotard and Adorno. Rothberg says he can bridge this gap. The result is that we get three simultaneous claims about the Holocaust: that it left an unproblematic trace, to protect against deniers, that its significance is an absence, to satisfy modernists, and that the movement between these two poles is governed by postmodern self-consciousness about the limits of the whole process.[46] "Traumatic realism is counterideological precisely because it does not produce an imaginary resolution, but rather programs readers to recognize the absence of the real" (104). By refusing to give referential weight to the languages of texts such as *Maus,* Rothman blocks out the transitional argument that they make for their own claim and prevents them from working with causal accounts of history.[47]

The different registers offered by philosophers and literary critics provide points of mutual interrogation. While philosophers, for instance, could ask whether the differences noted by literary critics are not simply variations on the same discursive formation that is itself suspect—e.g., liberal individualism for both Taylor and Foucault—literary critics challenge the sweeping descriptions of the governing assumptions of public imagination and their relationship to historical specifics.

While Foucault's own work offers several different historiographical points of entry, he cannot move from critique to an endorsement at the level either of problematic or of particular languages. Foucault's problematic cannot, for instance, endorse the languages of witnessing in *Beloved* or *Maus* versus their competitors. If Taylor does not develop the genealogical and critical historiography as much as he might—a point we will address momentarily—his problematic can accommodate moves from second-order characterization of institutions to first-order languages of literary texts. There is no necessary logic to such reasoning, but only the narrative argument about how the past has prepared for both this possibility and many others. By bringing narrative and institutions of meaning together,

Taylor's problematic will enable us to witness and work through historical damage and trauma in a way that poststructuralists and Habermasians, both of whom reject this kind of reasoning at the public level, cannot.

Taylor's Reasoning versus Rorty's Relativism

But doesn't Taylor fall into what Habermas calls Richard Rorty's "contextualism," in which all we have is "a historical-sociological description of the intuitions prevalent in the American population today" (Habermas 1996a, 62), a self-conscious ethnocentrism? After all, Rorty also thinks that we should give up looking for moral or epistemological foundations outside of cultural practices so that justification is "a matter of historical comparison with other attempts at social organization—those of the past and those envisaged by utopians" (1989, 53). He too is looking for "an improved self-description [of modernity] rather than a set of foundations" (52). Nonetheless, Rorty and Taylor offer starkly different understandings of subjectivity and rationality, and a brief comparison will clarify the distinctiveness of Taylor's position.

First, Rorty explicitly rejects Taylor's conception of the subject's relationship to institutions of meaning as "strong evaluations." Rorty wants to isolate and preserve two forms of rationality: "the ability to cope with the environment by adjusting one's reactions to environmental stimuli in complex and delicate ways" and "the ability not to be overly disconcerted by difference from oneself, not to respond aggressively to such differences," a commitment to "persuasion not force" (1998b, 186–187). What needs to be eliminated, in his view, is the idea of rationality that works through "strong evaluations"—that is, that sets "goals other than mere survival," that establishes "an evaluative hierarchy rather than simply adjusting means to taken for granted ends" (187). Evaluative frameworks are merely misguided self-understandings that clog rather than facilitate philosophical and political conversation. The only evaluative self-understandings that we should keep are those associated with democratic virtues listed above, while the rest should be rewritten in the Darwinian vocabulary of environmental coping. In this way, values become simply tools of desire, not part of the evaluative framework, "second-order desires," or the "world" that one inhabits.[48]

What also disappears with these hierarchies is the idea of historical transitional argument, including the argument for the democratic virtues that are tacked onto Darwinian social actors. By eliminating such hierarchies, we can, according to Rorty, think of the "triumph" of one culture over another—either within a tradition or cross-culturally—not as "an indication of a special virtue" but as the "outcome of concatenations of contingent circumstances" (1998b, 187). Rorty explicitly rejects the idea that cultural changes can be argued about in terms of "transitional arguments" from one logical space to another: "Europe did not decide to accept the idiom of Romantic poetry, or of socialist politics, or of Galilean mechanics. That sort of shift was no more an act of will than it was a result of argument. Rather, Europe gradually lost the habit of using certain words and gradually acquired the habit of using others" (1989, 6). Two reasons can be unpacked from his account. First, he associates historical reasoning with a progressive Hegelian supersubject, and here Taylor would certainly agree that there is no collective singular subject who stands above the fray of reasons and causes, cashing out the bloodshed of modernity into new syntheses. Unlike Rorty, however, Taylor thinks that we can preserve a notion of subjectivity that is able to reason through its historically and culturally specific transitions. Indeed, Taylor's understanding of modernity is expressly developed against the homogenizing "acultural" accounts that dominate Western social/political theory, as we saw in chapter 1.

Rorty's other objection is quite different, and it follows from the split he drives between the world of reasons and the world of causes: "The world is out there, but descriptions of the world are not" (1989, 5). Given this picture of conversation, it is perhaps not surprising that actual historical forces make almost no appearance in his account. Indeed, he states clearly that the values or frameworks one advocates should be kept separate from explanatory historical thinking: "What middle ground is there between causal explanation and celebration, where celebration means telling a story about what the universe would have to be like to make a certain person, or epoch, tend to look really good?" (1999, 214). He calls himself a celebrator.

The world of reasons is a self-contained logical space, a space that is so narrow that aberrant speech, such as metaphors, cannot be said to "persuade" listeners through the reasons of argument but to strike them as causes: "New metaphors are causes not reasons for changing belief" (Rorty 1989, 50). Hence, getting someone to change his or her mind in any substantive way cannot be called "argument," since this "requires that the same vocabulary be used in premises and conclusions" (Rorty 1991a, 125). In Rorty's view, a change in beliefs is such a radical deracination from the past, such a profound transfiguration of the identities of individual or collective subjects, that reasoning through the histories of such journeys through incommensurate packages of beliefs is impossible.[49] Unlike Taylor in his idea of best account and his moral realism, Rorty is unwilling to give any particular vocabulary moral or referential superiority.[50] The result is that our evaluative frameworks are simply ad hoc. They cannot be argued for or against other vocabularies or problematics, and they cannot be connected to any social history. As a result, Rorty separates political judgment from history just as much as Habermas does, though in different ways. Neither one gives us a problematic that engages the political arguments about history and memory.

One of the resources for Taylor against Rorty is that the former uses transcendental argument to open rather than close off his problematic from external challenge. By distinguishing between inescapable frameworks, the horizon of the intelligible, and the historical reconstruction of Western modernity, Taylor provides a space of dialogue unavailable to those who, like Rorty, conflate "the way we do things" in Western democracies and the intelligible. A Taylorian cannot simply shrug and claim to be merely a historical product, for she is obliged to characterize how moral languages fit within the larger horizon of the intelligible.[51]

Hence, Taylor's answer to Habermas's ethnocentricism charge is not to say with Rorty that this is inevitable. Instead, he begins by rejecting the idea that reason and universality stand or fall on an absolute claim. By making universality depend on absolute objectivity, one sets an impossible standard that ends up contributing to relativism. The usual scenarios that are evoked to produce the need for a standard outside all cultures are not only unrealistic—"do we really face people who quite lucidly reject the very principle of the inviolability of human life?" (Taylor 1995b, 35)—they undermine what they hope to prove. If we were to meet someone who really shared nothing of our moral intuitions, then we would have to worry about a huge range of concepts and self-understandings and not simply this person's conception of justice. Reasoning does not have to start without presupposition but instead shows how a particular "policy is unconscionable on premises that both sides can accept" (36). Taylor neither defines justice and autonomy through an extrahistorical appeal, nor does he fall back on adhocism.[52] Taylor's subject must recount how she arrives at her moral position and the goods (strong evaluations) that inspire it. Because this self is defined through rather than apart from its histories, it is vulnerable to challenge, loss, and negotiation in a way that the imperiously thin liberal self and the dialectically thick Hegelian selves are not.

Explanation and Practical Reason

That said, Taylor often understates important causal, interpretive, and moral questions. He has little to say about the historical horrors of modernity—the Holocaust, sexism, racism, imperialism, or the rise of global systems.[53] Further, he doesn't give space to the preoccupations of literary theory and criticism of the last twenty years: how literature is complicit with regimes of power and historical disasters or how it works to resist such pressures. Nor does his work look at the different sites of subjectivation according to different rules and practices. However, these objections to the way he develops the readings within his problematic are not knockdown objections to the problematic itself. Indeed, in his recent *Modern Social Imaginaries* (2004), Taylor gives a sociohistorical richness to his account of modernity that responds to some of these issues. Let's begin with the issue of causality.

The question of causal claims against Taylor—made in the most naked form by Quentin Skinner—won't hold. For Skinner, "The causal story [in *Sources of the Self*] tends to subvert Taylor's argument because we are faced with the disquieting implication that our forbearers may to some degree have been hoodwinked into exchanging their traditional picture of spirituality and citizenship for the very different one they in turn bequeathed to us. We become aware of contingency and loss" (Skinner 1991, 145). In response, Taylor says that he is offering not a causal account of the shifts in modern identity but an "interpretive one." This means "giving an account of the new identity which makes clear what its appeal was. What drew people to it? Indeed, what draws them to it today" (Taylor 1989, 203). To be sure, the force behind different evaluative frameworks in history comes not just simply from their persuasive appeal but from the interests of the powerful (Skinner, 145). Taylor's problematic does not eliminate causal forces in the complex twists of power or deny the role of unintended consequences of historical action; instead, he simply insists that we cannot stand outside all historical languages and intentions: "Only if we could show how relations of domination have totally invaded the world of everyday self-understanding could we adopt the neo-clausewitzean interpretation. The reality of historical change is messy, and the truth of ideas is neither decisive nor irrelevant" (1988, 226).[54] Taylor's point is that there is no way to generalize about the dominant causal features of any moment in history (2004, 33). In *Modern Social Imaginaries*, he devotes a chapter to "The Specter of Idealism," discussing the complex histories of how the idea of moral order that he finds at the heart of modernity "came to acquire the strength that eventually allowed it to shape the social imaginaries of modernity" (33). Tracing these modern imaginaries means looking at the historical emergence of three major institutional forms of self-understanding: "the economy, the public sphere, and the practices and outlooks of democratic self-rule" (69).

A different kind of causal critique could emerge for sociological critics in the line of Pierre Bourdieu, who would attack Taylor's neglect of the mediating institutions of public imagination and social reproduction, such as the school. This question is put most pointedly in John Guillory's widely praised *Cultural Capital,* where he claims that all sides of the canon debate confuse "culture as the study of preserved artifacts with the sense of culture as common beliefs, behaviors, attitudes" (1993, 40).[55] Preserved artifacts, the canon, and its institutional locus, the school, are then the objects of his analysis. He concludes that "the decline of the capital of literature" in the education system is the real subtext of the canon wars, and that the real function of the school is "the reproduction of the social order with all of its various inequalities" (ix).[56] Does Taylor's focus on the texts of high culture and his neglect of class issues invalidate his claims about the public imagination? To be sure, public imagination is shaped by the school, the media, and other institutions, but Taylor's philosophical focus is different from Guillory's but not incompatible with an institutional critique. Yes, Taylor does give a causal force to ideas and social imaginaries that Guillory would not. What distinguishes the two approaches is that Guillory's assumes that one can avoid reasoning through the social imaginary by turning it into an object and explaining it. In concentrating on the unmasking of institutional forces, he never addresses the question of how public imagination, and its literary component, inform his own project or those of citizens. The researcher's claim, implied or explicit, to be able to set aside his or her own conceptions of the good and public imagination in order to objectify culture is one of modernity's errors that Taylor attacks through his opening transcendental arguments.[57]

A broader form of causal criticism of Taylor's problematic is that such an interpretive approach makes meaning so context-dependent that all generalizations are impossible.[58] However, this objection confuses Taylor's concern with the proper language for discussing the shared imaginative furniture of the world with a rejection of generalizations. Although Taylor devotes most of his energies to articulating a language that lets Western modernity's divisions and problems appear, his problematic is compatible with explanatory approaches to historical forces.

Thus, in "Nationalism and Modernity," Taylor accepts Ernest Gellner's antihermeneutic functional explanations of nationalism that describe how the modern economy requires a flexible, mobile population with a largely homogeneous culture provided by a state system of education (Taylor 1997, 33). He pulls back, however, from making functionalism the whole story, insisting that the "moral thrust" of nationalist aspirations is not captured by such an account. For that, we have to come to terms with the social imaginaries of the cultures under consideration.[59] In sum, an interpretive history can revise itself in light of empirical and causal challenges, but it can never be evaporated into mere data or explained away as part of causal mechanisms. My point is not to sign on to a particular historical account of nationalism, modernity, and democracy, but rather to insist that practical reason in the present address its connection to such histories. In short, there is an ineliminable space of interpretive judgment in the employment of explanatory models, and this judgment depends on its historical debts to the past. Taylor's account is consistent with what I said earlier in connection with Ricoeur's *L'Histoire, la mémoire, et l'oubli,* about the interpretive judgment involved in the historiographical operations of the historian and the philosophical speculative moment of reflection on the historical condition.[60] No explanatory scheme can put philosophical articulation out of business since no account of hoodwinked subjects can be only explanatory.

Taylor's combination of transcendental argument, articulation, and the transitional arguments calls for a distinctive conception of deliberative exchange that is absent from both the discourse ethics of Habermas and from much contemporary theory that combines Foucauldian or neomarxist discussions of power with an appeal to the values of justice and equality.[61] In the space of global dialogue, the Taylorian self's heavy cultural baggage— which Habermas tries to shed through Kant, and which Rorty tries to shed through his Darwinian behaviorism—turns out to be a resource for flexibility and openness that is not available to the thin disenchanted self of Habermas's or Rorty's senses of modernity. By taking the short route of formal universalism to the cosmopolitan position, Habermas leaves out the hermeneutic labor through which understanding is reached by self-transformation. Rorty, on the other hand, short-circuits this work by envisioning a world of tool-users who work with incommensurate materials. In Taylor's view, the way to get an interlocutor to make her cultures vulnerable to dia-logue is not to begin by invoking a (liberal) standard that one side claims is external to both or by waving a liberal utopia in her face but to appeal to val-ues internal to the interlocutor's moral framework and tack forward and backward—if possible—to an intersubjectively acceptable conclusion.[62]

This dialogical conception of culture is urgent in the face of theories of globalization, which offer new versions of the Western metanarrative, except that the cunning of nature (Kant) or the cunning of reason (Hegel) that is working behind the backs of the self-understandings of cultures of the world is global capitalism. It is the new form of universal history in which global capitalism overpowers local cultures.[63] Beginning with a third-person constructivist problematic in which identities are defended only as strategic essentialism or with a purely formal defense of democracy only furthers this dissolution. In providing a transcendental defense of public imagination as the inevitable site of reasoning, Taylor counters wide-spread misdescriptions of how we think about the kind of world(s) we can share and provides news ways for clarifying, enriching, and negotiating multiple styles of political dialogue.

The Politics of Race and Imagination

ARENDT VERSUS ELLISON ON LITTLE ROCK

In this chapter I aim to enrich, extend, and exemplify my argument about public imagination and political dialogue by looking at the well-known dispute about race and education in Little Rock between Hannah Arendt and Ralph Ellison. I explore how the disagreement over desegregation opens onto a deeper disagreement between these thinkers about the way to understand the relationship of language, history, and political judgment. I am thus arguing for a mode of analysis that opens up the philosophical background of judgment in the public realm and for my specific conception of public imagination. The fact that this is an interdisciplinary exchange between a political philosopher who is well known for her sensitivity to language and narrative and a novelist does not limit the example; on the contrary, it helps me enrich the comments from the last chapter on the connections among everyday language, literature, and politics.

THE STAKES OF THE DEBATE

Few of Arendt's writings have drawn more criticism from her own supporters than "Reflections on Little Rock," in which she opposes the federally mandated desegregation of schools in Arkansas.[1] Seyla Benhabib, for instance, criticizes Arendt's failure to understand the function of public schools as well as her misguided attempt to employ her distinction between the social and the political.[2] While I agree with these criticisms, I want to take Arendt's comments as a way of opening up problems in her conception of the relationship among political storytelling, plurality, and judgment through comparison with Ellison's work. The differences between the two are not just about race or schools but about the proper conception of language in political judgment. From Ellison's point of view, Arendt's understanding of language is hamstrung by Kantian and phenomenological commitments that prevent her from giving a cognitive and ontological dimension to language that deliberative politics requires.

Arendt takes a Third Critique approach to narrative, similar to that of Ricoeur, in which the resources of Husserlian phenomenology are brought together with Kantian reflective judgment. For her, narrative is formal rather than substantive, and the emplotment emerges from a reflective rather than determinant referential judgment. As we recall, for the Third Critique view, narrative does not organize intuition but rather puts together particular, already cognized facts and events. Narrative is not woven into the fabric of everyday life; rather, it is a retrospective reflective construction. Action, says Arendt, "reveals itself fully only to the storyteller, that is, to the backward glance of the historian, who indeed always knows better what it was all about than the participants" (1958, 192).

Ellison's thinking on language and narrative is closer to Taylor's than to Arendt's. Ellison implicitly rejects four important and interrelated features of the Kantians: subject/object vocabulary, formalism, aesthetic separatism, and methodological individualism. Unlike the Third Critique Husserlian phenomenologists, Ellison does not keep a formal space of reflection or a material space of reference outside language. Narrative is less an ordering of the subjective or objective world than the reinterpretation of the existing narratives and symbols that always already inform one's self-understanding. That is, narratives, both literary and nonliterary, are part of the preunderstanding of our being in the world, part of the medium through which we live.[3]

Unlike Taylor, however, Ellison is highly suspicious of the existing languages of his culture, so he develops a form of novelistic genealogy as a way of criticizing existing linguistic and social structures of intersubjectivity. In Ellison's genealogies, we see the protagonist peel away existing languages and rewrite the past. For Ellison, unlike Foucault, genealogical analysis is tied to judgments about the present in the first person. Race is not a topic that can be addressed in existing identities and discursive patterns. However, instead of doing third-person exposures of these patterns, Ellison shows how first-order narrative can do genealogical work.

Arendt's phenomenology draws on Kant's *Critique of Judgment* and the Kantian distinction between reason (thinking) and intellect (knowing) to block out the question of our being in language. By contrast, the model of interpretive judgment that I will be developing through Ellison shows that the way we bring the question of our being in language and narrative into interpretive judgment is not decided in advance as either part of the development of tradition (Taylor) or the ontology of power (Foucault). One of the central problems of judgment is to decide how to interpret one's historical and cultural embedding; hence, narrative choices themselves call on political judgment. This question is perspicuously thematized in Ellison's account while it must struggle to appear through Arendt's Kantian presuppositions. The dispute over Little Rock will serve as a point of entry to these differences and their significance.

In her essay on Little Rock, Arendt opposed federally ordered desegregation for three reasons: (1) it asked children to take on political activities that were the province of adults; (2) it confused the social and the political— "what equality is to the body politic discrimination is to society" (1959, 51); and (3) it violated states' rights. I will focus on the second in connection to language and storytelling.[4]

For my purposes, Arendt's most revealing comments come when she tells us the two questions that she asked herself when formulating her essay: "What would I do if I were a Negro mother?" (1959, 179) and "what would I do if I were a white mother in the South?" (180). Here, Arendt assumes that the question is a private one and that she has access to the self-understanding of African American political thought that informs the judgment of black families. Certainly, her misreading is reinforced by her racism, which leads her to treat her differences with the NAACP over the social and the political not as a difference of equals but as a symptom of the damaged judgment of "oppressed minorities [who] were never the best judges on the order of priorities in such matters" (46).[5] However, I want to push beyond racism—Arendt's kind of misreading is parodied in the Prologue to Ellison's *Invisible Man*, as we'll see later—and her particular understanding of the role of education, which is quite interesting and controversial but beyond my subject.[6] Rather, I explore how Arendt's judgment points to problems in the way she conceives of the relationship among the public world, plurality, and language, relationships that Ellison's work addresses more successfully.

Ellison responds to Arendt by saying that she "has absolutely no conception of what goes on in the minds of Negro parents when they send their kids through those lines of hostile people" (1965, 344). Parents "are aware of the overtones of a rite of initiation which such events actually constitute for the child." The black child is "required to master the inner tensions created by his racial situation [. . .]. It is a harsh requirement, but if he fails this basic test, his life will be even harsher" (344). Ellison foregrounds the "implicit heroism of people who must live within a society without *recognition*" (342, my emphasis). Agreeing to participate peacefully in such a society means agreeing to sacrifice: "I believe that one of the clues to the meanings of [American Negro] experience lies in the idea, the ideal of sacrifice. Hannah Arendt's failure to grasp the importance of this ideal among Southern Negroes caused her to fly way off into left field" (343).[7] Arendt replies with a cryptic concession that takes little back: "It is precisely the ideal of sacrifice that I didn't understand" (cited in Young-Bruehl 1982, 316).

Unfortunately, there is no evidence that they continued this dialogue. However, there is an important biographical incident that Arendt never mentions in her letter but that she revealed in a television interview in 1964—her own experience with the drama of recognition at school, for school was the place where Arendt came to self-consciousness about herself as "a Jew." She says, "The word 'Jew' was never mentioned at home. I first encountered it—though it is hardly worth recounting—in the anti-Semitic remarks of children as we played in the streets" (cited in Young-Bruehl 1982, 11). Although Arendt states that "the 'Jewish Question' had no relevance" in her home, she describes how her family dealt with anti-Semitism: "All Jewish children encountered anti-Semitism. And the souls of many children were poisoned by it. The difference with me lay in the fact that my mother always insisted that I not humble myself. One must defend oneself!" (cited in Young-Bruehl 1982, 11). Developing the biographical, cultural, and psychological dimensions of this denial of her own experience would take this essay in another direction. What is important from my point of view is that this denial—this blind spot—appears in her political philosophy as well as in her particular judgment in this case.

ARENDT'S SEPARATION OF LANGUAGE FROM
TRUTH AND APPEARANCE

In her dispute with Ellison, Arendt assumes the existence of a common world that is in good enough shape to articulate and draw together her own position and that of black mothers. Arendt's idea of the world includes plurality but presupposes that there is a language and intersubjective visibility that provide adequate resources for the articulation of difference. She says, "The reality of the public realm relies on the simultaneous presence of innumerable perspectives and aspects in which the common world presents itself and for which no common measurement or denominator can ever be devised [. . .]. Being seen and being heard by others derive their significance from the fact that everybody sees and hears from a different position" (1958, 57). This idealized assumption inscribed in the metaphorics of vision and aestheticized appearances operates in her judgment about black mothers, who cannot "appear" in the world, except as the objects of white media. Her understanding of the world is reinforced by a subject-to-subject theory of judgment, as we'll see later on, in which the imagination "goes visiting" without interrogating the historical medium of language and culture. Arendt vacillates between a transhistorical philosophical conception of the public realm as part of the human condition and particular analyses of sociohistorical institutions of modernity that have eroded this realm's historical possibilities. However, Arendt does not integrate history and the institutions of meaning into her conception of judgment.[8] Thus, Ellison contests not only her particular assumption about the American public realm but her way of conceiving of the relationship of language to the public world.

To understand Arendt's privileging the fullness of the space of appearances over language, we must step away momentarily from her conception of judgment to examine another Kantian dimension of her thought, the distinction between reason and intellect. Reason addresses the unknowable but important questions of meaning while the intellect addresses cognitive questions of truth: "The need of reason is not inspired by the quest for truth but by the quest for meaning. And truth and meaning are not the same. The basic fallacy, taking precedence over all specific metaphysical fallacies, is to interpret meaning on the model of truth" (1978, I, 14). She clarifies this later in the text: "Truth is located in the evidence of the senses. But that is by no means the case with meaning and with the faculty of thought, which searches for it" (57). In making this Kantian distinction, Arendt keeps a firm wedge between truth and linguistic, interpretive practices. This wedge, which will have important consequences for her idea of political dialogue, is one that Ellison, like Taylor and Foucault, challenges.[9]

For Arendt, truth is of two kinds, rational and factual, and what lies behind these distinctions is her understanding of totalitarianism, in which distinctions between facts and lies and between rational and empirical truths are destroyed by the loss of the public sphere. The public sphere provides a place for different opinions about the facts: "Facts inform opinions, and opinions, inspired by different interests and passions, can differ widely and still be legitimate as long as they respect factual truth [. . .]. Factual truth informs political thought just as rational truth informs philosophical speculation" (Arendt 1977, 238). Totalitarianism deprives its citizens of "the distinctions between fact and fiction (i.e., the reality of experience) and the distinction between true and false (i.e., the standards of thought)" (1973, 474; also 1977, 249–254).

By "rational truth," she means "mathematical, scientific, and philosophical truths rather than factual truth" (1977, 231). Arendt wants to keep truth and meaning distinct because she sees a disastrous philosophical tradition that denigrates the public world by putting truth beyond appearance and common sense, beyond the realm of judgment. This tradition, which begins with Plato and continues through Hegel and Marx, finds contemporary articulation in Heidegger. "The modes of thought and communication that deal with truth, if seen from a political perspective, are necessarily domineering; they don't take into account other people's opinions, and taking these into account is the hallmark of all strictly political thinking" (241).

From my point of view, what is important in this discussion is Arendt's separation of language/narratives from factual and rational truth. In challenging this separation, my point is not the fungibility of facts, once we accept that interpretation goes "all the way down," but the irreality she assigns to narrative and language, an irreality that follows from her Kantian presuppositions, as we will see. In her view, facts are not linguistically and narratively mediated by the actors' self-understandings but stand outside narrative emplotment: "Truth," says Arendt, "is what we are compelled to admit by the nature either of our senses or of our brain" (1978, I, 61).

Arendt wants to keep a space between language and the world, for giving language greater purchase on experience opens the door to philosopher/storyteller with a truth behind appearance and to homo faber who confuses politics and fabrication: "Was it not precisely the discovery of a discrepancy between words, the medium in which we think, and the world of appearances, the medium in which we live, that led to philosophy and metaphysics in the first place?" (1978, I, 8). Because Arendt wants to preserve the priority of the world over language, she reverses philosophy's typical unmasking operation, so that everyday self-understanding unmasks the thinking self, which "is unaware of its own withdrawal from the common world of appearances"

(87). Reciprocally, she must plunge everyday self-understanding into an unre-flective certainty: "The quest for meaning [is] absent from and good for noth-ing in the ordinary course of human affairs, while at the same time the results remain uncertain and unverifiable" (88).

Arendt's conception of the world deflates the self-creating pretensions of both the literary and the philosophical storyteller from Plato to Marx who puts "an actor behind the scenes who, behind the backs of acting men, pulls the strings and is responsible for the story" (1958, 185). Thus, "although everybody started his life by inserting himself into the human world through action and speech, nobody is the author or producer of his own life story. In other words, the stories, the results of action and speech, reveal an agent, but this agent is not author or producer" (184). What such narrative strategies reveal is the equation of meaning and truth, such as Hegel's "Science of the Experience of Consciousness," which "eagerly blurs Kant's distinction between reason's concern with the unknowable and the intellect's concern with cognition" (1978, I, 16).

ELLISON ON PUBLIC LANGUAGES

Ellison is sensitive to these arguments, and he too affirms the priority of the historical actors' self-understanding to third-person Hegelian or Marxist transsubjective accounts. He lashes back at Irving Howe's Marxist reading of the politics of African American representation since Howe's reading disregards the agency and achievement of African American culture, "When he [Howe] looks at the Negro he sees not a human but an abstract embodiment of hell" (Ellison 1995, 159). Ellison insists that a "Negro" is "no product of the socio-political predicament" (112), and he develops this point in *Invisible Man* through the protagonist's relationship to the Brotherhood (Communist Party). But spontaneity here is not opposed to a historical understanding of one's linguistic and cultural constitution; it is made pos-sible by these languages.

Both Arendt and Ellison are committed to a phenomenology as the first step in historical understanding, for this approach preserves two interre-lated features of subjectivity that are dear to them: freedom and difference. For both, liberty has to be maintained not only in the face of explanation, as we saw above, but also in the face of homogenizing liberalism. In an inter-view, Richard Stern asks Ellison directly about the liberal tenet of neutrality toward the good, "The familiar liberal hope is that any specialized form of social life which makes for invidious distinctions should disappear. Your view seems to be that anything that counts is the result of such specialization" (1995, 78). Ellison replies at first with a simple "yes" and then develops his critique of liberalism when Stern asks about what equal access to all aspects of society would mean to African Americans: "Most Negroes would not be nourished by the life white Southerners live. It is too hag-ridden, it is too obsessed" (80). Like Arendt, Ellison is not interested in homogenizing public life whether through the schools or other means. He too wants a common world, not a common will. For Ellison, liberalism and Marxism fail to recognize African Americans despite their "good intentions" because both focus on the conditions of oppression rather than the self-understandings of either the oppressor or the oppressed.

However, unlike Ellison, Arendt believes that the kind of interpretive reflection that we find in works of art should be conceived of as "thought" rather than "cognition," since the former "has neither an end nor aim outside itself" (1958, 170; 1978, I, 13–15). Storytelling is closer to thought than to knowing, for stories perform a "desensing operation" on the phenomena and on common sense (1978, I, 87). "Even the simple telling of what has happened, whether the story tells it as it was or fails to do so, is preceded by the de-sensing operation" (87). Because Arendt accepts the epistemological tradition of philosophy that locates truth outside language and symbols, "she must," as Albrecht Wellmer says, "locate the human world, that is, the common world of men opened up by speech, the world of politics and poetry, of thinking and judging, beyond or above the sphere of cognition" (Wellmer 1996, 42).

The result is that culture is deprived of any constitutive dimension: "Culture and politics then belong together because it is not knowledge or truth which is at stake but rather judgment and decision" (Arendt 1977, 223). What this understanding ignores is the movement in the other direction, in which stories inform experience, which the hermeneutic understanding of language makes available. Arendt's statement denies the ontological and politically ambiguous force of culture (and art) to constitute identities in different ways. Thus, for Ellison, Arendt's conception denies the constitutive public force of the stories that his work thematizes, a force that makes the characters in the novel invisible to each other and that infects the relationship between text and reader. Ellison foregrounds the role of language and art in the public sphere by giving narrative a referential dimension. In speaking of his relationship to Richard Wright, particularly Wright's naturalism, Ellison says that his books would be implicit criticisms of Wright's, just as "all novels of a given historical moment form an argument over the nature of reality and are, to an extent, criticisms of each other" (1995, 165). Ellison's commitment to a relentless stripping away of the Invisible Man's sense of reality is a critique of the referential languages available at the time. Truth, not just meaning, is part of public political deliberation. This truth appears not simply as an appeal to the world but as a historical argument against or with his predecessor's language, the interpretive medium. Obviously, this view of history is principally "interpretive" rather than causal.

My Ellisonian critique of Arendt is that she employs a phenomenological vocabulary that misdescribes the linguistically informed heterogeneity and historicity of the public world as well as the dynamics of our dialogic interaction. We are gripped and transformed by our experiences with language and stories in a way that Arendt never makes available. Ellison's point is twofold. First, we cannot wish into existence a prelinguistic space so as to separate "the medium in which we think" from "the world of appearances" (Arendt 1978, I, 8). Second, we do not need to because the political problem that Arendt sees in the relationship between language and making is not a global problem that haunts all abstraction from the prepredictive world; rather, the problem of construction is a particular instrumental, antidialogical understanding of our being in language. Moreover, the possibility of transformation in language is not necessarily something that philosophers and politicians do to "remake" the lifeworld; rather, there is a transformative dimension to the first-order dynamics of dialogue. What her phenomenology keeps out is a constitutive conception of language either from the Taylorian side, in which "language itself serves to set up spaces of common action" (Taylor 1995b, 173), or the genealogical side, in which language forecloses such spaces. In her effort to avoid philosophy's habitual denigration of appearance—and to avoid Heidegger's conception of being in the world, in which Dasein seeks isolated authenticity in the midst of idle talk—Arendt is forced to flatten all language's unavoidable influence over the constitution of the world into the neutral vocabulary of appearances; hence, she leaves undeveloped the question of our being in language.[10]

ARENDT'S PUBLIC REALM AND REFLECTIVE JUDGMENT

Ironically, one of the ideas that drives language into exile is Arendt's understanding of a common, public realm and how it becomes available. Although "the public realm, as the common world, gathers us together and yet prevents our falling over each other, so to speak" (1958, 52), we do not access the space of appearances through a straightforward perception in the "natural attitude," to speak as a phenomenologist. Instead, the space of appearances emerges when we adopt the stance of Kantian aesthetic judgment, which does the work of a kind of phenomenological epoche by shifting us from determinant to reflective judgments: "In order to become aware of appearances we first must be free to establish a certain distance between ourselves and the object, and the more important the sheer appearance of a thing is, the more distance it requires for its proper appreciation. The distance cannot arise unless we are in a position to forget ourselves, the cares and interests and urges of our lives, so that we will not seize what we admire but let it be in its appearance" (1977, 210). In brief, "common sense [. . .] discloses to us the nature of the world insofar as it is a common world" (221). Arendt thinks that this is an appropriate model for political judgment since this model gets us beyond the self-interests and moral interests that constrict our appreciation of the world: "Taste judges the world in its appearance and in its worldliness [. . .] neither the life interests of the individual nor the moral interests of the self are involved here. For judgments of taste, the world is the primary thing, not man, neither man's life nor his self" (1977, 222). Abandoning the legacy of the Second Critique, in which the solitary subject "consulting nothing but his own reason, finds the maxim that is not self-contradictory" (1982, 49), Arendt urges us to attend to "men in the plural as they really are and lives in societies" (1982, 13). The issue is what she calls, after Kant, "enlarged mentality," the ability to "think in the place of everybody else" (1977, 220, 241).[11]

The focus of Arendt's conception of judgment has been her reading of Kant's *Critique of Judgment,* which has received so much sensitive and detailed commentary recently. What underwrites Arendt's idea of judgment amidst the particularities of the world is Kant's idea of sensus communis: Common sense is assumed "as the necessary condition of the universal communicability of our cognition, which is presupposed in any logic and in any principle of knowledge that is not skeptical" (Kant 1987, 88). Kant's common sense articulates the transcendental conditions of traditional common sense: "The idea of a sense shared [by all of us], i.e., a power to judge that in reflecting takes account (a priori), in our thought, of everyone else's way of presenting [something], in order as it were to compare our own judgment with human reason in general and thus escape the illusion that arises from the ease of mistaking subject and private conditions for objective ones" (160). This characterization presupposes an arena of consensus in which differences can appear. Kant goes too far when he moves from the need for common sense to the conclusion that reflective judgment can adopt a universal perspective ("human reason in general"). To be sure, Arendt's move to reflective judgment opens up the question of shared meaning in a way that is unavailable in Kant's practical philosophy, in which historical meanings are driven out by the rules of determinant judgment.[12] She thus seeks to minimize the objectification mistake common to Kantian liberalism in which shared meanings, languages, and facts are simply assumed.[13] She nonetheless does not leave a place for an ontological interrogation of our being in language, which is what is required for her to avoid a misreading of the African American mothers.

Arendt wants to keep reflective judgment apart from the concept, the domain of determinant judgments about truth (and morality) with its attending anti-political, nonpersuasive forms of argument rather than having reflective judgment go "all the way down" so as to place the terrain of the First Critique within the horizon of reflective, interpretive judgment. Hence, she must separate art and politics from truth: "Taste judgments [unlike demonstrable facts or truths demonstrated by argument] [. . .] share with political opinions that they are persuasive; the judging person—as Kant says quite beautifully—can only 'woo the consent of everyone else' in the hope of coming to an agreement with him eventually" (1977, 222).

ELLISON'S CRITIQUE OF KANTIANISM

Ellison's disagreement with Kant shares much with Gadamer's reading of "the Kantian subjectivization of aesthetics," in which art is sequestered from the historical dialogues in which it is passed down, dialogues that both inform and make claims on the subject of interpretation (Gadamer 1994, 42–55). To speak of "enlarged mentality" capable of appreciating a world ignores our being in language and the claims to truth, goodness, and the like made through these languages. The challenge of difference and otherness to judgment is better captured through a dialogical/genealogical model, in which the subject of judgment is made vulnerable through the linguistic tissues of his or her being by the appeal of the other. (I'll return at the end of the chapter to the question of historical consciousness.) The hope of *Invisible Man* is that the act of reading will produce such a public self-interrogation that a new dialogical space will be opened, a space that is currently foreclosed by the existing languages of self-understanding. "Who knows," says

Ellison's narrator, "but that on lower frequencies I speak *for* you" (1981, 568, my emphasis). The way to break out of the linguistic prison is not through an appeal to appearances—as Arendt says, "For us, appearance—something that is being seen and heard by others as well as ourselves—constitutes reality" (1958, 50)—but through a dialogical transformation that is possible only if we risk engaging the referential and ethical claims of the text, claims that Arendt's Kantian aesthetic blocks out.

In the opening scene of *Invisible Man*, the narrating self of the present—that is, the self that has been through the entire story that is about to be told—confronts the reader with an allegory of recognition. In this fable, the black protagonist is attacked by someone who does not see him. This initiates a drama of recognition, not just within the work but between text and reader. The text deliberately disorients the reader, playing off the slave narrative, *Notes from Underground*, and jazz traditions. This is a warning that readers will simply repeat the action of the assailant, commit a hermeneutic mugging of the text, if they are not prepared to give up the assumption of a shared linguistic world, which will mean giving up their self-understanding. Self-recognition has required transformation and loss for the narrator, and readers should expect a similar wrenching. Recognition of difference is not merely additive and synchronic but transformative and historical both individually and collectively. Ellisonian judgment does not ricochet between indeterminate "bannisterlessness" in politics and culture (to use Arendt's well-known phrase: 1979, 333–336) and determinacy in cognitive matters; rather, judgment emerges from dialogical reflection with the full range of experience. By making a common world a matter of aesthetic reflection rather than what emerges from a dialogical engagement about the true, good, and beautiful, Arendt shows that the danger of the Third Critique is not too much, but too little, agon.[14] The damage done to language and historical self-understandings by the forces of racism cannot be recognized or assessed by taking her aesthetic attitude.

Moreover, Ellison rejects any sequestering of aesthetics, in either its Arendtian or Habermasian versions, since "the work of art [. . .] is social action in itself" (1995, 91). Ellison is particularly sensitive to the way the category, "aesthetic," has been used to exclude African American literature and its overt social and political concerns—that is, such literature was/is concerned with matters that are "too prosaically political" and particularistic to be beautiful and universal.[15] For Ellison, language and art are politically important, not just on matters of equality and justice but also self-governance. A democracy is "not only a collection of individuals . . . but a collectivity of politically astute citizens . . . who would be prepared to govern" (Ellison 1981, xxi).

Arendt resists a conception of judgment informed by language and stories for several reasons. First, such a view threatens to make the subject of judgment into an artist who, by prospectively putting lives into narratives, turns people into things. Arendt thinks that work involves an instrumental relationship, in which an "element of violation and violence is present in all fabrication, and homo faber, the creator of human artifice, has always been the destroyer of nature [. . .]. [H]omo faber conducts himself as lord and master of the whole earth" (1958, 139). This is what Dana Villa calls the "Promethean" conception of authorship as willfulness against which Arendt reacts: "From Habermas to Marx, the hope has been to place human creations back under the will of their authors, and so to curtail the process of reification by which means become ends" (1996, 268). Arendt speaks of the "common error of regarding the state or government as a work of art" (1977, 153). The arts "bring forth something tangible and reify human thought to such an extent that the produced thing possesses an existence of its own"; hence, "politics is the exact opposite of art [. . .]. Independent existence marks the work of art as a product of making; utter dependence upon further acts to keep it in existence marks the state as a product of action" (153). Second, the artist, unlike the public, political actor, "must be isolated from the public, must be sheltered and concealed from it. Truly political activities, on the other hand, acting and speaking, cannot be performed at all without the presence of others" (217).

Arendt differentiates the perspective of the artistic creator from that of the perceiver: "The conflict, dividing the statesmen and the artist in their respective activities, no longer applies when we turn our attention from the making of art to its products [. . .]. These things obviously share with political 'products,' words and deeds, the quality that they are in need of some public space where they can appear and be seen; they can fulfill their own being, which is appearance, only in a public space which is common to all" (1977, 218). The reason Arendt can draw this line between reception and creation is because she does not think of the aesthetic observer as always already in narratives and symbols, as a being in language who risks her stories through dialogue with art or people.

From the Ellisonian perspective, Arendt gives a one-sided and ahistorical view of art as a thing rather than art as speech. To be sure, there is a long tradition of philosophical and literary thought that speaks of art in nondialogical terms—for example, as poesis. However, these accounts fail to describe the dialogical dynamics of the Western literary traditions. The most thorough articulation of this view is Mikhail Bakhtin's philosophy of the novel and of the subject. Bakhtin mounts a critique of the institutions of literary theory and criticism, which are set up only for poetry and poesis and which misunderstand the history of prose. (Aristotle's *Poetics*, formalism, and structuralism are the centerpieces of Bakhtin's critique.)[16] Three points about Bakhtinian/Ellisonian philosophy are relevant for contrast with Arendt. First, the author is not a maker who carves material into a shape but a speaker and listener whose medium (words) is already populated with the meanings and intentions of the speakers of the past and present. Bakhtin thus abandons the author as willful fabricator without giving up the constitutive dimension of language and narrative. Second, Bakhtin describes and valorizes the richness and multiplicity of everyday speech and writing so that the public space of intelligibility cannot be framed by such a global concept as "lifeworld." Such a frame is the first step in a process of creating unexamined presuppositions about the background necessary for intelligibility. Third, the relationship between the languages of daily life and the history of the novel is a fluid dialogical movement, not an opposition in which the fabricator carves out an object against the lifeworld.

Arendt's point, of course, is not about the history of literature but about politics, and how the importation of the metaphor of a constructed, fabricated society destroyed political freedom. This insight has no counterpart in Ellison's work, and it is of great importance, not just for understanding totalitarian regimes but for coming to terms with the paradoxes of the modern political project from Hobbes through liberalism.[17] Bakhtin's critique of this understanding of art acknowledges the force of Arendt's point as he dissents from this understanding of all of literature.

Thus, I am not denying that there is a relationship between art and the politics of making that is a danger. Rather, the danger of artifactual models that seek to coopt and deform political freedom can be better thematized through a dialogical understanding of subjectivity rather than by putting freedom beyond the reach of language. The interweaving of art and life is an important issue for political judgment, in which "art" is not precategorized as merely aesthetic, teleological, and reifying whether from the perspective of the speaker or the receiver.

The Taylorian line that I am following insists that storytelling is not just on the thinking side but on the knowing side precisely because it informs common sense. That is, we are always already in narratives that emerge from literary and nonliterary sources. Gadamer recognized the threat that Arendt sees in Plato's and Hegel's understanding of language: "What he [Hegel] calls dialectic and what Plato calls dialectic depends, in fact, on subordinating language to the 'statement,'" which is "antithetical to the nature of hermeneutic experience and the verbal nature of human experience of the world" (1994, 468). However, instead of driving a wedge between the speculative pursuits of philosophy and everyday speech, Gadamer finds speculation in our ordinary conversations: "Even in the most everyday speech there is an element of speculative reflection" since this happens any time that "words do not reflect being but express a relation to the whole of being" (469). The stories that inform our self-understandings open and foreclose experience (468–469). The history of the novel is about—among other things—differences in the relationship of language, fiction, and truth, in which art draws on and informs the common world. For Arendt, on the other hand, art only disengages from the world: "Art, therefore, which transforms sense objects into thought-things, tears them first of all out of their context in order to de-realize and thus prepare them for their new and different function" (1978, I, 49).

This dialogical understanding of our being in language also means that truth claims are not necessarily peremptory and anti-dialogic forms of speech, even if this has often been the historical practice. Hence, the problem is not the claim of truth but the linguistic practices that inform our dialogues. Moreover, these claims cannot and should not be excluded. (One afternoon with the discourse of *Oprah* illustrates how philosophical and metaphysical so-called ordinary conversation is.) Doxa does not always understand itself as mere opinion, but as a claim to truth. To characterize the views expressed in such forums as "doxa," "opinion," or "appearance" is to make a metaclaim about them, to take an unmasking philosophical stance toward these views, albeit a different one than the Platonic traditions Arendt notes. The differences between speakers in the public sphere are not just "horizontal" but also "vertical," even when the speakers are not philosophers. We are better off starting from the Gadamerian premise that all "understanding is [. . .] an encounter with something that asserts its truth" (1994, 489). Democratic institutions and virtues, not the exclusion of truth claims, preserve the plural public space of political action. The question is how to do public philosophy rather than whether to do it. In Ellison's case, this means that the new self-understanding that emerges during the course of the novel has political relevance because it reveals the oppressive shape to the public imagination that liberal and Arendtian concepts of freedom cannot bring out.[18]

Ellison's narrator gives us an example of this kind of interpretive judgment in the way he sets up his argumentative space with his audiences, with the languages of the past, and in the way he presents his protagonist's situations at different moments. That is, the narration of the story itself is about the exercise of political judgment. He tries to genealogize those constitutive elements he wants to slough off, while he narrativizes and incorporates those he wants to retrieve. Such judgment is neither determined nor "bannisterless."

Arendt, on the other hand, leaves us with a stark choice between Kant and Hegel: "Either we can say with Hegel: die Weltgeschichte ist das Weltgericht, leaving the ultimate judgment to Success, or we can maintain with Kant the autonomy of the minds of men and their possible independence of things as they are or as they have come into being" (1982, 5).[19] To say that we do not want historical success to replace judgment or a transsubjective spirit to absorb plurality does not require a rejection of any constitutive conception of language and the adoption of a Kantian conception. What is wrong with Hegel is not that he is speculative; rather, his ontology and the perspective of the absolute that informs it are unpersuasive as a public philosophy of democratic interpretation. Taylor, Bakhtin, and Ellison show us how situating the subject is not the same as determining judgment. Ellison's own practice of interpretive judgment shows how he engages with conflicting claims of different traditions—liberalism, Marxism, African American, canonical American—and he is certainly not the only novelist to do so. Indeed, one way of reading the nineteenth-century European novel is to see it as an argument about the legacy of the dispute between Kantians and Hegelians over how to tell the stories of embedded subjects concerned with freedom.

Thus, from Ellison's perspective, the problem with having the imagination "go visiting" (Arendt 1982, 43) is that it accepts a subject-to-subject model without interrogating the historical medium which articulates these subjects, the tissue of being that connects and fragments subjects. Ellison is forever interrogating the relationships among language, memory, and history as he moves through the world. He is sensitive to the resources and the oppressions of language and tradition in the articulation of the public realm—and the way African Americans are driven from it—in a way that Arendt is not. Arendt protects language from historical damage, as if language itself were not implicated in racial catastrophes of American life. Ellison portrays language as an ambiguous protean medium that articulates pain, triumph, love, and failure, a medium that connects and isolates us, enables and deprives, that shapes in a way that opens and forecloses the possibilities of the world: "If the word has the potency to revive and make us free, it has also the power to blind, imprison, and destroy. . . . The essence of the word is its ambivalence" (1995, 25). Ellison often speaks of the rituals of everyday life to talk about what I am calling "public imagination." Rituals are the politically ambiguous historical patterns of meaning. Ellison's work evokes and reworks such rituals throughout the novel—the opening scene of recognition in the Prologue, the Battle Royal scene in chapter 1, his encounters with all white leaders, his "romance" with white women. Events and actions are always already informed by patterns of language and action.[20]

No conception of the public/private distinction can keep these issues out of the public world, and Arendt's failure to see segregation's role in maintaining an exclusionary public sphere is remarkable. To be sure, Arendt describes the possibility of "worldlessness," to which persecuted minorities above all are subject when "the interspace we have called world [. . .] has simply disappeared" (1968, 21); however, her focus is on how modernity diminishes our world rather than the complex history of the languages of public imagination and institutions of meaning. These linguistic institutions, which long antedate modernity, have a continuity and durability that Arendt's fragile worlds do not.

Although Ellison never discusses directly the question of political judgment, I want to explore briefly how his work exhibits a philosophy of interpretive judgment. Ellison's story is of a nameless black protagonist's coming to see that he is invisible, and how he has internalized a self-understanding that makes him unaware of the problem. It is a first-person retrospective story of the meta-philosophical search for a site for telling the story, and there is a tension throughout between the language of the narrating self of the present and the series of experiencing selves of the past. The task of judgment I will pursue is how the narrating self interprets his relationship to his individual and collective histories, how he situates language with regard to the self-understanding of the character.

Often, Ellison employs a genealogical narrative that unmasks the racial vocabularies that inform both white and black self-understandings. He explains why such a genealogical strategy is necessary: "This unwillingness to resolve the conflict in keeping with his democratic ideals has compelled the white American, figuratively, to force the Negro down in the deeper level of his consciousness, into the inner world, where reason and madness mingle with hope and memory and endlessly give birth to nightmare and to dream; down into the province of the psychiatrist and the artist, from whence spring the lunatic's fancy and his work of art" (1995, 149). One of the effects of this inarticulate conflict is the unacknowledged presence of race in every facet of what white culture understands as "white": "It is practically impossible for the white American to think of sex, of economics, his children, womenfolk, or of sweeping sociopolitical changes, without summoning into consciousness fear-flecked images of black men" (149). Ellison does not subscribe to an essentialist identity politics of experience, even though he acknowledges the constitutive dimension of discourse, for the work of interpretation foregrounds the public possibilities of linguistic differences through the transformations of the narrator's identity and the structures of address to the reader.

Moreover, Ellison insists on the narrative understanding that must accompany any genealogical account. It is precisely here that Foucauldian and constructivist positions fall into a crisis of judgment, for they view narrative only as a factitious product of power and hence deprive themselves of the means of accounting for their own narrative/genealogical choices. For the narrating self, the experiencing self has internalized ideologies that have made him invisible to himself, not just others. To get beyond this, Ellison retrieves resources of African American traditions and American constitutional documents. Retrieval is predicated on the acknowledgment that racism and massive loss are inseparable from them. Ellison rejects any idealization of the past when he says, "The fantasy of an America free of blacks is at least as old as the dream of creating a truly democratic society" (1995, 577). Thus, he makes the question of our being in language one of interpretive judgment, in which dialogical retrieval (Taylorian strain) and genealogical unmasking make their claims on us and vice versa. Ellison thus asserts the worth of his claim against the claims of his historical predecessors.

HISTORY AND JUDGMENT

What accompanies Ellison's and Arendt's differences over language is a different conception of historical consciousness, even though they also share a great deal. In the interest of brevity, I will follow Benhabib's claim that Arendt's understanding of memory is pulled between a Husserl/Heidegger strain and a Benjaminian strain. In the former, we find "the mimetic recollection of lost origins of phenomena as contained in some fundamental human experience" (Benhabib 1996b, 95). Hence, in the *Human Condition*, we read of the "original meaning of politics" or of the "lost" distinction between "private" and "public" (Arendt 1958, 22ff., 68ff.).[21] In Benjaminian fragmentary history, the historian is the pearl diver or the collector who "select[s] his precious fragments from the pile of debris" (Arendt 1958, 200) of the past. As is well known, the pearls that Arendt recovers are the worlds of political action that were momentary achievements of Athenian democracy and the American Revolution. Benhabib praises the Benjaminian feature of her thought because it does not rely on a narrative of decline from some original way of being.

What interests me, however, is that both Benjamin and Heidegger understand modern historical consciousness in the context of catastrophe, in which modern subjects are so wrenched and deracinated from the resources of their cultural inheritance that the only task is to pull out moments from a distant past. For both thinkers, the lifeworlds of modernity are so damaged as to be unworthy of nuanced attention. Arendt thinks that tradition has lost its capacity to inform judgment because of two blows, the modern "'revolt' against the authority of tradition and the twentieth-century 'break' with tradition" (Benhabib 1996b, 91). "The thread of tradition is broken and we shall not be able to renew it [. . .]. What has been lost is the continuity of the past [. . .]. What you then are left with is still the past, but a fragmented past, which has lost its certainty of evaluation" (Arendt 1978, I, 212). With such an understanding of historical rupture, she is pushed into a transcendental reconstruction of the human condition and the idealized intersubjective world it requires rather than examining the ambiguous historical shifts in public meanings and imagination.

Arendt's storytelling follows these leads by giving rich, historically detailed accounts of the degradation of the world under totalitarianism, but historically thin and idealized discussions of the retrievals of the Greeks and the thinkers of the American Revolution for their momentary achievement of freedom. It is one thing to have these past moments enrich our understanding of political possibility, but quite another to overlook the failures of a Jeffersonian moment, which has also had its legacies. What is missing is a fine-grained account of historical consciousness of the subjects of the contemporary American public to whom she is speaking. Hence, the issue of what historical understanding of narratives and symbols informs the American public imagination at the time of her exchange with Ellison is not a question that Arendt's philosophy of judgment brings into play. Although she provides an extraordinary account of the losses of modernity, her particular form of historical consciousness is not suited to tracking the imbrication of racism even in democracy's great moments, to understanding the variegated linguistic medium that connects the rememberer to the remembered, or to providing a way of thematizing the workings of historical consciousness in everyday political life.

The politics of public memory, of how a particular democracy ought to remember its past, has been the subject of important debates about the interpretation of the Holocaust or slavery, debates that call on both Arendtian and Ellisonian forms of historical consciousness for thinking about catastrophe. Arendt focuses on modernity's power to impoverish and subject, while Ellison explores the specifics of what Saul Friedlander calls the historical working-through process.[22] What Ellison's texts dramatize are the deliberations of democratic historical consciousness and the revisions in public and private understandings that go with it. Ellison shows how we are in history and language in such a way that we spontaneously project the damage and resources of the past. His work is part of the American *Historikerstreit* over how to tell the story of American racism and the Civil War. This argument is taken up by contemporary novelists—from Toni Morrison's Beloved to Sherley Anne Williams's *Dessa Rose,* and Charles Johnson's *Middle Passage*—who retell and revise slave narratives because Americans of all races have not been able to bear witness and work through these issues. Thus, what Ellison does better than Arendt is help us think through the multiple ways our being in language informs political judgment so that it is neither determined by nor deracinated from the stories we tell ourselves.

Globalization and the Clash of Cultures

I looked at the problematic of public imagination in the context of national politics in chapter 4; this chapter will show how this problematic can clarify well-known disputes over the politics and rationality of culture in international debates. I pursue my examples in a developmental sequence, beginning with the work of Edward Said. Why is Said an important figure? First, his work has attracted the attention of scholars in literature, philosophy, and international relations.[1] Second, he proposes an understanding of literature and culture in which a text is not a mere reflection of a historical, material, or philosophical context, but is itself a dramatic participant—and, as such, a rival to my conception of public imagination.[2] Third, he exposes the ways that the moral ideals of modern Western political and cultural projects were imbricated with the practice of global imperialism and makes it clear that no appeal to democratic ideals can bypass a political witnessing to the disasters of European modernity outside, not just inside, its borders. Fourth, Said's achievements in opening up the politics of culture have, nevertheless, disguised important shortcomings of his interpretive philosophy that are symptomatic of certain strands of cultural studies. These failings derive from his treatment of culture as a constructed object for moral judgment and from his separation of culture both from practical reasoning and from explanatory analyses of social science.[3]

I dramatize these shortcomings and push my argument to the next level by examining Said's critique of Samuel Huntington's well-known thesis that global politics is driven by civilizational identity. Said's limited, empirical criticisms fail to address the challenge left by Huntington—can we reason through culture? I then look at one sophisticated positive answer to this question proposed by Amartya Sen's response to Huntington. Sen's proposal draws on empirical historical evidence from different cultures in order to advance the idea of the universality of freedom. What Sen leaves out of his model of reason, however, is public imagination, and I will bring this omission to the surface by looking at the challenge of Ashis Nandy to Sen's position.

SAID'S UNIVERSE OF CONSTRUCTED
OBJECTS AND COSMOPOLITAN SUBJECTS

Said's first important work for our purposes is *Orientalism*, in which he examines how the Western social imaginary in literature and the social sciences invented an Oriental other for purposes of invidious comparison or political exploitation. Social scientific studies and aesthetic texts work together to form a pervasive discourse.[4] In *Culture and Imperialism*, Said goes beyond *Orientalism* by adding the work of Third World writers to his critique of the West. In *Culture and Imperialism*, Said adopts the contrapuntal strategy of juxtaposing stories of imperialism (chap. 2) with stories of "resistance and opposition" (chap. 3). He wants to expose the ideologies of Western imperialism and of those cultures that fought against it. Said offers not a theory of imperialism but an account of the importance of culture in the study of politics. As he says, "Imperialism and the novel fortified each other to such a degree that it is impossible to read one without in some way dealing with the other" (1993, 71). These stories "become the method colonized people use to assert their own identity and the existence of their own history" (xii). These ideologies have prevented us from seeing how power and cultural identity work together to carve up the world into competing islands. He hopes to reconnect these islands by retelling their stories in a way that recognizes both Western culture and the marginalized cultures of the Third World. Imperialist and nationalist narratives that have been isolated by narrow self-understandings of identity and essentialism can be brought together: "My interpretive political aim (in the broadest sense) [is] to make concurrent those views and experiences that are ideologically and culturally closed to each other and that attempt to distance or suppress other views and experiences" (33). By bringing these together, Said hopes to open new empirical insights into the interconnectedness of the world's experiences: "To ignore or otherwise discount the overlapping experience of Westerners and Orientals, the interdependence of the cultural terrains in which colonizer and colonized co-existed and battled each other through projections as well as rival geographies, narratives, and histories, is to miss what is essential about the world in the past century" (xx).

Although Said gestures toward a variety of different approaches to culture, the consistent thread in his work from *Orientalism* and *Culture and Imperialism* to his final collection, *Reflections on Exile*, is a form of constructivism, in which he does an immanent critique of literary, social, and political discourses. In *Orientalism*, for instance, he says: "It is not the thesis of this book to suggest that there is such a thing as a real or true Orient (Islam, Arab, or whatever); nor is it to make the assertion about the necessary privilege of an 'insider' perspective over the 'outsider' one [. . .]. On the contrary, I have been arguing that the 'Orient' is itself a constituted entity" (1978, 54). In one sense, Said is doing a version of immanent critique that is reminiscent of Foucault's—that is, Said is interested in exposing previous accounts of the relations between the West and the East and their forms of power; he is not interested in writing a more adequate historical understanding of these relations.[5] However, what is very different from Foucault's archaeological or genealogical approaches is the way Said turns the "Orient" into a theme that runs from Aeschylus to the present.[6] Said does not do historically specific Foucauldian analyses. Instead, he takes the first-order languages of texts and shows "how all representations are constructed, for what purpose, by whom, and with what components" (1993, 314–315). His aim is not to place these texts in the context of historical forces or discursive systems but to point out the moral/political shortcomings that historical actors rationalized: "what appeared to be detached and apolitical culture disciplines [depended] upon a quite sordid history of imperialist ideology and colonialist practice" (41). Said's constructivism takes a third-person external perspective on historical agents and redescribes the workings of language and culture against the grain of their self-understandings, but remains agnostic about the self-understandings that underwrite critique. Hence, the study of "Orientalism" in the discourse of the West leaves out not just the self-understandings of the actual cultures in question but also those of the interpreter.

Said's analyses stop with the juxtaposition of the stories of colonizer and colonized and never get to a dialogue between these traditions and their ethical content. This is blocked in part because he understands traditions and cultures only as ideological traps to be exposed rather than as resources to be retrieved (1993, xii–xiii, 4–5, 15–16, 32–33). While Said is, of course, eloquent on his empirical positionality—that is, his upbringing in Palestine,

Egypt, and America—he says little about how he situates his thought in any traditions. "Culture" is one of the determinants of the subject that "critical consciousness" needs to watch, but it is defined only negatively as entrapment.[7] Said confesses that he is deeply suspicious of the concept: "As for me, though perhaps I am putting it too strongly, culture has been used as essentially not a cooperative and communal term but rather as a term for exclusion." His discussion of the concept of tradition is similar, for he considers it only as an ideological fabrication designed to produce a national or ethnic purity, not as a source of rationality (15–16). For Said, this concept of culture "is a source of identity, and a rather combative one at that," a conception that leads culture to separate itself from "the everyday world" (xiii).

Said is so concerned that any ethical/political shape, whether at the level of the individual or community, will become a reified enclave that he gives no theoretical, ethical, or narrative space to the positive construction of identity, including the identity of his ideal community. He assigns the pejorative adjective "religious" to all forms of cultural identity.[8] This use of the "secular" is a hallmark of liberal thought, and Said universalizes it in a theoretical and practical way.[9] For theoretical thought, the secular serves to note that we must take a third-person constructivist or explanatory stance toward identities and forms of reasoning. These must be explained functionally rather than treated as alternative reasonings: "Men and women produce their own history, and therefore it must be possible to interpret that history in secular terms, under which religions are seen, as you say as a token of submerged feelings of identity, of tribal solidarity" (1987, 232). Said seems to be asking us to evacuate all self-understandings by subjecting them to constructivist immanent critique; he is thus depriving us of any reality by evaporating all languages of reference and ethics.

With this epistemological objection to religious discourse comes the moral commitment to open, public discussion against any religious tendency to self-containment: "The importance of secularism is that it does leave open the space of discussion, whereas this is not true of the return to religion [. . .]. The secular at least gives one the opportunity to present, to talk, to discuss, and to change, which is the most important thing" (1994b, 24). Getting different cultures to make themselves vulnerable to dialogue at the same table is indeed a crucial issue; however, the question is whether we need to consider such a space as coming from moral/political ideals that are detached from all historical cultural and religious understandings.[10] In leaping to principles across history, Said is following the liberal tradition that we have seen.[11] Rawls and Habermas refer to history from very high up above the details because all they want from their accounts is the moral and political lesson, to which Said signs on directly.[12] Said thus joins liberals in missing the opportunity to examine the complex connections among public imagination, historical events, and political reasoning.[13]

In order to clarify this missed opportunity, I will look very quickly at a study that has similarities to *Orientalism* and *Culture and Imperialism*—a sweeping historical study of political imagination that seeks to change how we think about how our current modes of political reasoning. Stephen Toulmin's *Cosmopolis* explores the rise of modern European secular political philosophy, not only to clarify the genesis and details of the relationship among forms of public imagination and historical events but to retrieve forms of political reasoning that were lost or decanonized after the rise of formalist universalism. My point is not to endorse the details of Toulmin's argument but to bring out why changes in public imagination are an important touch point in public reasoning.[14]

The focus of Toulmin's study is the familiar terrain of political theory— the end of the Thirty Years War, the Peace of Westphalia, and the beginning of the idea of the modern liberal nation state. During this period, as the story goes, "the idea of a united Christendom was replaced by a Hobbesian scientific political philosophy and a new understanding of nationality in which each sovereign chose the official religion of his own State" (1990, 91). An international society of nation states arose. Toulmin revises the story of modernity in order to make three key points: 1. "Instead of regarding Modern Science and Philosophy as the products of leisure [. . .] we will do better to turn the received view upside down and treat them as a response to a contemporary crisis" (16). 2. Instead of telling a single story about this period, we need to separate the modernity of the humanist Renaissance of Montaigne, Shakespeare, and Henry IV that preceded the rise of science from the fundamentally different formalist modernity of science and politics that followed. The prescientific Renaissance had a sensitivity to and a tolerance for the diverse heterogeneity of the world that scientific modernity shut down. 3. Instead of canonizing and identifying with the scientific self-understanding as we do today, we need to recover these earlier resources of rationality. While we may certainly have reservations about his reading of Hobbes or where Toulmin comes out, any philosophy of deliberation ought to be able to engage the claims of this argument, for it touches the inescapable features of historicized public reasoning: What are the shifts in the shapes of key institutions of meaning for the time in question? What are the causal forces at stake in these meanings? What is the connection of current reasoning to the past?[15] Said's problematic gives us no way to engage these questions, for it reduces institutions of meaning to ideological smoke that obscures social reality and political judgment.

Said's Kantian cosmopolitan political aims not only put him at odds with historical philosophers such as Toulmin; they also separate him from Foucault.[16] Said's insights about the construction of public imagination are brought out in the context of a democratic forum, an international public sphere that "bind[s] the European as well as the native together in a new non-adversarial community of awareness and antiimperialism" (1993, 274). Thus, Said builds his idea of community, an international public sphere, on an empirical unmasking of destructive and interrelated stories and an appeal to a Kantian noumenal moral/political world that drops from the sky untainted by the blood of history. "The liberation of all mankind from imperialism" (1993, 274) requires "reconceiving of human experience in non-imperialist terms" (276). The word "experience," missing in Said's analyses of history, appears as a utopia so remote as to be inconceivable, for we never read about what such an experience might look like. What Said means by "noncoercive knowledge" is developed into a Kantian regulative ideal, even though Said never invokes Kant's name. By resorting to this formulation, Said seeks to avoid narrative and hermeneutics, which, for him, serve all too often to rationalize oppressive desires for national or ethnic identity. Unlike Habermas, Said does not theorize his political ideals or his conception of public reason. What he shares with Habermas is the location of his political ideals outside of history and its cultural documents. Indeed, it seems as if Said's attentiveness to the destructiveness of post-Enlightenment European culture pushes him to separate these ideals from any residual Hegelian elements that we find in Habermas's reworkings of Kant. Kantian formalism is the perfect pendant to constructivist distance, since neither offers us a subject of interpretation who reasons through rather than against his or her historico-linguistic embedding.[17]

What is left out here is precisely what Kant's analysis calls for—a way to stop dividing the political spaces of the world into ethnic nations by opening up political space to multiple identities. For all of his critique of modernity, Said stays in the grip of the old opposition between abstract cosmopolitanism and rooted nationalism. To be sure, his constructivism opens up universalism in a way that Kant never did. However, the horrors of modernity require specific witnessing and naming—languages of identity, reference, ethics, and politics. Many of the ills of nationalism that Said identifies cannot be chalked up simply to a morality of nationalism but must be ascribed to a host of complex causal and cultural issues that political judgment needs to address. Such issues include, for example, the functional needs of the modern economy (Gellner) and the problems of cultural and political integration within and between nations(Calhoun). Thus, when Said recoils from the horror of nationalism into abstract universality, he simply selects another of Western modernity's damaged strands. Instead, we need to learn to negotiate politically with our cultural identities, histories, and visions of the good, including religious ones.

To describe his ideal subject of political deliberation and that subject's interpretive labor, Said cites a passage from Hugo of St. Victor, a twelfth-century monk from Saxony, as a model for someone "wishing to transcend the restraints of imperial or national or provincial limits" (1993, 335): "The tender soul has fixed his love on one spot in the world; the strong person has extended his love to all places; the perfect man has extinguished his" (335). Said likens this process to a transitional argument, a Freudian working through: A "person achieves independence and detachment by *working through* attachments, not by rejecting them" (336). He goes on to endorse this attitude for the politically astute cultural historian: "Only through this attitude can a historian, for example, begin to grasp human experience and its written records in all their diversity and particularity; otherwise one would be more committed to the exclusion and reactions of prejudice than to the *negative freedom* of real knowledge" (335–336, my emphasis). This tale about monkish ethical work shows precisely how practical reason is divorced from history and the complexities of public imagination. Love is not given content except through its opposition to distance. In Said's description, the content of one's cultural inheritance and its ideas of reasoning are reduced to an escape to principle. In Said's version of Rawls's original position, the subject arrives at detachment through an ascesis, not just a thought experiment.

This passage illustrates beautifully one of the connections between Western secular cosmopolitanism and its Christian antecedents. The very particular historical trail behind this anecdote disappears once the insight about equal love and detachment appears. This trail takes on special importance because Said wants to detach his political claims from the histories of public imagination. What disappears in Said's moral critique is the specificity of Western modernity as well as the specificity of other cultures.[18]

Said's notion of the exiled deliberator causes problems when he tries to distinguish his position on agency from those of the antihumanist ontologies of Foucault and Derrida, which have been so influential in the postcolonial work of Gayatri Spivak and Homi Bhabha. Said rejects them because they ignore the agency of the oppressed and the responsibility of the oppressor. Thus, Said rejects Spivak's hypothesis that imperial discourse does not just oppress but completely coopts the native subject into complicity with his own oppression. National resistance, in her view, provides evidence of how thoroughly the hegemonic discourse has been internalized: "No perspective critical of imperialism can turn the Other into a self, because the project of imperialism has always already historically refracted what might have been the absolutely Other into a domesticated Other that consolidates the imperial self" (cited in Parry 1992, 36).[19] Said rejects postmodernist ontologies of power that rewrite agents as movements of signification. The problem is that Said does not give moral agency any historical force, and he does not connect the ideals of the actors to his own narrative position. Agency and recognition become merely formal requirements detached from any particulars.

The closest he comes to affirming the shape of a particular narrative is in his essay "Permission to Narrate." In this text, he affirms that the existence of a Palestinian narrative is crucial to the constitution of a political identity and that this narrative has not "drawn any acknowledgement from Israel or the United States, which have restricted themselves to nonnarrative and indefinite formulae" (1994a, 255).[20] Instead, Western media have turned the actions of Palestinians into the image of terrorism, which is "anti-narrative" (257). Yet here narrative is just a formal right that demands recognition: "The power to narrate and to block other narratives from forming and emerging is very important to culture and imperialism, and constitutes one of the main connections between them" (1993, xiii). Though Said is not for or against narrative in politics per se, he never sees narrative as a form of reasoning whose content needs to be addressed, whether in the texts he studies or in the ones he writes. For Said, narrative, like tradition, is a holistic notion, and Said, like Foucault, wants to dissolve all connections between judgment and history.[21] To clarify these broad criticisms, I will look at two readings from *Culture and Imperialism*, one from "within" the Western tradition and one from "outside."

In his discussion of Jane Austen's *Mansfield Park,* Said focuses on the connection between the Bertram family's life in England and the estate in Antigua from which the family draws its income. He then isolates a moment of silence in the novel when Sir Thomas is asked about the slave trade: "In order more accurately to read works like *Mansfield Park,* we have to see them in the main as resisting or avoiding that other setting which their formal inclusiveness, historical honesty, and prophetic suggestiveness cannot completely hide" (1993, 96). Said juxtaposes, in his typical contrapuntal fashion, this silence about Sir Thomas's activities in the colonies to the textual richness of his appearances at Mansfield Park: "From our later perspective, we can interpret Sir Thomas's power to come and go in Antigua as stemming from the muted national experience of individual identity, behavior, and 'ordination,' enacted with such irony and taste at Mansfield Park. The task is to lose neither a true historical sense of the first, nor a full enjoyment or appreciation of the second, all the while seeing both together" (97). Said's description of the task of the critic reveals his methodological problem. The truth of history is the imperialism in the text; what saves the text from being merely an instrument of oppression is its aesthetic dimension that we "appreciate" rather than "know," another Kantian echo. Instead of addressing the central question posed in his book—what does the recognition of imperialism in a major work in democratic ethical/political traditions do to the self-understanding of those traditions and those of the interpreter?—Said avoids confronting the different history in the object and subject of judgment.[22]

Moreover, Said remains silent about what is left to retrieve from Austen's work and the diverse strands of ethical and aesthetic European culture that inform it.[23] What is the relationship between his own ethical/political understandings and this historical moment? Instead, he offers us a Kantian moral lesson. By stating no account of how to work through the ethical and historical complexities of the past, he gives a reductive portrait of the West and the nonwest. We see here how the ahistorical, noumenal requirements of Kantian justice and autonomy and the good can have consequences for one's reading of history. To turn culture into a constructed object for the application of noumenal moral standards is to give no place to the work of interpretive political judgment. Said reads like a judge who puts these works on trial rather than a cultural/political historian. The procedures of Kantian justice and autonomy require and justify this abstraction. The task of critics, I would maintain, is rather to situate *Mansfield Park* and themselves in the cultures and languages they wish to defend in order to argue with the claims it makes on all of us as readers. In what sense does Austen's complicity with imperialism vitiate the positive claims her text makes on us, and in what sense does it not? What other strands of the social imaginary are being reinforced or revised by Austen's work?

These problems in Said's model are not rectified in his discussions of Third World writers, such as Fanon and C. L. R. James. Said celebrates these thinkers because they anticipate his own empirical insight that "Western and non-western experiences" belong "together because they are connected by imperialism" and because of their methodologies, which have "nomadic, migratory, and anti-narrative energy" (1993, 279). Yet his discussion of James does not sort through the different strains in James's thought; instead, Said praises him only for his ability to juxtapose discrepant experiences, praise which is all too thin. To retrieve a work because it is "heteroglot" or "hybrid" runs together facts about discourse with an assessment of discourse in order to celebrate multiplicity per se.[24] In the same way, "contrapuntalism" evacuates interpretive judgment, for it simply urges us to juxtapose previously separated narratives and discourses without offering guidelines about how to read them, about what the ensuing dialogue might look like, or what the consequences of this confrontation might be for each side.[25]

Moreover, Said's constructivism not only excludes such comparative thinking; it also gives no place to explanatory causal accounts of cultural processes that contribute to the production of culture. He implies that the hegemony of Western ideas comes from their single-minded moral depravity rather than the material and social forces of global capitalism.[26] In devoting himself to immanent textual critique, Said does not try to explain how certain cultural practices came about. This is not a particular choice on Said's part but a methodological stricture that follows from constructivism (and Foucault). Giving causal accounts of historical events or processes commits the theorist to saying what is really going on and why—precisely what constructivists refuse to do. Thus, to understand India's distinctive movement toward modernity requires understanding the dynamics of its reflexive interaction with British colonialism in such a way that the complexities of its modes of thinking and self-revision emerge.[27]

To highlight what is missing from Said's contrapuntal model, I would like to consider briefly Anouar Majid's *Unveiling Traditions: Postcolonial Islam in a Polycentric World*, which addresses the question of cross-cultural political reasoning in the context of Islam.[28] Majid's work has two main goals: to show the force of capitalism in generating global political and cultural conflicts and to show the modes of reasoning among different Islamic thinkers. For him, these texts are not constructed objects to be unmasked but dialogical partners whose languages are in touch with his own site of judgment. His analysis shows what "hybrid" thinkers look like from the inside and how the different strains interact. Thus, in his discussion of the feminist sociologist Fatima Mernissi, Majid articulates different assessments of specific strands of her thought. He agrees that "restoring women into the political arena becomes the necessary condition for the restoration of the long-eclipsed democratic spirit in Islam" but insists that "she fails to connect gender to capitalism" (2000, 105–108). He wants to highlight strains of contemporary thought that develop how Islam is compatible with democracy, not just with secular democracy. "The struggle in the Islamic world today is, in fact, over democratizing decision making and wresting the state from the hands of regimes that have ossified religion" (108).

Thus, while Said's work opens new insights into the interconnections of culture and imperialism, it offers no way for us to reason within or across cultures. My point about the importance of public imagination brings together all the conventional counters of reason—the empirical, the normative, and the explanatory. The political stakes of reasoning across cultures are articulated most bluntly by Samuel Huntington, who rejects any appeal to universals.

HUNTINGTON ON HISTORICAL AND CROSS-CULTURAL REASONING

There have been many criticisms of Huntington's well-known thesis that a "clash of civilizations" will replace the conflicts of the Cold War. My purpose here will not be to address the empirical critiques of his account of the state of world cultures but to examine the philosophical assumptions he makes about public imagination and reasoning. He defines "civilization," as "the common objective elements, such as language, history, religion, customs, institutions, and the subjective self-identification of people" (Huntington 1996, 43) and discusses them from a historical skycam ten miles up. Directing his analysis to foreign policy makers in the United States, he urges his audience to give up hope in the appeal to universal values. There are no such values for Huntington, and nonwesterners rightly see the appeal to these "universals"—and their embodiment in such institutions as the United Nations—as the instruments of Western power.[29]

Many critics—including Said—pour scorn on Huntington for his misleading generalizations about culture—for instance, his neglect of cultural hybridity and exchange—and his politics of power and self-interest.[30] As Said says, "[Huntington's] use of the words 'culture' and 'civilization' [is] sloppy precisely because for him the two words represent reified objects rather than the dynamic, ceaselessly turbulent things that they in fact are" (2000, 581). However, these empirical points do not address the question of culture and rationality.

From the point of view of my argument, the philosophical problem with Huntington's organic concept of culture is not just the way it homogenizes, but the way it denies the significance of reasoning done by cultures and polities about their identities and histories through time. He characterizes the dynamics of historical change in a civilization through the organic metaphors of growth and death (1996, 44). Civilizations (cultures) do not reason with themselves through time; they unfold according to a dynamic of internal and external forces. In his view, historical change can and should be characterized from the outside so that civilizations stand before one another as monoliths. Such sphinx-like beings can be dealt with only strategically. Since the internal histories of cultural identities are not accessible to dialogical reason, we cannot expect to be able to reason across cultures either. This inaccessibility of culture to reason seems to be attributed to the idea that questions of identity for Huntington are answered by religion, which offers only a dogma. "For people facing the need to determine Who am I? Where do I belong? Religion provides compelling answers" (97). Identities are facts to be accepted. To be sure, societies change "if the religious needs of modernization cannot be met by their traditional faiths" (100), but these changes are addressed not in terms of social forms and their historical possibilities but only from the functionalist perspective of an outsider who posits unmet "needs." Religion (culture) still stands opposed to rationality in this positivist epistemology. Moreover, there is a species of what philosophers call "emotivism" here, in which needs, feelings, aspirations are consigned to a subjective irrationality. While Huntington's organic cultures may seem an easy target for my philosophy of public imagination, the subtle analyses of culture and politics by Amartya Sen are not.

Amartya Sen's work covers an enormous range of subjects. For the sake of convenience, I will limit myself to Sen's critique of Huntington and to his debate with Ashis Nandy on secularism, for these two examples will enable me to show the value and limit of his work on public imagination.

Sen seizes on Huntington's assertion that Western notions of freedom are alien to Asia by opening up the history of both the West and the East. For Sen, one grasps a culture not by generalizing from present phenomena but by investigating the history of the public imagination of that culture. First, he says that it is shortsighted to see a Western tradition as embodying centuries of political philosophies of freedom. Instead, the liberal democratic ideas that we now take as "Western" are a very recent achievement of the last two hundred years. If we go back beyond these dates, we find that, by its own standards, the West doesn't look very progressive on freedom. Second, he implicitly criticizes Huntington for drawing superficial conclusions about Asian traditions. Huntington tends to dismiss other traditions as top-to-bottom authoritarian when he finds particular features that contradict contemporary liberal democracy. He thus ignores the extensive treatment of important individual concepts—such as freedom: "the real issue is not whether these non-freedom perspectives are present in Asian traditions, but whether the freedom-oriented perspectives are absent from them" (Sen 1997, 36). Asian cultures are complex and diverse, and they demand a reading that takes their reasoning seriously rather than consigning it to organic or constructivist development. Sen discusses two Indian thinkers: the emperor Ashoka from the third century B.C., and the philosopher Kautilya, whose Arthashatra ("economic science") comes from the fourth century B.C. The point, Sen insists, "is that the heterogeneity of Indian traditions contains a variety of views and reasonings, and they include, in different ways, arguments in favor of tolerance, of freedom, and even (in the case of Ashoka) of equality at a very basic level" (37). If mere writings are not enough to be convincing, Sen continues with the example of the political practices of Akbar, the Mogul emperor of the sixteenth century, who emphasized diversity of religions and rights of expression. He then reminds us that "while Akbar was making these pronouncements on religious tolerance, the Inquisition was in full throttle in Europe" (38). Hence, Sen concludes, "It is hard to make sense of the view that the basic ideas underlying freedom and rights in a tolerant society are 'Western' notions, and somehow alien to Asia, though that view has been championed by Asian authoritarians and western chauvinists" (39).

Despite these insights, Sen's problematic blocks out public imagination in important ways. He uses empirical points about the presence of reasoning about freedom and tolerance in nonwestern traditions to leap directly to the universality of freedom as capability.[31] In other words, he is not talking about shifts in the social imaginary through time and connecting it to practical reason, as I would do. Instead, he wants to show that the idea of freedom is sufficiently shared by most cultures to enable him to develop freedom as capability as a viable global universal: "this book is informed by a belief in the ability of different people from different cultures to share many common values and to agree on some common commitments. Indeed, the overriding value of freedom as organizing principle of this work has this feature of a strong universalist presumption" (2000, 244).[32] But so what if he does not address the problem of public imagination? Isn't traveling light in controversial areas such as our relationship to language an advantage in global politics? Ashis Nandy's reading of many of the same thinkers from Indian political history brings out exactly why we need a conception of public imagination if we are to hear and articulate political questions.

The key difference between Nandy and Sen from my perspective emerges in the way they articulate their positions on secularism and modernity. For Sen, it is a question of norms and developmental facts. For Nandy, the modern secular social imaginaries are under investigation. To understand their differences, we need a very brief background on the secularism debate.[33]

Two of the West's most powerful readings of secularism are to see it as an independent ethic and as common ground.[34] We have seen examples of the independent ethic in the work of Habermas and Said, but the tradition goes back to Hobbes. In this view, we "abstract from religious beliefs altogether [. . .] and look for certain features of the human condition which allow us to deduce certain exceptionless norms" (Taylor 1998b, 33). The other approach is "the common ground" perspective, which tries to be equidistant from established religious communities—a reading of the American separation of church and state, for example, as "one nation under God" but not bound to any particular church. Religious diversity obviously challenges the common ground approach and can push a culture toward the independent ethic. But the independent ethic is then subjected to a challenge of partisanship, not only from those with different religious beliefs, but also from those with conflicting comprehensive views—ecologists, feminists, and others—who claim that the principles invoked by the independent ethic are not neutral and universal.

Sen defines his own version of political secularism as "the separation of the state from any particular religious order." Such a position does not insist that "the state must steer clear of any association with any religious matter whatsoever." Instead, "there must be symmetry of treatment" (1998, 456). In making this move, Sen is trying to finesse both of these readings. He departs from the independent ethic approach in that he does not seek to push religion out of public life; he avoids the common ground approach in that he does not make his position emerge from the existing religious doctrines. Rather, he argues for the universality of freedom and tolerance and then tries to find examples in different traditions. This move enables him to avoid characterizing the public imaginations of competing political communities.[35] Thus, in his view, secularism does not have to take sides on modernity: "modernism is not really the issue at all" (481).

Nandy, on the other hand, uses "secularism" in a broad way to designate Western liberalism and modernity as a worldview rather than contenting himself with the question of norms and ideals. He wants to recover the lifeworlds of premodern South Asia from the vocabularies of Western social science. In "The Politics of Secularism and the Recovery of Political Toleration," Nandy cites some of the same examples of "premodern" freedom and tolerance as Sen does in the response to Huntington (e.g., Emperor Ashoka); however, Nandy takes these examples to argue that premodern religious communities dealt with questions of difference and tolerance in a way superior to that of the modern nation state. These are not examples of "tolerance" common to premodern and modern political culture, as they are for Sen, but examples of different forms of reasoning about culture, difference, and politics. For Nandy, such an empirical reading that looks for common values leaves in place "the hegemonic language of modern secularism popularized by the West" (321). To let Indian culture appear requires reconstructing the category of religion from its Western, Christian, post-medieval imbrication with the rise of the state. This narrowing of the concept of religion—which he calls "faith as ideology" (322)—is to be distinguished from a different understanding of religion that is more applicable to the lifeworld of South Asia—faith "as way of life" (322). Religion as a way of life has a record of tolerance toward difference, and it is especially open to the fluid conceptions of self that contrast with the model of Western autonomy. Religion as ideology and the idea of the nation state are part of the colonial project that South

Asian elites have internalized. He proposes that South Asia abandon seeking religious tolerance by having elites impose a Western model; instead, societies should "explore the philosophy, the symbolism and theology of tolerance in the faiths of the citizens and hope that the state systems in South Asia may learn something from the tolerance of everyday Hinduism, Islam, Buddhism or Sikhs" (338).

In order to learn through a comparative political exploration of the symbols, myths, and stories of different religions, we need to break the grip of Western modernity's historical self-understanding. Breaking this grip begins not just with reaching toward others for common values but with interrogating the emergence of the positions in question. Like Toulmin, Nandy asks the West to reexamine the historical trauma of "uprooting" (1995, 55) at the origin of modern historical, cosmopolitan consciousness. Placing itself beyond the grip of social imaginaries, this conception seeks an objective and universal reason that gives no stature to premodern modes of understanding that focus on the morality of the present rather than the facts of the past.[36] These premodern stories point to blind spots in historical and political reasoning that refuses to acknowledge the shaping presuppositions of its own social imaginary.

Nandy's mode of intervention in debate is not to march in with criteria but to pose a question that requires self-interrogation about the social imaginary that frames debate.[37] Thus, in the controversy surrounding the destruction of a mosque in Ayodhya by members of the Ramjanmabhumi movement, he questions the secularist claim that getting the history "right" is really going to be the decisive moment in what is a political argument about the present.[38]

Sen responds to Nandy only at the empirical level. Sen agrees about the important examples of tolerance before the advent of secularism as a political doctrine, but he denies on empirical grounds Nandy's claim that secularism has increased political violence. By avoiding the question of public imagination, Sen is not letting Nandy's argument appear. That is, he is not responding to Nandy's claims about the shaping of the social imaginary—that modernity and the nation state have damaged forms of life, that Western secular "tolerance" is more coercive than the premodern forms of "tolerance."[39] In other words, only through a conception of public imagination, such as I have argued for here, can the stakes of the argument between Sen and Nandy be fully articulated.[40] The apparent "overlapping consensus" between Sen and Nandy on premodern forms of religious tolerance could serve as a point of departure, but it cannot substitute for engaging the different public imaginations of citizens, as Sen, like Rawls, seems to hope.

Moreover, thematizing public imagination would change not just Sen's argument but Nandy's as well, for it would force him to discriminate among different strands of the West and articulate the social imaginaries of democratic communities of faith. Can secularism be reduced to Nandy's reductive portrait? Pushing both sides to articulate their positions more fully may not make them agree, but it would give them more to argue with and about.

The lesson of this chapter is that many thinkers in cultural studies and political philosophy have tried to ground and frame political dialogue by putting its fundamental principles and its construction of the facts beyond the historicity and complexity of public dialogue. The drive to move beyond the historicized medium of public imagination as the locus of reasoning into the specious clarity of facts and ideals is not a mistake of either the Left or the Right. It crosses the political spectrum.

One of the great contributions made by the studies of Said, Toulmin, Sen, and Nandy is that they show how important a historical understanding of institutions of meaning is to public reason. Public reason must not only bear witness to the specific horrors that continue to haunt the institutions of meaning; it must also return to previous configurations of institutions of meaning for resources in renegotiating the intersections of cultures and civilizations. The familiar vocabulary of liberalism and constructivism—abstract principle, negative liberty, homogenized cultures, and difference per se—do not open up a dialogical historicized space of public imagination; instead, these notions become part of a project for putting ideals beyond the damaged stories in question. Cultural ideals are bound up with complex movements of public meanings and imaginings as well as with historical forces. This does not mean public reasoning collapses into historical context. Political reasoning has no Archimedian point in the airtight meanings of principles. Rather than view this as a loss, however, I am showing how giving up such a quest can release the resources of comparative political reasoning. Such reasoning will make new demands on citizens to negotiate their public meanings rather than retreating to the false certainty of ideals. In the conclusion I sharpen and summarize my argument about how they can do this by looking at perhaps the best-known advocate of dissolving principles into history, Stanley Fish.

Conclusion

Is There No Such Thing as Principle?

The conclusion falls into two parts. In the first, I give a brief, abstract philosophical summary of the argument of the book, while in the second, I activate this summary through a critique of Stanley Fish's rival historicist account of political reasoning. Fish is a perfect interlocutor for two reasons. First, he, like liberals and Habermas, agrees to frame the question of public rationality on the opposition of principle and history; however, Fish grabs the history prong rather than the principle prong and argues that the particularities of the subject's historicity block any theorizing about the logic of principles independently from the context in which they are used.[1] Second, Fish argues primarily at the metaphilosophical level against competing conceptions, which lends his work to summary treatment. This rival account of public imagination—developed with concrete examples from liberalism's preferred tribunal of reason, the court—provides a foil to my alternative picture of public imagination and practical reason, in which the public mind is neither an abstract original position nor a series of unique historical particularities.

The argument of this book is that existing theories of practical reason, politics, and cultural history have circumscribed their areas of investigation in ways that hamstring political dialogue. The result is that public reasoning is either reduced to questions of principle or dissolved into historical multiplicity. In order to break the grip of these theories, I introduced the idea of public imagination to discuss the subject's relationship to the historical meanings of a political culture. Opening up this ontologically and politically ambiguous medium enabled us to give citizens in political dialogue the kind of interpretive agility they need to bring practical reasoning together with the critical and explanatory concerns of historians and theorists. The approaches to political thinking that currently oppose each other simplify the subject's complex embeddedness in institutions of meaning by objectifying them (Foucault), pushing them into normative irrelevance (Habermas), or phenomenologically idealizing them (Ricoeur).

Political reasoning cannot escape either the general condition of the historicity of meaning or the specific historical legacies that haunt political communities—the Holocaust, slavery, imperialism, and others. The history debates that have in recent years erupted in both general media and the professional outlets of the social sciences and the humanities show that public reason can no longer hide from history. Instead, we should read them as opportunities to bring together the divided zones of research and enrich political dialogue.

Chapters 1 and 2 looked at the division that structures much of contemporary debate: the split between philosophers of principle, such as Habermas, who put public imagination out of play, and philosophers of historical public imagination who do not give an adequate description of the subject's complex relationships to the social imaginaries they articulate. Chapter 3 developed an account of the subject of judgment that opens the interpretive dimension of everyday reasoning. My account of public imagination began with the transcendental level of interrogation. Everyday citizens, like Kantians, pragmatists, and Derridians, make grand presuppositions about language, subjectivity, and history that structure the ways they formulate political questions. Even those who explicitly reject transcendental arguments for historical descriptions, such as Foucault, implicitly make broad assumptions about their sites of historicization. In the account of the subject I put forward, I did not try to isolate the normative and political dimension from other evaluative languages of existence, as the liberal tradition does; rather, I redescribed the political subject's linguistic and historical constitution in such a way as to articulate the relationships among hermeneutic, genealogical, and causal modes of reasoning.

Once the ideals and principles of a political culture are understood as part of historical institutions of meaning rather than as a tribunal that frames debate, comparative evaluation and reflective judgments move into the place of the judgment of facts and norms. These comparisons are not just synchronic and internal to a polity; rather, they are historical and cross-cultural. In chapters 3, 4 and 5, I developed how the concept of public imagination works by examining the ways literary texts engage with the historical public languages of debate. That is, the literary texts are discussed not as "literature" but as political speech. I selected literary texts for several reasons. First, they thematize the diverse commitments of public speech—such as the writer's view of language, subjectivity, and the good—in ways that other forms of political speech do not. Second, literature is both an agent and an object. It has an agency at multiple levels, arguing not only with literary texts but also with the ideas and images of other public discourses. The literature argues with specific philosophical concepts in a society's past or present, such as justice or the idea of personhood, while also intervening in the social imaginary of the time through its configuration of images, situations, themes, and styles. Moreover, literature is not just a discrete act but also an object that has continuing consequences for the world. Literature thus captures nicely the ontological ambiguity of public meaning, in which it constitutes and shapes subjects and yet is also an object that can be thematized and contested. My analysis is a lesson in how citizens need to unpack the commitments of their diverse interlocutors so that political reasoning does not back away from actual differences into differences per se. Throwing up our hands at diversity pushes us toward transcendental norms that try to frame all positions rather than engaging with the particular commitments, strands of meaning, common assumptions, and social imaginaries that accompany them. What is now called "context" is misdescribed as the application of normative principles. However, once we have a concept of the social imaginary that is deeper than normative rules, that specifies modes of realization, then context is not just on the object side anymore but also on the "subject" side of the equation. It is virtual, imaginary.

This reading of literature as political speech has implications not only for philosophy and literary theory but also for history. Literature is often thought to intersect with the historian's idea of "mentalité," a historiographical approach that seeks out the collective patterns of everyday thinking that are often unconscious. My analysis of the dynamics of literature shows how we can avoid the well-known problems of the mentalities genre of history, in which the social imaginary is treated as a static, unified construct that does not account for change. A literary text is not just folded into the mentality of a particular period in a given society; rather, literature shows how political speech acts can have specificity and agency at the time as well as providing resources for future interpretive communities.

The readings of Arendt, Said, and Sen in chapters 4 and 5 showed the costs of trying to isolate principles from the histories of meanings with which they are bound up. The language of political dialogue cannot be sequestered from a wide-ranging engagement with the common ground of fictional and nonfictional speech—public imagination. The argument of this book is that these languages can be given a central place in political dialogue without abandoning rationality. What I mean by "rationality" here is that these languages must justify themselves in public dialogue against various challenges: transcendental challenges (e.g., "this self-articulation is in a misguided philosophy of language"); empirical challenges (e.g., "the description of your cultural identity ignores the diversity within your group"); causal challenges (e.g., "the institutions you want to create will crumble under the force of globalization"); and political challenges (e.g., "the languages and principles you promote have excluded and denigrated another group").

The usefulness of the problematic emerges nicely through a contrast with Fish's well-known polemic against principle. Liberal political principles, such as fairness or impartiality, Fish maintains, claim to be independent of any particular agenda, to be beyond politics, often resorting to such counterfactual devices as the original position to ground this neutrality. For Fish, such a fantasy can never work, for once we try to define principles, we "will always and necessarily proceed from the vantage point of some currently unexamined assumptions about the way life is or should be, and it is these assumptions contestable in fact but at the moment not contested or even acknowledged, that will really be generating the conclusions that are supposedly being generated by the logic of principle" (1999, 2–3). Instead of deriving a principle from an a priori logic, we should see it as emerging "from a set of historical circumstances to which it was a response" (6). Thus, Plessy v. Ferguson did not violate a logic of principle that Brown v. Board of Education then got right; rather, these were just different moments in the history of the principles of justice and equality, a history that is political all the way down. Principle is a matter not of "logic" but of rhetoric, in which public debaters are always trying to hijack the respected principles of the polity to their own agenda. Liberals thus should not criticize the Right for violating their principles; rather, they should devote their energies to wrapping these principles around their agendas in a convincing way. Instead of constantly turning back to the analytic question of principle—"what is its essence?"—we should ask the historical question—"where did it come from?" (1999, 6).

For Fish, this historical construal of principle permits us to get a better understanding of what is happening when the court seems to "resurrect" the Plessy decision by characterizing affirmative action as "reverse discrimination." The argument of the Right on reverse discrimination hinges on its claim to separate principle from historical contexts so that all acts that take race into account are made equivalent: "The assertion that any action tinged with race consciousness is equivalent to any other action tinged with race-consciousness [is] an assertion that makes sense only if historical differences are dissolved in the solvent of a leveling abstraction" (1999, 6–7). For Fish, liberals are making a philosophical and strategic mistake if they insist on tying reasoning to the logic of principle, a move that lets others equate Jim Crow with affirmative action. The conclusion Fish draws from the collapse of principle is precisely the one that liberals fear. Political debate is simply about marshaling power in the service of desires, a kind of Hobbesian war of meaning: "There is nowhere to go except to the goals and desires that already possess you, and nothing to do but try to implement them in the world" (8). Here we see Fish move from an argument for the inevitability of historicity to the inevitability of his version of philosophical pragmatism that drives a wedge between language and the world, much like Rorty, and unlike those we looked at in chapter 2.[2] My argument follows his in the claim about historicity but offers a completely different problematic for understanding what it means to be a historical linguistic being. In other words, puncturing the liberal conception of neutrality does not entail Fish's description.[3]

Fish blocks out the subject's relationship to historical institutions of meaning not only through his pragmatist conception of meaning but also through his employment of a subject position ten miles up, which permits him to give a purely external third-person account of change in the institutions: "The community is always engaged in doing work, the work of transforming the landscape into material for its own project, but that project is then itself transformed by the very work it does" (1990, 150). He thus closes a space for interrogating and arguing through self-understandings. Instead, the community (or individual subject) becomes a self-contained synchronic collection of beliefs, whose history is a series of leaps from one incommensurate package of beliefs to another.[4] Fish's own examples—as well as mine—show that the claim of radical incommensurability through time is empirically false—as well as suspect from the transcendental point of view; that is, such a radically fragmented subject is not intelligible.

The absence of a concept of public imagination shows up well in his op-ed piece for the *New York Times*, collected in *The Trouble With Principle* in which he argues that the Right has stolen liberal rhetoric. He gives three examples—the Rodney King verdict, the Babbit v. Sweet Home Supreme Court decision on the laws governing the destruction of a bird habitat, and the Adarand Constructors, Inc. v. Pena decision on affirmative action. In all three cases, Fish finds a similar pattern in the American social imaginary surrounding questions of agency and responsibility. In the King case, the defense argued, "Blows can only kill one by one, and not in relation to other blows in a sequence." In an environmental case, the court thought that "birds can only be taken one by one, and not by the destruction of the environment essential to their survival." Discrimination, likewise, is an individual question, and "the massive effects of longstanding structural racism" (1999, 311) should be ignored. Why, Fish wonders, don't people see through this? "Because it is performed with the vocabulary of America's civil religion—the vocabulary of equal opportunity, color-blindness, race neutrality, and above all, individual rights. This is also the vocabulary of civil rights activities, anti-McCarthyites and liberals in general" (312). Fish chides liberals for assuming "that the words mean what they did in 1960" (312) and, more generally, for placing their hope in the "true" meaning of their principles.

From my point of view, what we see here is not the disappearance of principle into historical contexts so minute and complex that they defy characterization. Instead, we see how our imagination of justice itself has been locked into atomistic, legalistic plot constructions within limited time focus. How can we conceive of environmental damage when we don't have a way of figuring the agents and the temporality of such actions?[5] The King verdict shows the continuing grip of long-standing patterns in the United States' racial imagination.[6] While the environmental case shows why practical reason needs to find future forms of imagination for its principles, this case shows the cost of having philosophies of justice that do not give a proper place to the consideration of the contours of inherited public meanings. We saw the consequences of this exclusion in our discussion of hate speech (chapter 2)—which the court system treated as the discrete act of an individual rather than as the long-standing traditions of a political community—and in the dispute between Arendt and Ellison in chapter 4. Ellison's intervention in the social imaginary of his time showed us why public debate cannot do without the full range of resources offered by plots, symbols, and characters that shape the lives of everyday citizens.

Reasoning in the manner that we have examined here will not be as neat and focused as arguments about the logic of principle and the nature of the facts apart from their dependence on historical social imaginaries. Defending a claim will involve articulating complex cultural and historical issues so that imaginary identities are not simply facts but part of a conception of public reasoning that includes different disciplines and different political cultures. The idea of public imagination developed here shows how the ideals of political dialogue can be historically informed without descending into the war of meaning that liberals and their critics such as Fish see. The hope that emerges from my argument is not that citizens will now come to a consensus; rather, the hope is that their political dialogues will be more productive because citizens will bring a more perspicuous understanding of their relationship to social imaginaries.

Such a conception of reasoning means that we no longer think of imagination as the faculty of poets or as a matter of strategic planning against an external enemy, as the 9/11 Commission does.[7] Moving beyond the signposts of facts and abstract norms does not just mean developing a new philosophical problematic; it also means accepting a new interpretive vulnerability, accepting the risk that public reasoning entails the potential loss of a self-understanding. Such a loss can be painful, but it can also be more fulfilling and less risky than hiding from history.

Notes

Introduction

1. See Steele, "Concept of Public Morality Missing from Flag Controversy" (1997a).
2. The resolution took place only six weeks after the first black student applied for admission to Clemson College, now Clemson University. See Walter Edgar, *South Carolina: A History* (1998, 538).
3. After surveying public school teachers in South Carolina, Paul Tosto concluded, "It's the most talked about piece of the state's history, heard in board rooms and bars, churches and on the street, yet rarely in the state's public schoolrooms" ("The History We Don't Teach").
4. There were many admirable political voices whose concerns were about recognition of the violence of the past and a political working through of these interpretive issues. The NAACP continues to call for an economic boycott of South Carolina.
5. John Rawls invokes the original position, in which citizens are asked to abstract from the historical particulars of their lives (1993, 22–28), in order determine what justice requires. Jürgen Habermas appeals to transcendental normative presuppositions about language. See chapter 1 below.
6. As Rawls says, "Political liberalism looks for a conception of justice that can gain the support of an overlapping consensus of reasonable religious, philosophical, and moral doctrines in a society regulated by it" (1993, 10). This consensus is not a mere modus vivendi or compromise but a source of legitimacy with moral force (147).
7. As Rawls notes, "In a democratic society there is a tradition of democratic thought, the content of which is at least familiar and intelligible to the educated common sense of citizens generally [. . .]. Thus, justice as fairness starts from within a political tradition and takes as its fundamental idea that of society as a fair system of cooperation over time" (1993, 14). He thus assumes that there is a consensus about justice that there isn't on other values.
8. While Rawls's model of public reason is the Supreme Court—"To check whether we are following public reason we might ask: how would our argument strike us presented in the form of a Supreme Court opinion?" (1993, 254)—I will be urging that public reason needs to be construed much more broadly.
9. See David Blight, *Race and Reunion: The Civil War in American Memory*: "In the half century after the war, as the sections reconciled, by and large, the races divided" (2001, 4).
10. In "Patriotic History," Robert Fullinwider divides the roles of the historian, so that the historian's professional role is kept apart from his/her role as educator

and citizen. Fullinwider defends "patriotic history," which "proceeds on the premise that children need a common, usable past if they are to be formed as citizens willing to make the sacrifices necessary to support and improve the nation's political institutions" (1996, 207). Thus, he joins William Galston in divorcing political commitments from historiographical issues. As Galston writes, "Very few individuals will come to embrace the core commitments of liberal societies through a process of rational inquiry [. . .]. Civic education [. . .] requires a more noble, moralizing history" (1991, 243). In my view, what students and adult citizens need is an understanding of public reasoning that can acknowledge the missteps of their nation and the historicity of its ideals.

11. The bibliography on transitions to modernity is massive. Two recent examples are *Alternative Modernities,* ed. Dilip Parameschwar Gaonkar, and "Multiple Modernities," *Daedalus* 129.

12. This identification of reason and rules goes beyond Kantians. For instance, in "Public Practical Reason: An Archaeology" (1995), Gerald Postema defines theoretical and practical reasoning as rule-following and then seeks to deduce the capacities of the subject that make such rule-following possible. Historical meanings are not an issue.

13. This is not to say that judges ignore history, of course, but that there is a strong tendency to keep principle from being absorbed into politics and history. This tendency has been opposed by other movements, such as Legal Realism and Critical Legal Studies. For a brief statement on the difference between lawyers and historians, see Cass Sunstein, "The Idea of a Usable Past," where he says that "constitutional lawyers, unlike ordinary historians, should attempt to make the best constructive sense out of historical events associated with the Constitution [. . .]. This idea points to the goal of finding elements in history that can be brought fruitfully to bear on current problems" (1995, 602–603). In this compromise, historical intentions are not allowed to determine norms and norms are not allowed to float free of history. See chapter 1 for Habermas's critique of such proposals.

14. Political sociologists have challenged the constructivist evaporation of agency. See, for instance, Anthony Smith, "The Nation: Invented, Imagined, Reconstructed?" (1991),and Partha Chatterjee, "Whose Imagined Community" (1991), who criticize Anderson for not recognizing the way political cultures self-consciously address the reproduction of their historical imagination. I address historians on public imagination in chapters 2 and 3.

15. "It is not the thesis of this book to suggest that there is such a thing as a real or true Orient [. . .]. On the contrary, I have been arguing that the 'Orient' is itself a constituted entity" (1978, 54).

16. There are exceptions, of course, such as Habermas, as we will see.

17. This common hostility has laid the ground for some thinkers to bring together normative universalism with a constructivist approach to historical meaning— e.g., Edward Said's *Orientalism* and Seyla Benhabib's *The Claims of Culture*—as we'll see later in the introduction and in chapter 5.

18. See Charles Taylor, *Modern Social Imaginaries*: "The notion of moral order goes beyond some proposed schedule of norms that ought to govern our mutual relations and/or political life [. . .]. The image of order carries a definition not only of what is right, but of the context in which it makes sense to strive for and hope to realize the right"(2004, 8–9).

19. I will discuss these technical issues in philosophy of language in chapter 1 on Habermas and again in chapter 3 in the work of Richard Rorty and Taylor.

20. For a sociological approach that seeks to overcome the split between the external approach to political sociology and the "internal" approach of political philosophy, see Craig Calhoun, especially "Constitutional Patriotism and Public Sphere" (2002), where he criticizes Habermas's views.

21. I owe the phrase "institutions of meaning" to Vincent Descombes's work *Les Institutions du sens* (1996), which seeks to bring philosophy of mind and language out into the world.

22. For genealogical and explanatory approaches to literature, see Jonathan Arac's study of the racial politics of reception in the canonization of *Huckleberry Finn*, *Huckleberry Finn as Idol and Target* (1997), and John Guillory's *Cultural Capital* (1993).

23. Richard Rorty captures the speculative dimension of philosophy, history, and literature nicely: "If [a work of literature, history, or philosophy] is to have inspirational value, a work must be allowed to recontextualize much of what you previously thought you knew" (1998a, 133). I discuss my reservations about Rorty's views in chapter 3.

24. For an analysis of the political arguments of *Forrest Gump*, see Thomas Byers, "History Re-membered" (1996).

25. My point here is not to draw analogies between literary judgment and legal or political judgment, as Ronald Dworkin does in *Law's Empire* (1986). Rather, I refer to literature because it articulates the argumentative and speculative character of an aspect of everyday speech (and language itself) that I want to bring out.

26. Hobsbawm and Ranger, eds., *Invention of Tradition* (1983). My conception of public imagination has some similarities with what Claude Lefort and Hannah Arendt call "the political," but I have a very different conception of public imagination from Arendt's. See chapter 4.

27. Paul Ricoeur shows how the speculative historical questions of the citizen and philosopher can never be driven out by the historiographical operations of historians; rather, they must accompany such explanatory concerns. Thus, the epistemological operations of explanation open onto "a second-order reflection

on the conditions of possibility of this [historiographical] discourse, . . . a reflection destined to occupy the play of a speculative philosophy of history" (2000, 373).

28. I include in the "public imagination" all the institutions of meaning that make up modern, Western, democratic societies—public schools, religious institutions, media of the public sphere, etc.—but my focus will be philosophical rather than historical or sociological.

29. I will defend this claim with specific discussion of each of these figures.

30. Larmore says: "Habermas has missed the relevant feature of modern experience. It does not lie in the demise of metaphysical and religious worldviews [. . .]. [Rather], the expectation of reasonable disagreement is the phenomenon that ought to guide our political thought today" (1996, 215). Rawls writes, "Justice as fairness [. . .] springs from and belongs to the tradition of liberal thought and the larger community of political culture of democratic societies. It fails then to be properly formal and truly universal, and thus to be part of the quasi-transcendental presuppositions (as Habermas sometimes says) established by the theory of communicative action" (1995, 179).

31. Thus, Habermas says that Rawls cannot avoid questions of rationality and truth that he claims to bypass (1995, 126).

32. For instance, White says, "Placed before the alternative visions that history's interpreters offer for our consideration, and without any apodictically provided theoretical grounds for preferring one over another, we are driven back to moral and aesthetic reasons for the choice of one vision over another [. . .]. We are free to conceive 'history' as we please" (1973, 433).

33. Butler, for instance, puts a transcendental question at the heart of her work, "Could language injure us if we were not, in some sense, linguistic beings, beings who require language in order to be?" (1997a, 1–2). Transcendental arguments are widespread among contemporary thinkers, from Hans-Georg Gadamer to Richard Rorty and Stanley Fish. I discuss the transcendental dimension of these various thinkers in chapters 2 and 3.

34. "What I mean by the term is an a priori that is not a condition of validity for judgment, but a condition of reality for statements" (1972, 127).

35. "I try to historicize to the utmost in order to leave as little space as possible to the transcendental" (1989, 79).

36. By "third-person" here, I refer to researcher's languages that aspire to stand outside of the language of the historical actors and of the evaluative languages of the present. I develop this distinction in *Theorizing Textual Subjects*(1997c).

37. Ontological approaches to the imagination—found in hermeneutic as well as post-structuralist thinkers—are to be distinguished from Nussbaum's, Ricoeur's, and Arendt's, which lean on methodological individualism and ignore the shaping power of language. See Stephen White's *Sustaining Affirmation: The Strengths of*

Weak Ontology in Political Theory (2000), which does a sympathetic reconstruction of ontological thinkers in political philosophy.

38. I will engage Taylor's principal historical critic, Quentin Skinner, in the course of my argument.

39. In the recently published *Modern Social Imaginaries*, Taylor addresses the charges of historical thinness and traces the formation of deep, widely shared social imaginaries that emerge over long stretches of time.

40. I discuss Fish in the conclusion.

1. Eliding Public Imagination

1. "On How Postwar Germany Has Faced Its Recent Past" (1996b), 1.

2. See Martin Matutstik, *Jürgen Habermas: A Philosophical-Political Profile* (2001), and Robert Holub, *Jürgen Habermas: Critic in the Public Sphere* (1991), for two accounts.

3. In his recent work, he gives a functional, constructivist explanation of nationalism: "Only national consciousness, crystallized around the notions of common ancestry, language and history [. . .] makes subjects into citizens of a single political community " (1998, 109). The public sphere is also crucial to the modern social imaginary, and Habermas's contribution to our understanding is central.

4. For a critique of the homogenizing grand theories of Western modernity and an exploration of alternatives that permit the specificity of changing forms of modern life to appear, see Pascal Michon, *Eléments d'une histoire du sujet* (1999).

5. Although my criticism of Habermas shares some points with Hans Kögler's excellent hermeneutic critique, my concern is not simply with the reflexive thematization of the ideologies and the power of the social imaginary, which is Kögler's focus, but with a conception of public reason.

6. See "Philosophy as Stand-In Interpreter," *Moral Consciousness and Communicative Action* (1990b), for Habermas's clearest description of philosophy's two roles: reconstructive and normative.

7. This framework is empirically dubious and philosophically contested.

8. See *Between Facts and Norms* (1996a), chapter 8, "Civil Society and the Political Public Sphere."

9. Habermas begins *Between Facts and Norms* with a similar attack, in which he assumes philosophy of history means teleology: "The philosophy of history can only glean from historical processes the reason it has already put into them with the help of teleological concepts" (2).

10. *The Theory of Communicative Action*, II, 383. Habermas says that he had to abstract "the development of cognitive structures from the historical dynamic of events" and from "the historical concretion of life forms" (II, 383).

11. See his "Universal Pragmatics" (1979c), and volume 1 of *The Theory of Communicative Action*.

12. "The nation . . . provided the cultural basis for the constitutional state" (1998, 109). I will consider his account of nationalism later. We can contrast this with Taylor's articulation of the long-term development "of the forms of social imaginary that have underpinned the rise of western modernity" (2004, 2) or Foucault's exposure of modern practices. Taylor and Foucault—in very different ways—give the historical languages and practices of modernity an ontological, constitutive force missing from Habermas's account.

13. "There is a universal core of moral intuition in all times and all societies and this is because there are unavoidable presuppositions of communicative activity" (1986a, 206).

14. Religion is thus tied to Habermas's division of the tasks of reason: "Neither science nor art can inherit the mantle of religion; only a morality, set communicatively aflow and developed into a discourse ethics, can replace the authority of the sacred" (1983,II, 92). For an excellent discussion of Habermas on religion, see Eduardo Mendieta's introduction to Habermas's *Religion and Rationality: Essays on Reason, God, and Modernity.*

15. The quotations are from Habermas, "The Hermeneutic Claim to Universality," and "A Review of Truth and Method," both collected in *The Hermeneutic Tradition* (1990a), 266, 239. I limit myself here to a quick summary of Habermas's views rather than trying to recapitulate his well-known debates with Gadamer and the poststructuralists.

16. While I am on the hermeneutic side, I do not endorse Gadamer's unnuanced position on language. For an outstanding critique of Gadamerian philosophy of language, see Pascal Michon, *Poétique d'une anti-anthropologie* (2000).

17. See Alessandro Ferrara's *Justice and Judgment* (1999), chapter 2 and chapter 6, 156–164, for a careful study of Habermas's efforts to soften the role of determinant moral judgments in his philosophy by incorporating aspects of reflective judgment. Ferrara concludes that Habermas never lets go of this determinant dimension.

18. I offer specific critique of Ricoeur's and Arendt's notions of reflective judgment in chapters 2 and 4, respectively.

19. "What raises us out of nature is the only thing whose nature we can know: language. Through its nature autonomy and responsibility are posited for us" (1973, 314).

20. "The unbridgeable gap Kant saw between the intelligible and the empirical becomes in discourse ethics a mere tension manifesting itself in everyday conversation as the factual force of counterfactual presuppositions" (1990b, 203).

21. As Seyla Benhabib explains, "These rules of fair debate can be formulated as 'the universal-pragmatic presuppositions' of argumentative speech and these can be stated as a set of procedural rules" (1992, 31).

22. Maeve Cooke, *Language and Reason* (1994), and Cristina Lafont, *The Linguistic Turn in Hermeneutic Philosophy* (1999).

23. Paraphrasing Frege, the initiator of this philosophical line, Habermas says, "Thoughts are propositionally structured" (1996a, 11). I say more on semantics below.

24. I will consider an alternative semantic view below.

25. While I agree with Lafont's criticism, I do not follow her solution.

26. Habermas insists that we cannot articulate and reason through any aspects of the lifeworld: "The unproblematic character of the lifeworld has to be taken in a radical sense: qua lifeworld it can never become problematic, it can at most fall apart" (1983, II, 130). His conception of the lifeworld has remained consistent through his current work: "As we engage in communicative action, the lifeworld embraces us as an unmediated certainty, out of whose proximity we live and speak [. . .] we make uses of such knowledge without the awareness that it could be false" (1996a, 22).

27. I agree with Benhabib's sharp critique: Reconstructions "begin to speak in the name of a fictional collective 'we' from whose standpoint the story of history is told. The fictive subject appears both as the subject of the past and the future; it is empirical and normative at once" (1986, 331). Moreover, "the very project of discursive argumentation presupposes the ongoing validity of reconciled subjectivity" (321). However, Benhabib's modifications to Habermas's project do not save it from the criticism I am offering. For a critique of Benhabib, see my "Three Problematics of Linguistic Vulnerability: Gadamer, Benhabib, and Butler" (2003b).

28. Setting up presuppositions of communication as ahistorical noumena makes easy pickings for Butler, who celebrates the oppressed for contradicting the historical meaning of universality. "Subjects who have been excluded from enfranchisement by existing conventions governing the exclusionary definition of the universal seize the language of enfranchisement and set into motion a 'performative contradiction,' claiming to be covered by that universal, thereby exposing the contradictory character of previous conventional formulations of the universal" (1997a, 89).

29. I draw my distinction between cultural and acultural accounts of the transitions to modernity from Charles Taylor. "A cultural theory of modernity is one that characterizes the transformations which have issued in the modern West mainly in terms of the rise of a new culture [. . .] [that is,] with its own specific understandings (e.g., of person, nature, the good), to be contrasted to all others, including its own predecessor civilization." An acultural account, on the other hand, "describes these transformations in terms of some culture-neutral operation [. . .] [that is,] an operation which is not defined in terms of specific cultures

it carries us from and to, but rather seen as of a type which traditional culture would undergo" (1993b, 205).

30. Michael Halberstam expresses this Arendtian point succinctly: "Liberal politics wants to take over this space [the public space of meanings] entirely, wants to frame it, where in truth this space frames the liberal framework of political association" (1999, 129).

31. As Craig Calhoun says, "Neither change nor reproduction in social forms simply works out the potential embedded in social imaginaries. Rather, imaginaries offer a repertory of resources for making sense of the world" ("Emergency Imaginaries," forthcoming).

32. I am pushing Taylor's idea of background beyond his footnotes to Hubert Dreyfus, *Being-in-the-World*, and John Searle, *The Construction of Social Reality*. Since Habermas also footnotes Searle, there can be legitimate confusion here. Also, my concern is different from Taylor's. Whereas he is interested in the long-term development of the modern social imaginary, I want to emphasize conflicts in the social imaginary in current debates and how we can argue through them.

33. See Pascal Michon, "Strata, Blocks, Pieces, Spirals, Elastics and Verticals: Six Figures of Time in Michel Foucault" (2002).

34. To speak the language of semantic philosophy proposed by Robert Brandom, we could say that we are "changing the inferential norms that govern the use of concepts" ("The Vocabularies of Pragmatism," 176). The consequence of accepting the constraints of new vocabularies is that they "enable one to make and understand an indefinite number of novel claims, formulate an indefinite number of novel concepts, frame an indefinite number of novel purposes." Hence, it "confers unparalleled positive freedom" (178). For the concept/conception distinction, see Hilary Putnam, *Reason, Truth and History* (116–117), where he uses this distinction to show that different conceptual schemes—e.g., various seventeenth-century theories of temperature—do not make the meanings of the concept "temperature" incommensurate.

35. The full citation reads as follows, "The fact that everyday communicative practice makes learning processes possible (thanks to built-in idealizations) in relation to which the world-disclosive force of interpreting language has in turn to prove its worth" (1987, 205).

36. Unfortunately, Rorty gives a merely external, behaviorist account of language and dialogue and is indifferent to the dynamics by which such texts reason. Thus, his analyses of literature are only thematic. I discuss Rorty at length in *Theorizing Textual Subjects*, 68–89, and in chapter 3 below.

37. Habermas says, "The explosive experiences of the extraordinary have migrated into art that has become autonomous" (1992b, 51). The opposition

of narrative (and literature) to argument is common in contemporary philosophy, as we will see in our discussion of Ricoeur in chapter 2. Jean-Marc Ferry begins his recent work *L'Ethique reconstructive* with the query, "Narration or argument?" (1).

38. My critique of Habermas is not just that he occludes the otherness coming from alternative cultures, as Kögler points out in *Power of Dialogue (1996)*. Rather, Habermas's problematic fails to grasp the multiplicity of argumentative spaces in the Western traditions.

39. For example, while discussion of human rights in the West often turns to a concept of human dignity, with all its individualistic implications, Thailand's Buddhist culture will have to look to a different package of beliefs, such as those around nonviolence. See Taylor's discussion of this example in "Conditions of Unforced Consensus on Human Rights" (1999a).

40. Thus, while I agree with Kögler point that Habermas "fails to capture the processes of power that operate on a transsubjective level within the historical-cultural lifeworld itself" ("The Self-Empowered Subject," *Philosophy and Social Criticism*, 21), my goal is not to argue only for the "possibility of the self-detachment from and critical inspection of social origins of one's own" (26), a hermeneutic reflexivity. Such a project assumes that there is consensus about what "seeing through" or "critical" might mean.

41. See Rawls (1993, 30) for a parallel claim about the need to separate public reason from everyday reasoning.

42. "The nation-state founded a domain of political communication that made it possible to absorb the advances in abstraction of societal modernization and to re-embed a population uprooted from traditional forms of life" (1998, 117).

43. In this essay, "Constitutional Democracy: A Paradoxical Union of Contradictory Principles," Habermas seeks to resolve the tension between the democratic will of citizens and their constitutional rights by making rights constitutive of democratic self-governance.

44. On Dworkin, see *Between Facts and Norms*, 205–225. For an incisive reading of the American Constitution and Bill of Rights that insists on the historical circumstances of their genesis and on an interpretive assessment of the worth of these original intentions, see Akhil Reed Amar, *The Bill of Rights: Creation and Reconstruction*.

45. Habermas defines this as a double identification: "identifications with one's own forms of life and traditions are overlaid with a patriotism that has become more abstract, that now relates not to the concrete totality of a nation but rather to abstract procedures and principles" (1989a, 261).Even if we consider such patriotism as "a collectively shared mentality," in Max Pensky's felicitous phrase, rather than as only a political value, we are still left with "a locationless network

of competencies"—such as taking the position of others—that stand apart from one's lifeworld (69–70).

46. In the next section, we'll see him speak of particulars that "nourish" universals and of universals forming a "hard substance" that are pervaded by the "rays of national traditions."

47. For a discussion of Anzuldúa's texts in the context of historical trauma and working through, see Cassie Premo Steele, *We Heal from Memory*.

48. See "Struggles for Recognition in the Democratic Constitutional State" (1994a). He says that fragmentation and multiplicity of cultures may make "us skeptical about universalist claims" (121) and that these concerns have implications "for the concepts of the just with which we operate when we examine the conditions of a politics of recognition"; however, he never develops those implications because the essay to which he is responding poses the problem of recognition at "the level of law and politics" (121).

49. Habermas's attempt to make the politics of difference an "external" issue has a long heritage in political theory that goes back to the standard readings of the Treaty of Westphalia. See David L. Blaney and Naeem Inayatullah, "The Westphalian Deferral" (2000), where they say, "The Peace was an attempt to formally contain difference within states so as to avoid the destruction of international war. The price of this move was to sanctify the continuation of conquest, purification, and conversion within a ruler's realm" (33).

50. Dole said, "There is a shocking campaign afoot among educators at all levels—most evident in the national history standards [. . .] to disparage America and disown the ideas and traditions of the West" (cited in Nash, 245).

51. Hence, from the point of view of my argument, the debates surrounding the politics of recognition misphrase the issues at stake because the questions raised by the historicity and multiplicity of meaning do not stand or fall on empirical claims about the integrity of particular "cultures." This is why I use the phrases "public imagination" and "institutions of meaning," instead of "culture," to discuss the citizen's deliberative situation. For a recent critique of the politics of recognition, see Seyla Benbabib's *The Claims of Culture* (2002). Although I agree with some of her critique, the solution she proposes—a constructivist approach to historical meaning married to an interactive universalism—leaves out precisely what I am thematizing here.

52. This kind of reasoning can apply at the international level as well. On the neglected role of the public sphere in European integration, see Craig Calhoun, "The Democratic Integration of Europe: Interests, Identity, and the Public Sphere" (2003).

53. One of the best accounts of the link between linguistic homogeneity and the nation as imagined community is Eugen Weber's *Peasants into Frenchmen: The Modernization of Rural France, 1870–1914* (1976).

54. "Whereas the voluntary nation of citizens is the source of democratic legitima-tion, it is the inherited or ascribed nation founded on ethnic membership that secures social integration" (1998, 115).

55. Nolte's *Der europäische Bürgerkrieg: 1917–1945: Nationalismus und Bolschewismus* (1987).

56. "[T]he abstract idea of the universalization of democracy and human rights forms the hard substance through which the rays of national tradition—lan-guage, literature, and history of one's own nature—are reflected" (1989a, 262).

57. See Carlo Ginsburg, *The Judge and the Historian*, and Paul Ricoeur, "L'historien et le juge," in *La Mémoire, l'historie, l'oubli*, 413–436, as well as Cass Sunstein, "The Idea of a Usable Past."

58. See, for instance, *Nazi Germany and the Jews*.

59. See Robert Shandley's discussion of the reception in his introduction to *Unwill-ing Germans: The Goldhagen Debate*. For a detailed attack, see Norman Finkel-stein's *A Nation on Trial: The Goldhagen Controversy and Historical Truth*.

60. The full citation reads: "In public discourses of self-understanding which can be touched off by films, television series, or exhibitions just as much as by historical works or 'affairs,' we argue not so much over short-term goals and policies as over the forms of a desired political existence [. . .]. This connec-tion between political self-understanding and historical awareness also deter-mines the point of view from which Goldhagen's book is relevant to us" (1997b, 2).

61. See Bartov's "Ordinary Monsters" (1996b), for his comments on Goldhagen.

62. "What Does Working Off the Past Mean Today?" *Berlin Republic*, 17–40. "Pub-licly conducted ethical–political self-understanding is the central—although only one—dimension of what Adorno called 'working off the past'" (19).

2. Avoiding Judgment

1. I introduce some of Habermas's concerns when I look at Seyla Benhabib's criti-cisms of Judith Butler, but I defer most of them until chapter 3.

2. Lacan, following the Lévi-Strauss line, develops an account of the symbolic that severs it from the social. The symbolic is the condition of the possibility of the social.

3. Structuralism, of course, was not the only antihumanist understanding of his-tory in France at the time. The Annales School, led by Fernand Braudel, also repudiated an event-based history and its narrative recounting: "Social science virtually detests the event. Rightly so: the short time period is the most capacious and most deceptive of durations" (1969, 46). Braudel adds, "All the new research done by Lévi-Strauss [. . .] is successful only when his models sail on the water of the long duration" (114).

4. See, for instance, Sartre's idea of the "universal singular": "Man is never an individual; it would be more fitting to call him a universal singular. Summed up and for this reason universalized by his epoch, he in turn resumes it by reproducing himself in it as singularity" (1981, ix).

5. In response to Lévi-Strauss, Sartre says, "I am in complete agreement that social facts have their structure and laws that dominate individuals, but I see in this the replay of worked matter to agents who work it. [. . .] Structures are created by activity which has no structure, but suffers its results as structure" (cited in Poster 1975, 335).

6. Frank Ankersmit also accepts this position: "Saying *true* [i.e., factually correct] things about the past is easy [. . .] but saying *right* things about the past is difficult" (1990, 209). See his "Historiography and Postmodernism" (1989) and Peter Zagorin's "Historiography and Postmodernism: Reconsiderations" (1990), both in *History and Theory,* for a good representation of the debate between textualists, such as White and Ankersmit, and those who view the historian's language as "largely subservient to the historian's effort to convey [. . .] an understanding or knowledge of the past" (Zagorin 200).

7. For White's Kantianism see Hans Kellner, "Hayden White and the Kantian Discourse: Tropology, Narrative, and Freedom" (1992). Kellner says, "The tropes, however often they are called conventional or arbitrary, look very much like a mental structure, a natural part of human cognition" (253). White is upfront about this: "I will not apologize for this Kantian element in my thought, but I do not think modern psychology, anthropology or philosophy has improved upon it" (1978, 22).

8. "The socially responsible interpreter can do two things: (1) expose the fictitious nature of any political program based upon appeal to what history supposedly teaches; 2. remain adamantly 'utopian' in face of any criticism of political realism" (White 1988, 227). Utopian thought is understood not in a dialectical way but as a way to "goad living human beings [. . .] to endow their lives with a meaning for which they alone are fully responsible" (72).

9. White says a "historical narrative does not, as narrative, dispel false beliefs about the past, human life [. . .]; what it does is test the capacity of a culture's fiction to endow real events with the kinds of meaning that literature displays to consciousness through its fashioning of patterns of imaginary events" (1988, 46).

10. "Precisely insofar as historical narrative endows sets of real events with the kinds of meaning found otherwise only in myth and literature, we are justified in regarding it as a product of allegoresis. Therefore, rather than read every historical narrative as mythic or ideological in nature, we should read it as allegorical, that is, as saying one thing and meaning another" (White 1988, 45).

11. Martin Jay also notes how White neglects the institution of history: "History isn't a single historian emplotting the past but the institution of history" (1992, 105).

12. See C. Behan McCullagh, *Justifying Historical Descriptions* (1984), for a careful analysis of the presuppositions of historical arguments.

13. Arendt and Taylor criticize specifically this Kantian move of setting up of the subject of freedom outside the world, as we'll see.

14. Kant himself does not present historical judgment this way.

15. He is widely regarded as the great mediator of philosophy and the social sciences. See in particular François Dosse, *L'Empire du sens*.

16. Ricoeur is frequently placed together with hermeneutic thinkers, such as Taylor, on the issue of language and narrative. For instance, Richard Kearney says, "Ricoeur's stance on narrative identity receives support from a number of contemporary quarters—including recent works by Charles Taylor, Alasdair MacIntyre, and Seyla Benhabib" (1996, 181). See also Nicholas Smith, *Strong Hermeneutics: Contingency and Moral Identity* (1997, chap. 2). An exception is Gary Aylesworth's "Dialogue, Text, Narrative: Confronting Gadamer and Ricoeur" (1991) in which he discusses the difference between Ricoeur's continuance of the epistemological tradition and Gadamer's ontological hermeneutics.

17. See David Carr, who makes this point nicely in *Time, Narrative, and History.* David Pellauer responds to Carr's criticisms of Ricoeur in "Limning the Liminal: Carr and Ricoeur on Time and Narrative" *(1991)*. For my purposes here, what is crucial is the point he concedes at the end of the essay: "Carr, it seems to me, is correct, when he emphasizes the importance of narrative as part of everyday life and activities [. . .]. This is an aspect of narrative that Ricoeur has not explored, again for reasons of method, since he confines himself to the formal narrative plane and its two major forms" (61).

18. Reflective judgment has generated a lot of interest recently, which I can hardly address here. I will simply point out that reflective judgment has provided a bridge between Kant and Husserl that has come to prominence in Hannah Arendt's understanding of narrative, which I will discuss in chapter 4.

19. I develop what I mean by "transitional" in chapter 3. Ricoeur presents "traditionality" as our only recourse between "the contingency of a mere history of genres, or types [. . .] and an eventual logic of possible narratives that escape history [i.e., structuralism]" (1984–88, II, 14–15). However, this conception cannot do the work he assigns it unless the substantive issues he has abstracted find their way back in. Ricoeur follows the reductive structuralist distinction between *histoire* (content of the story) and *récit* (specific narrative realization of this content). This opposition eliminates the way ideas and languages are articulated through narrative so that "content" becomes unshaped material. For a discussion of this

distinction and its problems for hermeneutics, see Meili Steele, "The Dangers of Structuralist Narratology: Genette's Misinterpretation of Proust" (1986).

20. Ricoeur tries to downplay the significance of the ontological turn: "I have tried to set my analyses of the 'sense' of metaphorical statements and of that of narrative plots against the background of *Verstehen,* limited to its epistemological usage, in the tradition of Dilthey and Max Weber." This understanding of meaning, according to Ricoeur, "remains unaffected by its later development in Heidegger and Gadamer, in the sense of the subordination of the epistemological to the ontological theory of *Verstehen*" (1983, 195). Taylor, like Gadamer, gives a central place to this distinction.

21. Ricoeur seeks a middle ground between the "exalted subject" (Descartes) and the "humiliated subject" (Nietzsche) (1992, 16) through "attestation." Similarly, in his work on metaphor and narrative, he moves between "the irrationalism of immediate understanding, conceived as an extension to the domain of texts of the empathy by which a subject puts himself in the place of a foreign consciousness in a situation of face-to-face intensity [. . .]. I am equally unable to accept a rationalistic explanation which would extend to the text the structural analysis of sign systems that are characteristic not of discourse but of language as such [. . .]. To these two one-sided attitudes, I have opposed the dialectic of understanding and explanation" (1983, 194).

22. By contrast, Ricoeur says, "Hermeneutics begins where dialogue ends" (1976, 32).

23. I will focus on *Excitable Speech* and Butler's contribution to *Feminist Contestations: A Philosophical Exchange,* in which she debates with Benhabib, Drucilla Cornell, and Nancy Fraser.

24. A good example of such a history is Linda Gordon's *Heroes of Their Own Lives.* Later in this section, we will examine Gordon's exchange with Scott in *Signs* 15, 848–852.

25. Scott says, "Concepts of gender structure perception and the concrete symbolic organisation of all social life. To the extent that these [concepts] establish distributions of power (differential control over or access to material and symbolic resources), gender becomes implicated in the conception and construction of power itself" (1986, 45).

26. In *The Psychic Life of Power* and *Bodies That Matter: The Discursive Limits of "Sex,"* Butler develops the "constitutive outside" in psychoanalytic terms as the "degraded object" of same sex desire, which is denounced and internalized (1993, 3). Heterosexuality is thus melancholic since it cannot witness and mourn the loss of this desire.

27. Scott says, "Any unity concept rests on—contains—repressed or negated material and so is unstable, not unified." Deconstruction "undermines the historians' ability to claim neutral mastery or to present any particular story as if were complete,

universal and objectively determined. Instead, if one grants that meanings are constructed through exclusions, one must acknowledge and take responsibility for the exclusion involved in one's own project" (1986, 7).

28. Like Derrida, Butler thinks that the hermeneutic idea of "understanding" is too grandiose and opts for a minimalist idea of sense. As Derrida says, "One of the things SEC [his essay "Signature Event Context"] was driving at is that the minimal making sense of something (its conformity to the code, grammaticality, etc.) is incommensurate with the adequate understanding of intended meaning" (1977, 203).

29. I discuss the Derrida/Searle debate in the context of hermeneutics in *Critical Confrontations* (1997b), 47–57.

30. In the introduction to *The Psychic Life of Power*, Butler speaks of the tensions between two temporal modalities of subjection, between the transcendental condition and the self-understanding: "First, as what is for the subject always prior, outside of itself and operative from the start; second as the willed effect of the subject" (1997b, 14).

31. This same problem of interpretive judgment undermines Joan Scott's deconstructive "history" of feminism in France, *Only Paradoxes to Offer*. Scott's transcendental generator is a formal paradox produced by the demands of equality and difference. This paradox is then reinscribed by the particular historical languages employed through time: "To the extent that feminism acted for 'women,' feminism produced the sexual difference it sought to eliminate. This paradox— the need both to accept and to refuse sexual difference—was the constitutive condition of feminism as a political movement through its long history." Although "the terms of her [the subject of feminism] representation shifted" (14), they nonetheless illustrate a nontranscendable paradox: "Feminism is not a reaction to republicanism, but one of its effects, produced by contradictory assertions about the universal human rights of individuals, on the one hand, and exclusions attributed to 'sexual difference,' on the other. Feminist agency is constituted by this paradox" (168).

32. Benhabib refers here to a debate between Joan Scott and Linda Gordon over women's agency in *Signs* 15, 848–852. Although the debate began as a question over the specifics raised by Gordon's attribution of agency to the women in her book *Heroes of Their Own Lives,* the argument quickly escalated into a question of what problematic should be used to read women's lives throughout history. Scott's recent book is a sequel to this argument. I discuss Benhabib's dilemmas at greater length in "Interpreting Our Linguistic Vulnerability: Gadamer, Benhabib, and Butler."

33. She claims that this approach to the history of philosophy follows Walter Benjamin (1992, 239). Benjamin and Arendt shared a horror of Hegel's philosophy

of history, and, in Benhabib's view, "her response was the same as [his]: "to break the chain of narrative continuity [. . .] to stress fragmentariness, historical dead ends, failures, and ruptures" (1996b, 88).

34. By pulling out the stories of isolated individuals who assert liberal ideals, rather than having a hermeneutic engagement with the historical languages of public imagination, Benhabib leaves unexamined the symbolic and social inheritance that other feminists have found.

35. Scott also calls up the strawperson of "liberal agency" in order to justify her problematic: "Instead of assuming that agency follows from an innate human will, I want to understand feminism in terms of the discursive processes—the epistemologies, institutions, and practices—that produce political subjects, that make agency [. . .] possible" (1996, 15). She does exactly the same thing in her well-known argument for a constructivist view of "experience." She calls up the specter of a naive "appeal to experience as uncontestable evidence and as originary point of explanation" (1991, 777). But the rejection of "willful agency" and "experience as evidentiary bedrock" in no way entails her description.

36. See Lorraine Code's *Rhetorical Spaces* (1995) for a feminist philosophical exploration of "the epistemology of the everyday" (xi). Instead of deconstructing the typical philosophical subject of epistemology and morality—i.e., "the abstract, interchangeable individual whose monologues have been spoken from nowhere, in particular, to an audience of faceless, usually disembodied speakers" (xiv)—she explores the intersubjective particularities that are blocked out by such a view.

37. Scott also assumes that all first-order experience and the narrative/symbolic action through which it is made available merely reproduce rather than transgress or revise the reigning system of meaning (1991, 770). Moreover, she gives no way for texts that make "epistemological errors" to contribute to public imagination. Is the history of literature simply a list of philosophical mistakes? All Scott ever argues for is more scrutiny of the processes by which subjects are produced (780), but who is opposed to opening up these processes? Isn't the next level of argument about how to scrutinize and to what end?

38. *Words of Fire: An Anthology of African-American Feminist Thought.*

39. Scott says of the women she studies, "I do not think of these women as exemplary heroines. Instead I think of them as sites—historical locations and markers—where crucial political and cultural contests are enacted and can be examined in some detail. To figure a person—in this case, a woman—as place or location is not to deny her humanity; it is rather to recognize the many factors that constitute her agency, the complex and multiple ways in which she is constructed as a historical actor" (1996, 16). Fair enough. But the language through which we characterize these "locations" is not a positivistic one but one imbued with the hopes and ideals of the speaker.

40. While I agree with Fraser that both deconstruction and identity politics fail "to link struggles for recognition to struggles for redistribution," my focus is on the philosophical problem of interpretive judgment, which cannot be solved by an appeal to redistribution.

41. See also Saul Friedlander's *Memory, History, and the Extermination of the Jews in Europe.*

42. Toni Morrison's *Beloved* offers an excellent example of trauma and witnessing, both within the novel—e.g., Sethe and Paul D—and between the text and reader. Morrison retells the slave narrative because of the failure of American society to witness the trauma of slavery. Interestingly, Butler discusses Morrison in *Excitable Speech* only to illustrate the thesis that the subject does not control language, and not for the intersubjective achievements in Morrison's work. In the next chapter, I look at Dominick LaCapra's efforts to mediate what he calls the dispute between the "structural" trauma, which is Butler's concern, and particular historical trauma.

43. See, for instance, Michael Kelley, ed., *Critique and Power: Recasting the Foucault/Habermas Debate.*

44. Foucault calls into question the movement between the empirical and the transcendental, which is the hallmark of Kantian critique and Husserlian phenomenology. This "transcendental/empirical doublet" is where "the threshold of our Modernity is situated [. . .] by the constitution of an empirco-transcendental doublet that was called man" (1970, 19).

45. Foucault comments on this process: "The analysis of actual experience is a discourse of mixed nature: it is directed at a specific yet ambiguous stratum, concrete enough for it to be possible to apply to it a meticulous descriptive language, yet sufficiently removed from the positivity of things for it to be possible, from that starting point, to escape from that naivete, to contest it and seek foundations for it" (1970, 321).

46. In the *Crisis*, Husserl speaks of the philosophical and historical reduction. See David Carr's discussion of the "historical" reduction in chapter 5 of *Phenomenology and the Problem of History.*

47. "Self and world belong together in the single entity of Dasein" (Heidegger, 297).

48. See *Being and Time*, 194–195, for Heidegger's discussion of the hermeneutic circle.

49. "Our being amidst the things with which we concern ourselves most closely in the 'world' [. . .] guides the everyday way in which Dasein is interpreted and covers up ontically Dasein's authentic being, so that the ontology which is directed toward this entity is denied an appropriate basis" (Heidegger, 359).

50. Heidegger does not try to make a historical argument for his language, e.g., "fallenness," "guilt," and "anxiety"; thus the relationship between the transcendental and the historical is obscured.

51. "Husserl and Heidegger bring up for discussion again all of our knowledge and its foundations, but they do this by beginning from that which is original. This analysis takes place, however, at the expense of any articulated historical content" (Foucault 1989, 77).

52. See *Michel Foucault: Beyond Structuralism and Hermeneutics*, 2nd ed. I use Dreyfus and Rabinow here because I want to separate their reading of Foucault and hermeneutics from my own in chapter 3.

53. Heidegger says, "Existential analysis, therefore, constantly has the character of doing violence whether to the claims of everyday interpretation, or to its complacency and its tranquilized obviousness" (359).

54. He uses "episteme" in *The Order of Things* to play a role similar to that of archive as the new site of analysis; "it is not men who constitute [the human sciences] and provide them with a specific domain; it is the general arrangement of the episteme that provides them with a site, summons them and establishes them" (1970, 364).

55. François Dosse notes that this is a source of confusion for historians who took his conception of statement [*énoncé*] as empirical: "The discursive sphere is what interests Foucault, not the referent, which remains the privileged object of the historian" (1992, II, 278).

56. Historical a priori "is defined as the group of rules that characterize a discursive practice; but these rules are not imposed from the outside on the elements that relate together; they are caught in the very things that they connect" (Foucault 1972, 127).

57. Archaeology is "nothing more than a rewriting: that is, in the preserved form of exteriority, a regulated transformation of what has already been written. [. . .] It is the systematic description of a discourse object" (Foucault 1972, 140).

58. "My aim was to analyze this history, in the discontinuity that no teleology could reduce in advance; to locate it in dispersion that no preestablished horizon could embrace; or allow it to be deployed in an anonymity on which no transcendental constitution would impose the form of the subject" (Foucault 1972, 203).

59. Foucault is offering a critique here of the very idea of an event, not just the Revolution: "The idea of a single break suddenly, at a given moment dividing all discursive formations, interrupting them in a single moment and reconstituting them in accordance with the same rules—such an idea cannot be sustained" (1972, 175).

60. As Roger Chartier says, Foucault blocks out two recurrent ideas in the historiography of the Revolution: "that it is possible to deduce the practices from the discourse that serve as their foundation and justification; second, that it is possible to translate the latent meaning of social operations into the terms of an explicit ideology" (1997, 59).

61. Pascal Michon(2002, 7): "Time is [no longer] in blocks but in pieces."

62. In another formulation, he says, "In short, with this genealogy the idea was to investigate how individuals were led to practice, on themselves and others, a hermeneutics of desire" (1985, 5).

63. "One might have changed point of view, one has gone round and round the problem, which is still the same, namely, the relations between the subject, truth and the constitution of experience" (Foucault 1990,48).

64. I take up the problematic of "practice" in the next chapter.

65. Foucault explicitly connects thinning out universals to revealing historical specificity: "to dispense with universals as much as possible in order to interrogate their historical constitution" (1994, IV, 634).

66. In the interview cited above, he does not refer to his own change of judgment but to a change in subject matter—from coercive practices to practices of the self—as reason for the change.

67. Certainly, one could read modernity using the problematic of the later Foucault.

68. Foucault wants to analyze "the kind of relationship you ought to have with yourself, a rapport à soi [. . .] and which determines how the individual is supposed to constitute himself as a moral subject of his own actions" (1984, 352).

69. I explain my use of the term in the next chapter.

70. On this point, see Richard Bernstein, "Foucault: Critique as Philosophical Ethos" (1991).

71. Foucault seems to give modern literature a kind of transgressive power, but does not characterize it beyond an allusion to Roland Barthes's intransitive writing: "Literature is the contestation of philology [. . .]. From the romantic revolt against a discourse frozen in its own ritual pomp, to the Mallarmean discovery of the word in its impotent power, it becomes clear what the function of literature was, in the nineteenth century, in relation to the modern mode of being of language. [L]iterature becomes progressively more differentiated from the discourse of ideas and encloses itself within a radical intransitivity" (1970, 300).

3. Reasoning through Public Imagination

1. See, for instance, Will Kymlicka, *Contemporary Political Philosophy*, chap. 6, "Communitarianism," and Gary Gutting, *Pragmatic Liberalism and the Critique of Modernity*, section III, which I discuss below.

2. In *New Literary Histories*, a survey of recent work, Claire Colebrook cites *Sources of the Self* as a foil to the work of Foucault and New Historicism. "Such histories rely upon a notion of continuity, such that the concept of 'self' is said to have gradually altered its meaning through time. The alterations in meaning are attributed to a logical process of human development or fall (from ancient times to modernity) and it is assumed that the phenomena of the present can be

explained and made meaningful by a historical narrative which reveals its origin" (1989, 48).

3. Taylor's emphasis on epiphantic poetry in the last part of *Sources of the Self* has led to confusion about the status of the good because his religious interests emerge there in an overt way. For example, Frederick Olafson reads Taylor as saying "that it is only in the medium of epiphantic art that his own deepest philosophical convictions find expression" (1994, 196). In reply, Taylor says that the end of the book "contains [. . .] hints of affirmation which go beyond what I make any systematic attempt to argue for" (1994, 203).

4. Quentin Skinner, for instance, accuses Taylor of "reckless a priorism," for *Sources* "assumes all societies have a strong sense of self" (1991, 137).

5. Transcendental argument can be used to close down the space of argument and reinforce ethnocentrism, as we see in Stanley Fish's well-known antitheory polemic and in Rorty's postmodern liberalism, considered later in the chapter. William Connolly assimilates Taylor to this tendency when he says, "The drive to knockdown argument in onto political interpretation is a corollary to the drive to fundamentalism in political life" (1995, 16). For a defense of transcendental inquiry in history, see Reinhart Koselleck's *The Practice of Conceptual History* (2002), where he says that "the discipline of history today has conceptualized historicity as the outlining of the conditions of possibility both for history in general and for the discipline of history more narrowly defined" (3).

6. For instance, Taylor says, "Our whole notion of negotiation is bound up [. . .] with the distinct identity of the parties, with the willed nature of the relation; it is a very contractual notion" (1985b, 32).

7. Taylor's recent work has moved into comparative political reasoning. See, for instance, his discussion of Thailand in "Conditions of an Unforced Consensus on Human Rights" (1999a). I will address cross-cultural dimensions of Taylor's problematic in chapter 5.

8. Taylor takes a Heideggerian insight and develops it in a distinctive way. He says that one of Heidegger's crucial ideas is "that grasping things as neutral objects is one of our possibilities only against the background of a way of being in the world in which things are disclosed as ready-to-hand [. . .]. [H]ence [. . .] this comportment could not be original or fundamental" (1993a, 333).

9. Hobbes says, "Whatsoever is the object of a man's appetite or desire, that is it which he for his part calleth good" (1968, chap. 6). Rorty says, "The question of what propositions to assert, which pictures to look at, what narratives to listen to [. . .] are all questions about what will help us get us what we want" (1982, xliii). I return to Rorty's naturalism later in the chapter.

10. The moral subject in Kant and Rawls is someone "who is prior to the ends, which are affirmed by it" (Rawls 1971, 560; Sandel 1998, 54), not constituted by

them. As Michael Sandel says, "Since for Rawls the faculty of self-reflection is limited to weighing the relative intensity of existing wants and desires, the deliberation it entails cannot inquire into the identity of the agent" (1998, 160).

11. Taylor writes, "The agent of radical choice would at the moment of choice have *exhypothesi* no horizon of evaluation. He would be utterly without identity [. . .]. [T]he subject of radical choice is another avatar of that recurrent figure which our civilizations aspires to realize, the disembodied ego, the subject who can objectify all being [. . .] and choose in radical freedom" (1985a, 35).

12. Taylor is breaking down not just the distinction between description and evaluation but also that between theoretical language and the language of description. Raymond Guess defines scientific, objectifying theories as ones that "distinguish clearly between the theory and the 'objects' to which the theory refers" (1981, 55).

13. In the critique of individualism, Taylor would agree with the poststructuralist Butler, who says, "The linguistic domain over which the individual has no control becomes the condition of possibility for whatever domain of control is exercised by the speaking subject. Autonomy in speech is conditioned by dependency on language whose historicity exceeds in all directions the speaking subject" (1997a, 28).

14. "Only interpretive analytic such as Foucault's would enable one, at least retroactively, to understand how easily the countercultural movement was coopted and made to serve the very trends in the culture it opposed, those trends which produce both the object and subjective social sciences and which these sciences inevitably fail to grasp" (Dreyfus and Rabinow,165).

15. Dreyfus and Rabinow turn "interpretive analytics" into a Wittgensteinian description: "We no longer do theory. We are no longer searching for deep, hidden meaning." Instead, we try to understand "our form of life [which] has no essence, no fixity, no underlying unity. But nonetheless has its own specific coherence" (1982, 125). This proposal is at odds with Taylor's idea of historical articulation and argument, as we'll see.

16. Gary Gutting, for instance, misreads Taylor's transcendental argument for the embedded subject as an empirical claim about a consensus on values: "Taylor is overoptimistic. We should not expect reflective scrutiny of each individual's moral experience to yield objective values" (1999, 155). Yet Taylor says the purpose of an ontological thesis "is to structure the field of possibilities in a more perspicuous way. But this does leave us with choices, which need some normative, deliberative arguments to resolve" (1995b, 183).

17. See in particular the critiques of Clifford Geertz in this regard: Giorgio Levi's "I pericoli del geertzismo" (1985), and Bernard Lepetit's "De l'échelle en histoire" (1996), especially 78–82. William Sewell sums up the historian's concern: "One reason Geertz's cultural systems appear impervious to change is that few of his

works explore differences or variations in the beliefs, values, or idioms embraced by different groups within societies" (1999, 49).

18. I cannot address here the extensive debate about the meaning of the term "practice" in contemporary philosophy of social science. See David Stern's excellent discussion of these issues in "The Practical Turn," *The Blackwell Guide to the Philosophy of Social Science,* 185–206. However, I do think Taylor shows how his version of practice avoids making it either purely subjective or purely objective.

19. See Ernest Gellner's critical paraphrase of Wittgenstein: "The custom of a community, expressed in speech, is the only law mankind can ever know or live by" (Gellner, cited in Stern, 199). Stern defends Wittgenstein against this charge.

20. Taylor distinguishes three levels of articulation. The first concerns the "explicit doctrine about society, the divine or the cosmos." The second is "the symbolic," which is found in art and ritual and is close to what historians call "mentalités," and the third is "embodied understanding," or "habitus" (1999c, 167). The idea of a social imaginary, which he develops in *Modern Social Imaginaries,* complements and enriches his previous work by moving beyond the concerns of philosophy and literature into social and cultural history.

21. Taylor's work parallels Lefort's effort to pry loose the social imaginary and the political from social scientific method. Lefort writes, "The opposition between philosophy and science is one between two intellectual requirements. For science [. . .] operates in accordance with an ideal of objectivity which introduces a sovereign distance between the subject and the social. The externality of the knowing subject is of necessity combined with the idea that the social can stand outside itself" (1988, 220–221).

22. See, for instance, Peter Burke, "The Strength and Weaknesses of the History of Mentalities," *Varieties of Cultural History,* 162–182.

23. In his account, Fish employs a subject position ten miles up and gives a purely external, third-person account of change in the institutions: "The community is always engaged in doing work, the work of transforming the landscape into material for its own project, but that project is then itself transformed by the very work it does" (1990, 150). He thus closes a space of interrogation and makes community a self-contained synchronic collection of beliefs, whose history is a series of leaps from one incommensurate package of beliefs to another. I discuss Fish further in the conclusion.

24. In Taylor's view, "it is only through their articulation in language that our norms and purposes can be changed [. . .]. This whole dimension of disclosure through language is left untouched by a theory of society geared towards a proceduralist ethics" (1986, 35).

25. Amartya Sen appeals to a similar idea of evaluation in his critique of rational choice theory. "We cannot rank-order individual preferences simply on the basis

of choices without an account of the evaluations that lie beneath choices" (cited in Nussbaum 1995, 131).

26. Thus, Benthamites appeal to nonutilitarian goods such as the "love of humankind" or the relief of suffering (Taylor 1989, 331). Kantians also are properly understood as strong evaluators: "In Kant's theory, rational agency is the constitutive good" because such agency "alone has dignity, brings with it an awe which empowers morally" (94). Foucauldians appeal to negative liberty.

27. Taylor's conception of "background" does not serve merely to situate and limit the subject, as James Bohman contends in his defense of Habermasian social science, but to enable: "The main problem with strong holism is that it confuses constraints with limits" (1993, 121).

28. Lorraine Code's chapter "Taking Subjectivity into Account" in *Rhetorical Spaces* develops the importance of articulating hidden gendered background of modern epistemology.

29. Taylor is not alone in linking everyday speech to the speculative dimension of language, but his understanding of it is distinctive.

30. See Gadamer's well-known attack on the Kantian legacy of "subjectivizing aesthetics," *Truth and Method*, which is the art world's counterpart to ethical "emotivism." Taylor's ontological conception of language, though indebted to Gadamer's, explicitly rejects the homogenizing dialogue of tradition that we find in *Truth and Method*. He insists on the multiplicity of languages and kinds of performances.

31. Rorty seizes on this exact passage to highlight his differences from Taylor: "Perhaps our most basic disagreement is whether poetry should be seen as 'a means of arranging the order of our internal lives by making an harmonious pattern of extremely complex attitudes, once thought to refer to an external order of metaphysics but now seen to be a symbolic order of our inner selves'" (I. A. Richards' view quoted by Stephen Spender and cited in Sources, 1989, 490–491). Taylor says that "'such a self-enclosed view will not do' [. . .]. I think it will do admirably" (Rorty 1998b, 84). I will return to Rorty later.

32. Larmore, for example, speaks of two distinct ways in which art may be seen as a vehicle of truth. According to one conception, "the function of art is to present in a particularly vivid form what we can recognize to be true by other, if less memorable, means. This is the mimetic conception of art, which holds that the beautiful imitates the true. But a different conception is that the work of art may be an indispensable means for grasping truths we cannot adequately express or, at least, would not have discovered by other means. In this view art is not imitation, but revelation" (1996, 198–199).

33. Gutting is clearly scrambling here, bringing in mathematical rather than moral and political reasoning. He says, "Poetic objectivity is quite different from mathematical or scientific objectivity" (1999, 135).

34. Gutting: "Individuals have the right to follow their own visions. But personal visions, even if objective in some sense, remain in the private domain and are not normative for public morality" (1999, 135).

35. By contrast, Gutting locates himself in the naturalist tradition that tries to eliminate this "third possibility" by separating desire from mediating institutions: "Ethical naturalism holds that morality makes sense even if it is grounded in nothing more than human desires" (1999, 156).

36. For "transitional justice," see Neil J. Kritz, ed., *Transitional Justice: How Emerging Democracies Reckon with Former Regimes*; Ruti Teitel, *Transitional Justice*; and Martha Minow, *Between Vengeance and Forgiveness: Facing History after Genocide and Mass Violence*.

37. See Thomas McCarthy, "Vergagenheitsbewältigung in the USA: On the Politics of the Memory of Slavery," and Andrew Vails, "A Truth Commission for the United States?" The flag debate in South Carolina, to recall our example from the introduction, could have been much more productive if it had led to a systematic engagement with the past instead of muted symbolic acknowledgment.

38. In chapter 4, I develop these ideas through Ralph Ellison's subtle dramatization of the dynamics of language, race, and memory. Throughout this chapter I am qualifying and expanding Taylor's rather narrow treatment of narrative. See Margaret Walker's critique of his emphasis on the quest and on life-transforming narratives in *Moral Understandings*, 143–147.

39. Lefort says, "The singularity of democracy does not become fully clear until we remember what the monarchical system of the Ancien Régime was" (*Essais politiques*, 26).

40. See chapter 2 above. Taylor has also not discussed their differences. See in particular, David Carr, Charles Taylor, and Paul Ricoeur, "Discussion: Ricoeur on Narrative," where Taylor says, "I find myself in substantial agreement with Ricoeur insofar as I grasp the major trajectory of his thought" (1992), 174).

41. Taylor sees Foucault's analysis as woven from strands of naturalism and the counter-Enlightenment.

42. I summarize here Greg Forter's argument in "Against Melancholy: The Antipathy to Mourning in Contemporary Theory and Literary Modernism."

43. I have given only a sketchy and partial summary of Arac's detailed study.

44. On the role of witnessing as means of coming to terms individually and collectively with trauma, see Dori Laub, "Truth and Testimony: The Process and the Struggle."

45. One could speak about a political community's "working through" its discursive inheritance, but the terms and temporalities would be different than in working through an event(s).

46. Rothberg calls the trace "an index" that "instead of indicating an object or phenomenon that caused it [. . .] points to a necessary absence" (2000, 104). By

146–148. See also Robert Bernasconi's "The Double Face of the Political and the Social: Hannah Arendt and America's Racial Divisions" (1991)and Kenneth Warren, "Ralph Ellison and the Problem of Cultural Authority: The Lessons of Little Rock."

3. Alasdair MacIntyre says, "Stories are lived before they are told" (1984, 212). The debate on whether stories are "lived" or "told" is nicely summed up in David Carr's *Time, Narrative, and History*. Most treatments of Arendt ignore this important issue and hence do not describe the role of language in judgment in a perspicuous way. Benhabib, for instance, says, "all action, including agonal action, is narratively constituted. The what of our actions and the who of the doer are always identified via a narrative" (1996b, 129). This sentence conflates precisely what Arendt is insistent in separating—that action is not prospectively constituted through narrative but only retrospectively cast this way. In a footnote, Benhabib cites MacIntyre's "narrative character of action" as "a more interesting account of the impossibility of a social science of a nomological and predictive nature" (96). MacIntyre's holistic elements contradict Arendt. In short, she leaves unanswered all the key philosophical questions posed by narrative itself. Lisa Disch's *Hannah Arendt and the Limits of Philosophy* (1994)and "More Truth Than Fact: Storytelling as Critical Understanding in the Writings of Hannah Arendt" (1993) look at Arendt's storytelling as an alternative to foundationalism and relativism: "Arendt's understanding of storytelling proposes an alternative to the Archimedean model of impartiality as detached reasoning" (1994, 109). However, she too cites MacIntyre's definition of narrative and does not address the questions of our being in language.

4. See James Bohman's "The Moral Costs of Political Pluralism: The Dilemmas of Difference and Equality in Arendt's 'Reflections on Little Rock'" *(1996)*, which goes beyond the social versus the political to examine "the problem of the moral and political costs of justice that include both equality and plurality" (57). This is an interesting but very different take from mine.

5. For a critique of Arendt's reading of African American thinkers, see Anne Norton, "Heart of Darkness: Africa and African Americans in the Writings of Hannah Arendt" (1995). Benhabib defends Arendt against Norton's charges in *The Reluctant Modern*, 85–86. A nuanced discussion of Arendt on race is beyond my scope, but I don't think we have to choose between Arendt's insight about the connections between European imperialism and the rise of totalitarianism, on the one hand, and the racism in her judgments about American political issues, on the other. For a discussion of Arendt in the wider context of race and philosophy, see Linda Alcoff, "Philosophy and Racial Identity" (1996).

6. Arendt thinks that "the function of school is to teach children what the world is like" (1977, 195) and "to prepare [children] in advance for the task of renewing a

common world" (195), a conception whose interest for the philosophy of education transcends this particular exchange.

7. In this same interview, Ellison says, "So today we sacrifice, as we sacrificed yesterday, the pleasure of personal retaliation in the interest of the common good" (1965, 342). See Danielle Allen's "Law's Necessary Forcefulness" (2001) and *Talking to Strangers* (2004). In these fascinating works, she explores the inescapabilty of sacrifice in democracy and uses Ellison's understanding of sacrifice as a touchstone for her argument.

8. Benhabib says, "The two phenomenological dimensions of the public realm are (a) its quality as a space of appearance and (b) its quality of being a common world. These dimensions are phenomenological in that they are aspects of the human condition per se, under whatever sociohistorical conditions in whatever epoch. Humans 'appear' to each in other in concentration camps [. . .]. But the aspect of the public realm as a common world is somewhat more fragile and more closely linked to sociohistorical conditions" (1996b, 128). She also notes that Arendt has not always kept "the categories of space, appearance, common world and public world" (129) distinct.

9. "In the realm of human affairs being and appearance are indeed one and the same" (Arendt 1965, 98). "But if it is true that thinking and reason are justified in transcending the limitations of cognition and the intellect—justified by Kant on the ground that the matters they deal with, though unknowable, are of the greatest existential interest to man—then the assumption must be that thinking and reason are not concerned with what the intellect is concerned with" (1978, I, 14).

10. Arendt says, "In his [Heidegger's] description of human existence everything that is real or authentic is assaulted by the overwhelming power of 'mere talk' that irresistibly arises out of the public realm, determining every aspect of everyday existence [. . .]. There is no escape, according to Heidegger, from the 'incomprehensible triviality of this common everyday world' except by withdrawal from it into that solitude which philosophers since Parmenides and Plato have opposed to the political realm" (1968, ix). Arendt is fighting off not just this aspect of Heidegger's thought—I agree with Arendt here—but also the Heideggerian account of embeddedness.

11. Kant explicates the critical role of sensus communis in relation to three maxims of the common human understanding: "1. To think for oneself; 2. To think from the standpoint of everyone else; 3. To think consistently" (1987, 160).

12. "The space of appearances comes into being wherever men are together in the manner of speech and action, [and] therefore predates and precedes all formal constitution of the public realm" (Arendt 1958, 199). For an incisive critique of Arendt's reading of Kant that helped clarify my argument, see

Alessandro Ferrara, "Judgment, Identity, and Authenticity: A Reconstruction of Hannah Arendt's Interpretation of Kant" (1998).

13. Michael Halberstam expresses this tendency well: "This disposition on Kant's part to posit a greater degree of consensus in matters of practical judgment than is warranted by the principles on which he bases such agreements" means that there "is a constant tendency to make objectification mistakes inherent in the Kantian position" (1999, 108).

14. Dana Villa asks, "How then does the appropriation of the Third Critique enable Arendt to escape the excess of an aesthetic, agonistic conception of politics?" (1996, 102).

15. As we saw in chapter 1, it is not that Habermas is simply wrong about art but that he simplifies the everyday by sequestering the radical questioning of language into art. See Paul Lauter's comparative reading of American literary history in which he urges that we "be aware not only of the varieties of artistic function but of their changing character over time" (1991, 67).

16. Bakhtin says, "The great organic poetics of the past—those of Aristotle, Horace, Boileau—are permeated with a deep sense of the wholeness of literature and of the harmonious interaction of all genres contained within this whole [. . .]. In this is their strength—inimitable, all-embracing fullness and exhaustiveness of such poetics. And they all, as a consequence, ignore the novel" (1981, 5). While the Russian Formalists and Heidegger find the everyday to be the place of automatized speech of the "they," Bakhtin finds a dynamism here that informs the novel. Moreover, Bakhtin's conception of authorship means that characters are "not only objects of authorial discourse but also subjects of their own directly signifying discourse" (1984, 7). This is not to say that Bakhtin's philosophy of language and literary histories provide a political philosophy or even an unproblematic literary theory. Bakhtin does not provide an account of historical argument that is important to Ellison and me.

17. Halberstam phrases this Arendtian insight as follows: "Liberalism and totalitarianism share the idea that society is an artifact and that politics is a species of making" (1998, 463).

18. Ellison and I are not following Habermas here, even though he too objects to the absence of a cognitive dimension in Arendt's judgment: "Arendt sees a yawning abyss between knowledge and opinion that cannot be closed with arguments" (Habermas 1994b, 225).

19. Arendt claims both Hegel and Heidegger base their projects on an attack on common sense: "Hegel testifies to the intramural warfare between philosophy and common sense" (1978, I, 90). Of Heidegger she says, "In other words, what for common sense is the obvious withdrawal of the mind from the world appears in the mind's own perspective as 'withdrawal of Being or oblivion of

Being. [. . .] And it is true, everyday life, the life of the 'They,' is present in a world from which all that is 'visible' to the mind is totally absent" (1978, I, 88). Despite her criticisms of *Being and Time* in "What Is Existenz Philosophy," *Essays in Understanding*, and in *Men in Dark Times*, she appropriates the late Heidegger's idea of thinking as separate from knowing and willing.

20. In differentiating his work from Eliot's and Joyce's use of ancient ritual, Ellison says that "it took [him] a few years to realize that myths and rites which we find functioning in our everyday lives could be used in the same way" (1995, 216).

21. Benhabib says, "There are two strains in Arendt's thought, one corresponding to the method of fragmentary historiography inspired by Walter Benjamin; the other, inspired by the phenomenology of Husserl and Heidegger, and according to which memory is the mimetic recollection of the lost origins of phenomena as contained in some fundamental human experience" (1996b,95).

22. See Friedlander, *Memory, History, and the Extermination of the Jews in Europe*, LaCapra, *Representing the Holocaust: History, Theory, Trauma*, and Ellison, "Harlem Is Nowhere," *Shadow and Act*.

5. Globalization and the Clash of Cultures

1. Said's work is so widely discussed that one hardly needs to cite critics in each of these fields. For a good overview of his work and the criticism surrounding it, see Valerie Kennedy's *Edward Said: A Critical Introduction*.

2. This claim is widespread in Cultural Studies and New Historicism. As Claire Colebrook says in her survey of New Historicism, "The text is not an expression or reflection of its world; it plays an active part in producing and acting with that world" (1997, 68).

3. I will focus on *Orientalism* and *Culture and Imperialism* as studies of public imagination and cultural theory rather than on his journalistic interventions in the politics of the Middle East.

4. Orientalism "is a distribution of geopolitical awareness into aesthetic, scholarly, economic, sociological, historical and philosophical texts" (Said 1978, 12).

5. He calls Orientalism "a discourse as described by [Foucault] in *The Archaeology of Knowledge* and *Discipline and Punish*" (1978, 3).

6. As James Clifford points out, Said, in fact, gives three competing definitions of Orientalism: 1. What orientalists do and have done. 2. A style of thought based upon an ontological and epistemological distinction between the orient and the occident. 3. a corporate institution for dealing with the orient (Clifford, 259). Clifford also discusses the ways in which Said is not Foucauldian.

7. "Critical consciousness stands between the temptations represented by two formidable and related powers [. . .]. One is the culture to which critics are bound filiatively (by birth, nationality, profession); the other is a method or

system acquired afiliatively (by social and political convention, economic and historical circumstance, voluntary effort and willed deliberation)" (1983, 24–25).

8. He introduces the opposition "secular/religious" in the first and last chapters of *The World, the Text, and the Critic.* "Religious criticism," for Said is not just about religion per se but a kind of discourse that surfaces in many secular forms, such as orientalism, nationalism, and literature. Thus, "orientalism" is understood as a secularized Christian story, as "structures inherited from the past, secularized, redisposed, and reformed by such disciplines as philology, which in turn were naturalized, and laicized substitutes for (or versions of) Christian supernatural-ism" (1978, 122). To say something is a "secularization" in Said's usage is always to delegitimize it.

9. I will look at secularism in the broader context of political philosophy later in the chapter. As a preliminary definition, secularism can be considered as the West-ern political response to the wars of religion, in which political norms were sepa-rated from particular Christian religious practices.

10. In "Modes of Secularism," Taylor distinguishes three principal modes of West-ern secularism: the independent ethic, initiated by Hobbes and continued in dif-ferent terms by neo-Kantians such as Habermas; the "common ground" approach to religious difference in the tradition of Locke; and the "overlapping consensus" advocated by Rawls.

11. Rawls says the "historical origin of political liberalism (and of liberalism more generally) is the Reformation and its aftermath, with the long controversies over religious toleration in the sixteenth and seventeenth centuries" (1993, xxiv–xxv). Habermas says, "The key historical events in establishing the principle of sub-jectivity are the Reformation, the Enlightenment, and the French Revolution" (1987, 17).

12. Rawls writes, "Something like the modern understanding of liberty of con-science and freedom of thought began then [. . .] the success of liberal constitu-tionalism came as a discovery of a new social possibility: the possibility of a reasonable harmonious and stable pluralist society" (1993, xxiv–xxv).

13. It is not just nonwestern thinkers, such as Nandy and Sen, whom I will discuss momentarily, who challenge Western modernity's epistemological and political definitions of the secular, but also those who seek to retrieve premodern western forms of political reasoning. In addition to Tully, *Strange Multiplicities,* see Awiakta's *Selu,* which explores Native American political thinking and its influ-ence on the American Founders.

14. See, for instance, Quentin Skinner's review of Toulmin, "The Past in the Pre-sent" *(1990),* which captures some of my reservations. I discuss my philosophi-cal criticism later.

15. While Toulmin offers an insightful critique of formalism, he does not give us much of an alternative beyond Montaigne. He thus falls into the alternative of formalism and contextual skepticism without linking history to his philosophical problematic or principles of deliberation. For a complication of Toulmin's picture, particularly with regard to Hobbes, see Richard Tuck's *Philosophy and Government*.

16. "*Orientalism* is theoretically inconsistent and I designed it that way: I didn't want Foucault's method [. . .] to override what I was trying to put forward. The notion of a kind of noncoercive knowledge, which I come to at the end of the book, was deliberately anti-Foucault" (1987, 134, 137).

17. In *The Claims of Culture*, Seyla Benhabib also combines a constructivist approach to culture with a dialogical universalism in the Habermas line. She argues against the politics of difference and the holistic hermeneutic approach to culture that she thinks goes with it because she believes that cultures are too heterogeneous and dynamic to be reduced to an overarching identity. While I agree that this argument does indeed work against some formulations of the politics of difference, the problem of difference, as I am presenting it here through public imagination, does not hinge on the empirical assertion of a unified identity—say, "Native American" or "African American"; rather, my claim is that "culture" or "public imagination" is philosophically prior to the division that she makes between empirical identities and universal principles.

18. See Marcel Gauchet's "Quand les droits de l'homme deviennent une politique," in *La démocratie contre elle-même* for an insightful analysis of how contemporary politics has been damaged by its exclusive focus on rights at the expense of historical/social questions.

19. Said is critical of postmodernism: "Cults like post-modernism, discourse analysis, New Historicism, deconstruction, neo-pragmatism" manifest "an astonishing sense of weightlessness with regard to the gravity of history" (1993, 366–367).

20. In literary and cultural theory, it is common to view a phenomenology of narrative as a wish fulfillment that satisfies a desire for coherence—as we saw in our discussion of Hayden White. Two years after "Permission to Narrate," Said published *After the Last Sky: Palestinian Lives*, in which he speaks of the possibility of entrapment by narrative. Palestinians debate "whether a clear, direct line can be drawn from our misfortunes in 1948 to our misfortunes in the present" (1986, 5), and he raises his voice to respond, "I don't think that such a line can be drawn; no clear and simple narrative is adequate to the complexity of our experience." Hence his text "do[es] not tell a consecutive story" (6).

21. "What I was trying to do in *Culture and Imperialism* was not to *narrate*; it's impossible to narrate so many narratives, even contrapuntally" (1994b, 24). Jonathan Arac captures the relationship of narrative to contrapuntalism nicely:

"Contrapuntal criticism is not itself narrative, but rather [. . .] a technique of theme and variations. Yet counterpoint may be established between different narratives, and if the book as a whole does not make a narrative, it makes a pattern of Western narrative challenged by the resistances of 'counter-narrative'" (Arac 1994, 11).

22. Aijaz Ahmad articulates Said's ambivalence well: "Said denounces with Foucauldian vitriol what he loves with Auerbachian passion" (1992, 168). Said's reading of Austen has been contested by those who claim that Austen's references to Antigua are self-conscious. See, for instance, Michael Steffes, "Slavery and Mansfield Park: The Historical and Biographical Context" (1996).

23. How to retrieve and discard damaged historical self-understandings is precisely the question that Ellison addresses so well, as we saw in chapter 4.

24. In postcolonial and cultural studies "hybridity" is associated with Mikhail Bakhtin and Homi Bhabha. Bakhtin defines it as "a mixture of two social languages within the limits of a single utterance, an encounter, within the arena of an utterance, between two linguistic consciousnesses, separated from one another by an epoch, by social differentiation or by some other factor" (1981, 358). Bhabha gives this linguistic ontology a political animation so that hybridity opens political possibilities: "If the effect of colonial power is seen to be the production of hybridization [. . .] [it] enables a form of subversion [. . .] that turns the discursive conditions of dominance into the grounds of intervention" (1985, 154). This animation of language and the unqualified valuation of subversion per se leave out interpretive judgment.

25. We can contrast Said here with a work such as Roxanne Euben's *Enemy in the Mirror: Islamic Fundamentalism and the Limits of Modern Rationalism* (1999), which criticizes Western social and political theory for failing to take Islamic self-understandings seriously and reductively explaining them as a reaction to social pressures. However, she does not simply unmask Western philosophy for misrepresenting Islam and demand formal recognition of its cultural and political rights; rather, she opens its modes of thinking through its distinctive historical imaginations. She sets up a conversation between Western critics of modernity and Islamic thinkers.

26. As Ahmad says, "All societies have prejudices about gender, class ethnicity, etc., but what makes European prejudices powerful is not ontological obsession but the power of colonial capitalism" (1992, 184). Said's silence on gender has been noted by many. See, for instance, Susan Fraiman's "Jane Austen and Edward Said: Gender, Culture, and Imperialism" (1995).

27. See Sudipat Kaviraj, "Modernity and the Politics of India" (2000), for an account of how models of Western rationality miss the uniqueness of India's transition to modernity.

28. I will treat this, and other works considered later for similar reasons, for the philosophical significance of their approaches and not comment on their empirical accuracy.

29. "Decisions made at the U.N. Security Council or in the International Monetary Fund that reflect the interests of the West are presented to the world as reflecting the desires of the world community. The very phrase 'the world community' has become the euphemistic collective noun (replacing 'the Free World') to give global legitimacy to actions reflecting the interests of the United States and other Western powers" (Huntington 1993, 39).

30. Huntington's argument has been widely discussed. See, for instance, *The Clash of Civilizations: Asian Responses*, ed. Salim Rashid (1997), and Roy P. Mottahedeh, "The Clash of Civilizations: An Islamicist's Critique" (1995).

31. "Capability is freedom to achieve alternative functioning combinations, or less formally to achieve various lifestyles" (2000, 75).

32. He articulates the distinctiveness of his approach by comparing the type of information on which it relies with the kind of information on which competing approaches to ethics and political philosophies (e.g., Rawlsian and utilitarian philosophies) rely (2000, chap. 3). For an excellent survey and critique of debate over Asian values and liberalism, see Surain Subramaniam, "The Asian Values Debate: Implications for the Spread of Liberal Democracy" (2000).

33. For purposes of this example, I will be drawing primarily on the excellent collection *Secularism and Its Critics*, ed. Rajeev Bharghava. The literature on secularization—e.g., Max Weber, Hans Blumenberg, Marcel Gauchet—is too vast for even the shallowest overview.

34. For the sake of brevity, I am following Taylor's division in "Modes of Secularism." For a provocative interpretation of religion and modernity that attends to the historical specificity of the West's peculiar "exit from religion" through Christianity, see interviews in *La Condition historique*, where Marcel Gauchet articulates clearly and briefly his extensive research on these issues.

35. In extracting common values from the public imaginations of different political cultures, he makes the same move he did in the debate with Huntington, where he pulled values and norms from the social imaginaries of different periods of Indian history.

36. Western historians assume that "the aim is to unravel the secular processes and the order that underlie manifest realities of past times, available in ready-made raw forms as historical data" (1995, 47).

37. For an extended development of Nandy's mode of questioning, see Blaney and Inyatullah, *International Relations and the Problem of Difference*.

38. The argument is between secular historians who believe that "secular faiths [. . .] more tolerant should correct that history" and Hindu nationalists, who "believe

that, except for Hinduism, most faiths, including secular ones, are intolerant" (Nandy 1995, 64).

39. Sen makes an analogous move in his misreading of Taylor's challenge to Rawls's conception of justice. Sen reads Taylor as calling for "a sense of communal solidarity" (1999, 12). As we saw in chapter 3, Taylor is rewriting the starting point for reasoning such that justice or any other value cannot be thought of apart from public imagination. This ontological claim must be kept distinct from his advocacy of a particular position.

40. In his critique of Nandy, Rorty too blocks out Nandy's appeal to public imagination. For Rorty, we should not try to think through the institutions of meaning we inhabit—i.e., not concern ourselves with "goals other than mere survival" and limit ourselves to our "ability to cope with the environment" and our "ability not to be overly disconcerted by differences from oneself" (1998b, 186).

Conclusion

1. My title responds to Fish's well-known denial of principle in both *The Trouble With Principle*—"The trouble with principle is [. . .] that it does not exist" (1999, 2)—and *There Is No Such Thing as Free Speech*.

2. "The world [that] pragmatism describes [. . .][is] the world we inhabit independently of its description" (Fish 1999, 308).

3. Fish's legal critics often charge that he ignores criteria and rules—e.g, Ronald Dworkin ("Law as Interpretation" and "My Reply to Stanley Fish"), Owen Fiss (*The Law as It Could Be*, 149–190)—and thus fail to attack Fish's transcendental argument about the conditions of interpretation. This lets Fish repeat his argument that such considerations are always already committed to the agenda of a particular interpretive community. See Fish, *Doing What Comes Naturally*, for his essays on Dworkin ("Working on the Chain Gang" and "Wrong Again") and Fiss ("Fish v. Fiss").

4. From the synchronic perspective, he also fragments the subject's self-understandings. See *The Trouble with Principle*, 279–308.

5. Nandy makes a similar point about the political understanding of historical processes: "While direct violence produces identifiable victims and refugees, social processes such as development produce invisible victims and invisible refugees" (1995, 55).

6. See Robert Gooding-Williams, *Reading Rodney King*.

7. Chapter 11, section 1 of *The 9/11 Commission Report* is entitled "Imagination," and in it the Commission's concern is why the bureaucracies of the United States did not see the attack coming and what can be done to prepare for such future incidents.

Works Cited

Ahmad, Aijaz. 1992. *In Theory: Classes, Nations, Literatures.* London: Verso.

Alcoff, Linda. 1996. "Philosophy and Racial Identity." *Radical Philosophy* 75, 5–14.

Allen, Danielle. 2001. "Law's Necessary Forcefulness: Ralph Ellison vs. Hannah Arendt on the Battle of Little Rock." *Oklahoma City University Law Review* 26, 857–895.

———. 2004. *Talking to Strangers. Anxieties of Citizenship since Brown v. Board of Education.* Chicago: University of Chicago Press.

Amar, Akhil Reed. 1998. *The Bill of Rights: Creation and Reconstruction.* New Haven: Yale University Press.

Anderson, Benedict. 1991. *Imagined Communities: Reflections on the Origin and Spread of Nationalism.* London: Verso.

Anderson, Joel. 1996. "The Personal Lives of Strong Evaluators: Identity, Pluralism, and Ontology in Charles Taylor's Value Theory." *Constellations: An International Journal of Critical and Democratic Theory* 3, 17–38.

Ankersmit, Frank. 1989. "Historiography and Postmodernism." In *History and Theory: Contemporary Readings,* ed. Brian Fay et al. Oxford: Blackwell.

———. 1990. "Reply to Professor Zagorin." In *History and Theory: Contemporary Readings,* ed. Brian Fay et al. Oxford: Blackwell.

Anzuldúa, Gloria. 1987. *Borderlands/La Frontera.* San Francisco: Spinsters/Aunt Lute.

Ansell-Pearson, Keith, et al., eds. 1997. *Cultural Readings of Imperialism: Edward Said and the Gravity of History.* New York: St. Martin's Press.

Arac, Jonathan. 1994. "A Symposium on Edward Said's *Culture and Imperialism.*" *Social Text* 40, 10–14.

———. 1997. *Huckleberry Finn as Idol and Target: The Functions of Criticism in Our Time.* Madison: University of Wisconsin Press.

Arendt, Hannah. 1958. *The Human Condition.* Chicago: University of Chicago Press.

———. 1959. "Reflections on Little Rock" and "A Reply to Critics." *Dissent* 6, 45–56, 179–181.

———. 1965. *On Revolution.* New York: Penguin.

———. 1968. *Men in Dark Times.* New York: Harcourt Brace.

———. 1973. *The Origins of Totalitarianism.* New York: Harcourt Brace Jovanovich.

———. 1977. *Between Past and Future.* New York: Penguin.

———. 1978. *The Life of the Mind.* 2 vols. New York: Harcourt Brace.

———. 1979. "On Hannah Arendt." In *Hannah Arendt: The Recovery of the Public World,* ed. Melvyn A. Hill. New York: St. Martin's.

———. 1982. *Lectures on Kant's Political Philosophy.* Chicago: University of Chicago Press.

———. 1994. *Essays in Understanding: 1930–1954,* ed. Jerome Kohn. New York: Harcourt Brace.

Awiakta. 1993. *Selu: Seeking the Corn-Mother's Wisdom.* Golden, Colorado: Fulcrum Publishing.

Aylesworth, Gary. 1991. "Dialogue, Text, Narrative: Confronting Gadamer and Ricoeur." In *Gadamer and Hermeneutics,* ed. Hugh Silverman. New York: Routledge.

Bakhtin, Mikhail. 1981. *The Dialogic Imagination,* trans. and ed. Caryl Emerson and Michael Holquist. Austin: University of Texas Press.

———. 1984. *Problems in Dostoevsky's Poetics,* trans. Caryl Emerson. Minneapolis: University of Minnesota Press.

Baldwin, Peter, ed. 1990. *Reworking the Past: Hitler, the Holocaust, and the Historians' Debate.* Boston: Beacon Press.

Barber, Benjamin. 1995. *Jihad vs. McWorld.* New York: Times Books.

Bartov, Omer. 1996a. *Murder in Our Midst: The Holocaust, Industrial Killing, and Representation.* New York: Oxford University Press.

———. 1996b. "Ordinary Monsters." *New Republic* 29, 32–38.

Bauman, Zygmunt. 1989. *Modernity and the Holocaust.* Ithaca: Cornell University Press.

Benhabib, Seyla. 1986. *Critique, Norm, and Utopia.* New York: Columbia University Press.

———. 1992. *Situating the Self.* New York: Routledge.

———. 1995. "Subjectivity, Historiography, and Politics: Reflections on the 'Feminism/Postmodernism Exchange.'" In *Feminist Contentions: A Philosophical Exchange,* ed. Seyla Benhabib et al. New York: Routledge, 1995.

———, ed. 1996a. *Democracy and Difference: Contesting the Boundaries of the Political.* Princeton: Princeton University Press.

———. 1996b. *Hannah Arendt: The Reluctant Modern.* Thousand Oaks, CA: Sage.

———. 2002. *The Claims of Culture.* Princeton: Princeton University Press.

Bernasconi, Robert. 1991. "The Double Face of the Political and the Social: Hannah Arendt and America's Racial Divisions." *Research in Phenomenology* 26, 3–24.

Bernstein, Richard. 1991. "Foucault: Critique as Philosophical Ethos." In *The New Constellation.* Cambridge: MIT Press.

Bhabha, Homi. 1985. "Signs Taken for Wonder: Questions of Ambivalence and Authority under a Tree Outside Delhi, May 1817." *Critical Inquiry* 12, 144–165.

Bharghava, Rajeev, ed. 1998. *Secularism and Its Critics.* Delhi: Oxford University Press.

Blaney, David L., and Naeem Inayatullah. 2000. "The Westphalian Deferral." *International Studies Review* 2, 29–64.

Blight, David. 2001. *Race and Reunion: The Civil War in American History.* Cambridge: Harvard University Press.

Bohman, James. 1993. *New Philosophy of Social Science: Problems of Indeterminacy.* Cambridge: MIT Press.

——. 1996. "The Moral Costs of Political Pluralism: The Dilemmas of Difference and Equality in Arendt's 'Reflections on Little Rock.'" In *Hannah Arendt: Twenty Years Later,* ed. Larry May and Jerome Kohn. Cambridge: MIT Press.

Brandom, Robert. 2000. "The Vocabularies of Pragmatism." In *Rorty and His Critics,* ed. Robert Brandon. Oxford: Blackwell.

Braudel, Fernand. 1969. *Ecrits sur l'histoire.* Paris: Gallimard.

Burke, Peter. 1997. "The Strengths and Weaknesses of the History of Mentalities." *Varieties of Cultural History.* Ithaca: Cornell University Press.

Butler, Judith. 1993. *Bodies That Matter: The Discursive Limits of "Sex."* New York: Routledge.

——. 1995. "Contingent Foundations." In *Feminist Contestations: A Philosophical Exchange.* New York: Routledge.

——. 1997a. *Excitable Speech: A Politics of the Performative.* New York: Routledge.

——. 1997b. *The Psychic Life of Power.* New York: Routledge.

Byers, Thomas. 1996. "History Re-membered: *Forrest Gump,* Postfeminist Masculinity, and the Burial of the Counterculture." *Modern Fiction Studies* 42, 419–444.

Calhoun, Craig. 2002. "Constitutional Patriotism and the Public Sphere: Interests, Identity, and Solidarity in the Integration of Europe." In *Global Justice and Transnational Politics,* ed. Pablo De Greiff and Ciaran Cronin. Cambridge: MIT Press.

——. 2003. "The Democratic Integration of Europe: Interests, Identity, and the Public Sphere." In *Europe without Borders: Re-Mapping Territory, Citizenship, and Identity in a Transitional Age,* ed. Mabel Berezin and Martin Schain. Baltimore: Johns Hopkins University Press.

——. Forthcoming. "Emergency Imaginaries." In *Secularization, Multiple Modernities, Social Imaginaries: Essays in Honor of Charles Taylor,* ed. Dilip Gaonkar and Thomas McCarthy. Minneapolis: University of Minnesota Press.

Carr, David. 1974. *Phenomenology and the Problem of History.* Evanston: Northwestern University Press.

——. 1986. *Time, Narrative, and History.* Bloomington: Indiana University Press.

Carr, David, Charles Taylor, and Paul Ricoeur. 1992. "Discussion: Ricoeur on Narrative." In *On Paul Ricoeur,* ed. David Wood. London: Routledge.

Carroll, Noel. 1998. "Interpretation, History, and Narrative." In *History and Theory: Contemporary Readings,* ed. Brian Fay et al. Oxford: Blackwell.

Caruth, Cathy. 1995. "Introduction: Trauma and Experience." In *Trauma: Explorations in Memory,* ed. Cathy Caruth. Baltimore: Johns Hopkins University Press.

Castoriadis, Cornelius. 1975. *L'Institution imaginaire de la société*. Paris: Seuil.

Chartier, Roger. 1997. *On the Edge of the Cliff: History, Language, and Practices*, trans. Lydia G. Cochrane. Baltimore: Johns Hopkins University Press.

Chatterjee, Partha. 1991. "Whose Imagined Community?" *Millennium* 20, 521–525.

Chopin, Kate. 1994. *The Awakening*. New York: Norton.

Clifford, James. 1988. *The Predicament of Culture*. Cambridge: Harvard University Press.

Code, Lorraine. 1995. *Rhetorical Spaces: Essays on Gendered Locations*. New York: Routledge.

Colebrook, Claire. 1997. *New Literary Histories*. Manchester: Manchester University Press.

Connolly, William E. 1985. "Taylor, Foucault, and Otherness." *Political Theory* 13, 365–376.

——. 1995. *Ethos of Pluralization*, Minneapolis: University of Minnesota Press.

——. 1999. *Why I Am Not a Secularist?* Minneapolis: University of Minnesota.

Cooke, Maeve. 1994. *Language and Reason*. Cambridge: MIT Press.

Dallmayr, Fred. 1998. *Alternative Visions: Paths in the Global Village*. Lanham, MD: Rowman and Littlefield.

Dean, Carolyn. 2002. "Traumatic Realism: The Demands of Holocaust Representation." *History and Theory* 41, 239–249.

Derrida, Jacques. 1977. "Limited Inc." *Glyph* 2, 162–254.

——. 1982. "Signature, Event, Context." In his *Margins of Philosophy*, trans. Alan Bass. Chicago: University of Chicago Press.

Descombes, Vincent. 1996. *Les Institutions du sens*. Paris: Minuit.

Disch, Lisa. 1993. "More Truth Than Fact: Storytelling as Critical Understanding in the Writings of Hannah Arendt." *Political Theory* 21, 665–694.

——. 1994. *Hannah Arendt and the Limits of Philosophy*. Ithaca: Cornell University Press.

Dosse, François. 1992. *Histoire du structuralisme*. 2 vols. Paris: La Découverte.

——.1994. *History in Pieces*, trans. Peter V. Connor. Urbana: University of Illinois.

——. 1995. *L'Empire du sens*. Paris: La Découverte.

Dreyfus, Hubert. 1991. *Being-in-the-World*. Cambridge: MIT Press.

Dreyfus, Hubert, and Paul Rabinow, eds. 1982. *Michel Foucault: Beyond Structuralism and Semiotics*. Chicago: University of Chicago Press.

Dworkin, Ronald. 1983. "Law as Interpretation," and "My Reply to Stanley Fish." In *The Politics of Interpretation*, ed. W. J. T. Mitchell. Chicago: University of Chicago Press.

——. 1986. *Law's Empire*. Cambridge: Harvard University Press.

Edgar, Walter. 1998. *South Carolina: A History*. Columbia: University of South Carolina Press.

Eisenstadt, S. N., ed. 2000. "Multiple Modernities." *Daedalus*, 1–29.

Ellison, Ralph. 1965. "Leadership from the Periphery." In *Who Speaks for the Negro?*, ed. Robert Penn Warren. New York: Random House.

——. 1981. *Invisible Man*. New York: Vintage.

——. 1995. *The Collected Essays of Ralph Ellison*, ed. John Callahan. New York: Modern Library.

Euben, Roxanne.1999. *Enemy in the Mirror: Islamic Fundamentalism and the Limits of Modern Rationalism*. Princeton: Princeton University Press.

Ferrara, Alessandro. 1998. "Judgment, Identity, and Authenticity: A Reconstruction of Hannah Arendt's Interpretation of Kant." *Philosophy and Social Criticism* 24, 1–24.

——. 1999. *Justice and Judgment: The Rise and the Prospect of the Judgment Model in Contemporary Political Philosophy*. Thousand Oaks, CA: Sage.

Ferry, Jean-Marc. 1996. *L'Ethique reconstructive*. Paris: Cerf.

Finkelstein, Norman. 1988. *A Nation on Trial: The Goldhagen Controversy and Historical Truth*. New York: Henry Holt.

Fish, Stanley. 1990. *Doing What Comes Naturally*. Durham: Duke University Press.

——. 1994. *There Is No Such Thing as Free Speech: And It's a Good Thing, Too*. New York: Oxford University Press.

——. 1999. *The Trouble with Principle*. Cambridge: Harvard University Press.

Fiss, Owen. 2003. *The Law as It Could Be*. New York: New York University Press.

Forter, Greg. 2003. "Against Melancholy: The Antipathy to Mourning in Contemporary Theory and Literary Modernism." *differences* 14, 134–170.

Foucault, Michel. 1970. *The Order of Things*, trans. Alan Sheridan. New York: Random House.

——. 1972. *The Archaeology of Knowledge*. New York: Pantheon.

——. 1977. *Discipline and Punish*, trans. Alan Sheridan. New York: Vintage.

——. 1978. *History of Sexuality*, trans. Robert Hurley. Vol. 1. New York: Vintage.

——. 1984. *The Foucault Reader*, ed. Paul Rabinow. New York: Pantheon.

——. 1985. *Uses of Pleasure*. Vol. 2 of *History of Sexuality*, trans. Robert Hurley. New York: Vintage.

——. 1988. *The Final Foucault*, ed. James Bernauer and David Rasmussen. Cambridge: MIT Press.

——. 1989. *Foucault Live: Interviews 1966–84*, trans. John Johnston, ed. Sylvère Lotringer. New York: Semiotext(e).

——. 1990. *Politics, Philosophy, Culture: Interviews and Other Writings 1977–84*, trans. Alan Sheridan et al., ed. Lawrence Kritzman. New York: Routledge.

——. 1994. *Dits et écrits, 1954–1988*. Vols. 1–4. Paris. Gallimard.

Fraiman, Susan. 1995. "Jane Austen and Edward Said: Gender, Culture, and Imperialism." *Critical Inquiry* 21, 805–821.

Fraser, Nancy. 1997. "Thinking the Public Sphere." In *Justice Interruptus*. New York: Routledge.

Friedlander, Saul, ed. 1992. *Probing the Limits of Representation: Nazism and the "Final Solution."* Cambridge: Harvard University Press.

———. 1993. *Memory, History, and the Extermination of the Jews in Europe.* Bloomington: Indiana University Press.

———. 1997. *Nazi Germany and the Jews.* New York: HarperCollins.

Friedman, Thomas. 2000. *The Lexus and the Olive Tree.* New York: Farrar, Straus, and Giroux.

Fullinwider, Robert. 1996. "Patriotic History." In his *Public Education in a Multicultural Society: Policy, Theory, Critique.* Cambridge: Cambridge University Press

Gadamer, Hans Georg. 1994. *Truth and Method,* ed. Joel C. Weinsheimer and Donald G. Marshall. New York: Continuum.

Galston, William. 1991. *Liberal Purposes.* Cambridge: Cambridge University Press.

———. 1995. "Two Concepts of Liberalism." *Ethics* 3, 516–534.

Gaonkar, Dilip Parameschwar, ed. 2001. *Alternative Modernities.* Durham: Duke University Press.

Gauchet, Marcel. 2002. "Quand les droits de l'homme deviennent une politique," in *La démocratie contre elle-même.* Paris: Gallimard.

———. 2004. *La Condition historique.* Paris: Stock.

Gellner, Ernest. 1983. *Nations and Nationalism.* Ithaca: Cornell University Press.

Ginzburg, Carlo. 1999. *The Judge and the Historian: Marginal Notes on a Late-20th-Century Miscarriage of Justice,* trans. Antony Shugaar. London: Verso Books.

Goldhagen, Daniel. 1996. *Hitler's Willing Executioners.* New York: Knopf.

———. 1998. "Modell Bundesrepublik: National History, Democracy and Internationalization in Germany." In *Unwilling Germans,* ed. Robert Shandley. Minneapolis: University of Minnesota.

Gooding-Williams, Robert. 1993. *Reading Rodney King/Reading Urban Uprising.* New York: Routledge.

Gordon, Linda. 1988. *Heroes of Their Own Lives.* New York: Penguin.

Guess, Raymond. 1981. *The Idea of Critical Theory.* New York: Cambridge University Press.

Guillory, John. 1993. *Cultural Capital.* Chicago: University of Chicago Press.

Gutting, Gary. 1999. *Pragmatic Liberalism and the Critique of Modernity.* Cambridge: Cambridge University Press.

Guy-Sheftall, Beverly, ed. 1995. *Words of Fire: An Anthology of African-American Feminist Thought.* New York: New Press, 1995.

Habermas, Jürgen. 1973. *Knowledge and Human Interests,* trans. Jeremy Shapiro. Boston: Beacon Press.

———. 1979a. "History and Evolution," trans. David J. Parent. *Telos* 3, 5–44.

———. 1979b. "Universal Pragmatics." In his *Communication and the Evolution of Society*, trans. Thomas McCarthy. Boston: Beacon Press.

———. 1983. *The Theory of Communicative Action*, trans. Thomas McCarthy. 2 vols. Boston: Beacon Press.

———. 1986a. *Autonomy and Solidarity: Interviews*, ed. Peter Dews. New York: Verso.

———. 1986b. "Questions and Counterquestions." In *Habermas and Modernity*, ed. Richard Bernstein. Cambridge: MIT Press.

———. 1987. *Philosophical Discourse of Modernity*, trans. Frederick Lawrence. Cambridge: MIT Press.

———. 1989a. *The New Conservatism: Cultural Criticism and the Historians' Debate*, trans. Shierry Weber Nicholsen. Cambridge: MIT Press.

———. 1989b. *The Structural Transformation of the Public Sphere: An Inquiry into a Category of Bourgeois Society*, trans. Thomas Burger with assistance from Frederick Lawrence. Cambridge: MIT Press (originally published 1962).

———. 1990a. "The Hermeneutic Claim to Universality" and "A Review of Truth and Method." In *The Hermeneutic Tradition*, ed. Gayle Ormiston and Allan Schrist. Albany: SUNY Press.

———. 1990b. *Moral Consciousness and Communicative Action*, trans. Christian Lendhardt and Shierry Weber Nicholsen. Cambridge: MIT Press.

———. 1992a. "Further Reflections on the Public Sphere." In *Habermas and the Public Sphere*, ed. Craig Calhoun. Cambridge: MIT Press.

———. 1992b. *Postmetaphysical Thinking: Philosophical Essays*, trans. William Mark Hohengarten. Cambridge: MIT Press.

———. 1992c. "Yet Again: German Identity—A Nation of Angry DM Burghers?" In *When the Wall Came Down: Reactions to German Unification*, ed. Harold James and Maria Stone. New York: Routledge.

———. 1993. *Justification and Application: Remarks in Discourse Ethics*, trans. Cioran F. Cronin. Cambridge: MIT Press.

———. 1994a. "Struggles for Recognition in the Democratic Constitutional State." In *Multiculturalism*, ed. Amy Gutmann. Princeton: Princeton University Press.

———. 1994b. "Hannah Arendt's Communications Concept of Power." In *Hannah Arendt: Critical Essays*, ed. Lewis Hinchman and Sandra Hinchman. Albany: SUNY Press.

———. 1995. "Reconciliation through the Public Use of Reason: Remarks on John Rawls's Political Liberalism." *Journal of Philosophy* 92, no. 3, 109–131.

———. 1996a. *Between Facts and Norms: Contributions to a Discourse Theory of Law and Democracy*, trans. William Rehg. Cambridge: MIT Press.

———. 1996b. "On How Postwar Germany Has Faced Its Recent Past." *Common Knowledge* 5, 1–13.

——. 1996c. "Three Normative Models of Democracy." In *Democracy and Difference,* ed. Seyla Benhabib. Princeton: Princeton University Press.

——. 1997a. *A Berlin Republic: Writings on Germany,* trans. Steven Rendall. Lincoln: University of Nebraska Press.

——. 1997b. "On the Public Use of History: Why a Democracy Prize for Daniel Goldhagen?" trans. Max Pensky. *Common Knowledge* 6, 1–9.

——. 1998. *Inclusion of the Other,* trans. Ciaran Cronin. Cambridge: MIT Press.

——. 2001. "Constitutional Democracy: A Paradoxical Union of Contradictory Principles?" *Political Theory* 29, no. 6, 766–781.

Halberstam, Michael. 1998. "Totalitarianism as a Problem for the Modern Conception of Politics." *Political Theory* 26, 459–488.

——. 1999. *Totalitarianism and the Modern Conception of Politics.* New Haven: Yale University Press.

Han, Béatrice. 2002. *Foucault's Critical Project: Between the Transcendental and the Historical,* trans. Edward Pile. Stanford: Stanford University Press.

Hegel, Georg W. F. 1977. *Phenomenology of Spirit,* trans. A. V. Miller. New York: Oxford University Press.

Heidegger, Martin. 1962. *Being and Time,* trans. J. Macquarie and E. Robinson. New York: Harper & Row.

Hobbes, Thomas. 1968. *Leviathan.* New York: Penguin.

Hobsbawm, Eric, and Terence Ranger, eds. 1983. *The Invention of Tradition.* Cambridge: Cambridge University Press.

Holub, Robert. 1991. *Jürgen Habermas: Critic in the Public Sphere.* New York: Routledge.

Huntington, Samuel. 1993 "The Clash of Civilizations?" *Foreign Affairs* 72, 22–49.

——. 1996. *The Clash of Civilizations and the Remaking of the World Order.* New York: Simon and Schuster.

Husserl, Edmund. 1970. *Crisis of the European Sciences and Transcendental Phenomenology.* Evanston: Northwestern University Press.

Inayatullah, Naeem. 2003. "Something There: Love, War, Basketball, and Afghanistan: An Antidotal Memoir." *Intertexts* 7, 143–156.

Inayatullah, Naeem, and David L. Blaney. 2004. *International Relations and the Problem of Difference.* New York: Routledge.

Jameson, Fredric, and Masao Miyoshi, eds. 1996. *The Cultures of Globalization.* Durham: Duke University Press.

Jay, Martin. 1992. "Of Plots, Witnesses, and Judgements." In *Probing the Limits of Representation: Nazism and the "'Final Solution,"* ed. Saul Friedlander. Cambridge: Harvard University Press.

Kant, Immanuel. 1987. *Critique of Judgment,* ed. and trans. Werner S. Pluhar. Indianapolis: Hackett.

——. 1991. "The Idea for a Universal History with a Cosmopolitan Intent." In his *Political Writings*. Cambridge: Cambridge University Press.

Kaplan, Steven. 1995. *Farewell, Revolution: The Historians' Feud, France 1789/1989*. Ithaca: Cornell University Press.

Kaviraj, Sudipat. 2000. "Modernity and the Politics of India." *Daedalus* 129, 137–162.

Kean, Thomas, et al. 2004. *The 9/11 Commission Report*. New York: Norton.

Kearney, Richard. 1996. "Narrative Imagination: Between Ethics and Poetics." In *Paul Ricoeur: The Hermeneutics of Action*, ed. Richard Kearney. Thousand Oaks, CA: Sage.

Kelley, Michael, ed. 1994. *Critique and Power: Recasting the Foucault/Habermas Debate*. Cambridge: MIT Press.

Kellner, Hans. 1992. "Hayden White and Kantian Discourse: Tropology, Narrative, and Freedom." In *The Philosophy of Discourse: The Rhetorical in Twentieth Century Thought*, ed. Chip Sills and George H. Jensen. Portsmouth, NH: Boynton.

Kennedy, Valerie. 2000. *Edward Said: A Critical Introduction*. Cambridge: Blackwell.

Kögler, Hans. 1996. "The Self-Empowered Subject." *Philosophy and Social Criticism* 22: 13–44.

——. 1996. *The Power of Dialogue: Critical Hermeneutics after Gadamer and Foucault*, trans. Paul Hendrickson. Cambridge: MIT Press.

Koselleck, Reinhart. 2002. *The Practice of Conceptual History: Timing History, Spacing Concepts*, trans. Todd Samuel Presner and Others. Stanford: Stanford University Press.

Kritz, Neil J., ed. 1995. *Transitional Justice: How Emerging Democracies Reckon with Former Regimes*. 3 vols. Washington, DC: United States Institute of Peace.

Kymlicka, Will. 1990. *Contemporary Political Philosophy*. New York: Oxford University Press.

LaCapra, Dominick. 1994. *Representing the Holocaust: History, Theory, Trauma*. Ithaca: Cornell University Press.

Lafont, Christina. 1999. *The Linguistic Turn in Hermeneutic Philosophy*, trans. José Medina. Cambridge: MIT Press.

Larmore, Charles E. 1996. *Morals and Modernity*. Cambridge: Cambridge University Press.

Laub, Dori. 1995. "Truth and Testimony: The Process and the Struggle." In *Trauma: Explorations in Memory*, ed. Cathy Caruth. Baltimore: Johns Hopkins University Press.

Lauter, Paul. 1991. "The Literatures of America—A Comparative Discipline." In *Canons and Contexts*. New York: Oxford University Press.

Lefort, Claude. 1988. *Democracy and Political Theory*, trans. David Macey. Minneapolis: University of Minnesota.

——. 2001. *Essais sur le politique*. Paris: Seuil.

Lepetit, Bernard. 1996. "De l'échelle en histoire." *Jeux d'échelle: La micro-analyse à l'expérience,* ed. Jacques Revel. Paris: Seuil/Gallimard.

Levi, Giorgio. 1985. "I pericoli del geertzismo." *Quaderni Storici* 58, 269–277.

Lévi-Strauss, Claude. 1963. *Structural Anthropology,* trans. Claire Jacobson and Brooke Grundfest. New York: Basic Books.

———. 1966. *The Savage Mind.* Chicago: University of Chicago Press.

Little, Daniel. 1991. *Varieties of Social Explanation.* Boulder: Westview.

MacIntyre, Alasdair. 1984. *After Virtue.* Notre Dame: University of Notre Dame Press.

Majid, Anouar. 2000. *Unveiling Traditions: Postcolonial Islam in a Polycentric World.* Durham: Duke University Press.

Matutstik, Martin. 2001. *Jürgen Habermas: A Philosophical-Political Profile.* Lanham, MD: Rowman & Littlefield.

McCarthy, Thomas. 2002. "Vergagenheitsbewältigung in the USA: On the Politics of the Memory of Slavery." *Political Theory* 30, 623–648.

McCullagh, C. Behan. 1984. *Justifying Historical Descriptions.* Cambridge: Cambridge University Press.

McGowan, John. 1998. *Hannah Arendt.* Minneapolis: University of Minnesota Press.

———. 2002. *Democracy's Children: Intellectuals and the Rise of Cultural Politics.* Ithaca: Cornell University Press.

Mendieta, Eduardo. 2002. Introduction to Habermas, *Religion and Rationality: Essays on Reason God and Modernity.* Cambridge: MIT Press.

Michon, Pascal. 1999. *Eléments d'une histoire du sujet.* Paris. Kimé.

———. 2000. *Poétique d'une anti-anthropologie. L'herméneutique de Gadamer.* Paris: Vrin.

———. 2002. "Strata, Blocks, Pieces, Spirals, Elastics and Verticals: Six Figures of Time in Michel Foucault." *Time & Society* 11, 163–192.

Minow, Martha. 1998. *Between Vengeance and Forgiveness: Facing History after Genocide and Mass Violence.* Boston: Beacon Press.

Morrison, Toni. 1988. *Beloved.* New York: Penguin.

Moses, A. D. 1998. "Structure and Agency in the Holocaust: Daniel Goldhagen and His Critics." *History and Theory* 37, 194–219.

Mottahedeh, Roy. 1995. "The Clash of Civilizations: An Islamicist's Critique." *Harvard Middle Eastern and Islamic Review,* no. 2, 1–26.

Nandy, Ashis. 1987. *Traditions, Tyrannies, and Utopia: Essays in the Politics of Awareness.* Delhi: Oxford University Press.

———. 1995. "History's Forgotten Doubles." *History and Theory* 34, 44–66.

———. 1998. "The Politics of Secularism and the Recovery of Political Toleration." In *Secularism and Its Critics,* ed. Rajeev Bharghava. Delhi: Oxford University Press.

Nash, Gary. 1997. *History on Trial: Culture Wars and the Teaching of the Past*. New York: Knopf.

Nolte, Ernst. 1987. *Der europäische Bürgerkrieg: 1917–1945: Nationalismus und Bolschewismus*. Berlin: Propyläen Verlag.

Norton, Anne. 1995. "Heart of Darkness: Africa and African Americans in the Writings of Hannah Arendt." In *Feminist Interpretations of Hannah Arendt*, ed. Bonnie Honig. University Park: Pennsylvania State University Press.

Nussbaum, Martha. 1995. *Poetic Justice: The Literary Imagination and Public Life*. Boston: Beacon Press.

Olafson, Frederick. 1994. "Comments on *The Sources of the Self*." *Philosophy and Phenomenological Research* 54, 191–196.

Parry, Benita. 1987. "Problems in Current Theories of Colonial Discourse." *Oxford Literary Review* 9, 27–58.

———. 1992. "Overlapping Territories and Intertwined Histories; Edward Said's Postcolonial Cosmopolitanism." In *Edward Said: A Critical Reader*, ed. Michael Sprinker. Cambridge: Blackwell.

Pavel, Thomas. 2001. *The Spell of Language*. Chicago: University of Chicago Press.

Pellauer, David. 1991. "Limning the Liminal: Carr and Ricoeur on Time and Narrative." *Philosophy Today*, 51–62.

Pensky, Max. 1995. "Universalism and the Situated Critic." In *The Cambridge Companion to Habermas*, ed. Stephen K. White. Cambridge: Cambridge University Press.

———. 2000. "Cosmopolitanism and the Solidarity Problem: Habermas on National and Cultural Identities." *Constellations* 7, no. 1, 64–79.

Postema, Gerald. 1995. "Public Practical Reason: An Archaeology." *Social Philosophy Policy* 12, 43–86.

Poster, Mark. 1975. *Existential Marxism in Postwar France: From Sartre to Althusser*. Princeton: Princeton University Press.

Premo Steele, Cassie. 2000. *We Heal from Memory*. New York: Palgrave.

Proust, Marcel. 1989. *A la recherche du temps perdu*. 4 vols. Paris: Gallimard.

Putnam, Hilary. 1981. *Reason, Truth, and History*. Cambridge University Press.

Rashid, Salim, ed. 1997. *The Clash of Civilizations: Asian Responses*. New York: Oxford University Press.

Rasmussen, David. 1990. *Reading Habermas*. Oxford: Blackwell.

Rawls, John. 1971. *A Theory of Justice*. Cambridge: Harvard University Press.

———. 1993. *Political Liberalism*. New York: Columbia University Press.

———. 1995. "Reply to Habermas." *Journal of Philosophy* 92, 132–180.

Ricoeur, Paul. 1983. "On Intepretation." *Philosophy in France Today*, ed. Alan Montefiore.

———. 1984–88. *Time and Narrative*, trans. Kathleen Blamey and David Pellauer. 3 vols. Chicago: University of Chicago Press.

——. 1990. *Soi-même comme un autre*. Paris: Seuil.

——. 1991. *From Text to Action*, trans. Kathleen Blamey and John Thompson. Evanston: Northwestern University Press.

——. 1992. *Oneself as Another*, trans. Kathleen Blamey. Chicago: University of Chicago Press.

——. 2000. *La Mémoire, l'historie, l'oubli*. Paris: Seuil.

Rorty, Richard. 1979. "Transcendental Arguments, Self-Reference, and Pragmatism." *Transcendental Arguments and Science: Essays in Epistemology*, ed. Peter Bieri, Rolf P. Horstmann, and Lorenz Krüger. Dortrecht: Reidel.

——. 1982. *Consequences of Pragmatism*. Minneapolis: University of Minnesota.

——. 1989. *Contingency, Irony, and Solidarity*. Cambridge: Cambridge University Press.

——. 1991a. *Essays on Heidegger and Others*. Cambridge: Cambridge University Press.

——. 1991b. *Objectivity, Relativism, and Truth*. Cambridge: Cambridge University Press.

——. 1993. "Feminism, Ideology, and Deconstruction: A Pragmatist View." *Hypatia* 8, 96–105.

——. 1994. "Taylor on Self-Celebration and Gratitude." *Philosophy and Phenomenological Research* 54, 197–204.

——. 1998a. *Achieving Our Country: Leftist Thought in Twentieth-Century America*. Cambridge: Harvard University Press.

——. 1998b. *Truth and Progress*. Cambridge: Cambridge University Press.

——. 1999. "Comment on 'Naturalness and Mindedness: Hegel's Compatibilism.'" *European Journal of Philosophy* 7, 213–216.

Roth, Michael. 1995. *The Ironist's Cage: Memory, Trauma, and the Constitution of History*. New York: Columbia University Press.

Rothberg, Michael. 2000. *Traumatic Realism: The Demands of Holocaust Representation*. Minneapolis: University of Minnesota Press.

Rubinstein, R. E., and J. Crocker. 1993. "Challenging Huntington." *Foreign Policy*, 113–128.

Said, Edward. 1978. *Orientalism*. New York: Pantheon.

——. 1983. *The World, the Text, and the Critic*. Cambridge: Harvard University Press.

——. 1986. *After the Last Sky: Palestinian Lives*. New York: Pantheon.

——. 1987. "Interview with Edward Said." In *Criticism in Society*, ed. Imre Salusinsky. New York: Methuen.

——. 1992. Interview with Edward Said." In *Edward Said: A Critical Reader*, ed. Michael Sprinker. Cambridge: Blackwell.

——. 1993. *Culture and Imperialism*. New York: Knopf.

——. 1994a. "Permission to Narrate." In *The Politics of Dispossession: The Struggle for Palestinian Self-Determination 1969–94*. London: Chatto and Windus.

——. 1994b. "Response: A Symposium on Edward Said's *Culture and Imperialism*." *Social Text* 40, 20–24.

——. 2000. *Reflections on Exile*. Cambridge: Harvard University Press.

Sandel, Michael. 1996. *Democracy's Discontent: America in Search of a Public Philosophy*. Cambridge: Harvard University Press.

——. 1998. *Liberalism and the Limits of Justice*. 2nd ed. Cambridge: Cambridge University Press.

Sartre, Jean Paul. 1981. *Search for Method: Family Idiot*. Chicago: University of Chicago Press.

Scott, Joan. 1986. *Gender and History*. New York: Columbia University Press.

——. 1991. "Evidence of Experience." *Critical Inquiry* 17, 773–797.

——. 1996. *Only Paradoxes to Offer: French Feminists and the Rights of Man*. Cambridge: Harvard University Press.

Searle, John. 1997. *The Construction of Social Reality*. New York: Free Press.

Sen, Amartya. 1997. "Human Rights and Asian Values," *New Republic*, July 14 and 21, 33–40.

——. 1998. "Secularism and Its Discontents." In *Secularism and Its Critics*, ed. Rajeev Bharghava. Delhi: Oxford University Press.

——. 1999. *Reason before Identity*. New York: Oxford University Press.

——. 2000. *Development as Freedom*. New York: Knopf.

Sewell, William H., Jr. 1999. "Geertz, Cultural Systems, and History: From Synchrony to Transformation." In *The Fate of "Culture": Geertz and Beyond*, ed. Sherry Ortner. Berkeley: University of California Press.

Shandley, Robert, ed. 1998. Introduction to *Unwilling Germans: The Goldhagen Debate*. Minneapolis: University of Minnesota Press.

Shklar, Judith. 1991. "Review of *Sources of the Self*." *Political Theory* 19, 105–109.

Skinner, Quentin. 1990. "The Past in the Present." *New York Review of Books*, April 12, 36–37.

——. 1991. "Who Are 'We'? Ambiguities of the Modern Self" *Inquiry* 34, 133–153.

——. 1999. *Liberty before Liberalism*. Cambridge: Cambridge University Press.

Smith, Anthony. 1991. "The Nation: Invented, Imagined, Reconstructed?" *Millennium* 20, 353–368.

Smith, Nicholas. 1997. *Strong Hermeneutics: Contingency and Moral Identity*. New York: Routledge.

——. 2002. *Charles Taylor: Meaning, Morals, and Modernity*. Cambridge: Blackwell.

Spiegelman, Art. 1986. *Maus: A Survivor's Tale. I: My Father Bleeds History*. New York: Pantheon.

——. 1991. *Maus: A Survivor's Tale. II: And Here My Troubles Began*. New York: Pantheon.

Spivak, Gayatri. 1988a. "Can the Subaltern Speak?" In her *Marxism and the Interpetation of Culture*. Urbana: University of Illinois Press.

——. 1988b. *In Other Worlds: Essays in Cultural Politics*. New York: Routledge.

Steele, Meili. 1986. "The Dangers of Structuralist Narratology: Genette's Misinterpretation of Proust." *Romance Notes* 26, 1–7.

———. 1997a. "Concept of Public Morality Missing from Flag Controversy." *The State* (Columbia, SC), March 3.

———. 1997b. *Critical Confrontations: Literary Theories in Dialogue.* Columbia: University of South Carolina Press.

———. 1997c. *Theorizing Textual Subjects: Agency and Oppression.* Cambridge: Cambridge University Press.

———. 2002. "Arendt versus Ellison on Little Rock: The Role of Language in Political Judgment." *Constellations* 9, 184–206.

———. 2003a. "Ricoeur versus Taylor on Language and Literature." *Metaphilosophy* 34, 425–446.

———. 2003b. "Three Problematics of Linguistic Vulnerability: Gadamer, Benhabib, and Butler." In *Feminist Interpretations of Hans-Georg Gadamer,* ed. Lorraine Code. University Park: Pennsylvania State University Press.

———. Forthcoming. "Ontologie linguistique et dialogue politique chez Bakhtine." *Bakhtine et la pensée dialogique,* ed. André Collinot and Clive Thomson. Atlanta/Amsterdam: Rodopi.

Steffes, Michael. 1996. "Slavery and Mansfield Park: The Historical and Biographical Context." *English Language Notes* 34, no. 2, 23–41.

Stern, Daniel. 2003. "The Practical Turn." In *The Blackwell Guide to the Philosophy of Social Science,* ed. Peter Machamer and Michael Silberstein. Cambridge: Blackwell.

Subramaniam, Surain. 2000. "The Asian Values Debate: Implications for the Spread of Liberal Democracy." *Asian Affairs: An American Review* 27, 19–35.

Sunstein, Cass. 1995. "The Idea of a Usable Past." *Columbia Law Review* 95, 601–608.

———. 1996. *Legal Reasoning and Political Conflict.* New York: Oxford University Press.

Taylor, Charles. 1984a. "Foucault on Freedom, and Truth." *Political Theory* 12, 152–183.

———. 1984b. "Philosophy and Its History." In *Philosophy in History,* ed. Richard Rorty et al. Cambridge: Cambridge University Press.

———. 1985a. "Connolly, Foucault, and Truth." *Political Theory* 13, 377–385.

———. 1985b. *Language and Human Agency.* Cambridge: Cambridge University Press.

———. 1985c. *Philosophy and the Human Sciences.* Cambridge: Cambridge University Press.

———. 1986. "Language and Society." In *Communicative Action,* ed. Axel Honneth and Hans Joas. Cambridge: Polity.

———. 1988. "The Hermeneutics of Conflict." In *Meaning and Context: Quentin Skinner and His Critics,* ed. James Tully. Princeton: Princeton University Press.

——. 1989. *Sources of the Self.* Cambridge: Harvard University Press.

——. 1991. "Comments and Replies." *Inquiry* 34, 237–254.

——. 1993a. "Embodied Agency and Background in Heidegger." In The *Cambridge Companion to Heidegger,* ed. Charles Guignon. Cambridge: Cambridge University Press.

——. 1993b. "Modernity and the Rise of the Public Sphere." *The Tanner Lectures on Human Values* 14, ed. Grethe B. Peterson. Salt Lake City: University of Utah Press.

——. 1993c. "The Motivation behind the Procedural Ethic." In *Kant and Political Philosophy,* ed. Ronald Beiner. New Haven: Yale University Press.

——. 1994a. *Multiculturalism and the Politics of Recognition.* Princeton: Princeton University Press.

——. 1994b. "Précis and Reply to Commentators in Symposium on *Sources of the Self.*" *Philosophy and Phenomenological Research* 54, 185–186, 203–213.

——. 1995a. "A Most Peculiar Institution." In *World, Mind, and Ethics,* ed. J. E. J. Altham and Ross Harrison. Cambridge: Cambridge University Press.

——. 1995b. *Philosophical Arguments.* Cambridge: Harvard University Press.

——. 1997. "Nationalism and Modernity." In *The Morality of Nationalism,* ed. Robert McKim and Jeff McMahan. Oxford: Oxford University Press.

——. 1998a. "Le Fondamental dans l'histoire." In *Charles Taylor et l'interprétation de l'identité moderne,* ed. G. Laforest and P. de Lara. Sainte Foy: Les Presses de l'Université Laval.

——. 1998b. "Modes of Secularism." In *Secularism and Its Critics,* ed. Rajeev Bharghava. Delhi: Oxford University Press.

——. 1999a. "Conditions of an Unforced Consensus on Human Rights." In *The East Asian Challenge for Human Rights,* ed. Joanne R. Bauer and Daniel Bell. Cambridge: Cambridge University Press.

——. 1999b. "Democratic Exclusion (and Its Remedies?)." In *Multiculturalism, Liberalism, and Democracy,* ed. Rajeev Bhargava et al. New Delhi: Oxford University Press.

——. 1999c. "Two Theories of Modernity." *Public Culture* 11, 153–174.

——. 2004. *Modern Social Imaginaries.* Durham: Duke University Press.

Teitel, Ruti. 2000. *Transitional Justice.* Oxford: Oxford University Press.

Tosto, Paul. 1997. "The History We Don't Teach." *The State* (Columbia, SC), January 26, p. 12.

Toulmin, Stephen. 1990. *Cosmopolis: The Hidden Agenda of Modernity.* Chicago: University of Chicago Press.

Tuck, Richard. 1993. *Philosophy and Government: 1572–1651.* Cambridge: Cambridge University Press.

Tully, James. 1995. *Strange Multiplicities.* Cambridge: Cambridge University Press.

Vails, Andrew. 2003. "A Truth Commission for the United States?" *Intertexts* 7, 157–170.

Villa, Dana. 1996. *Arendt and Heidegger: The Fate of the Political.* Princeton: Princeton University Press.

Walker, Margaret. 1998. *Moral Understandings: A Feminist Study in Ethics.* New York: Routledge.

Walker, R. B. J. 1992. *Inside/Outside: International Relations as Political Theory.* Cambridge: Cambridge University Press.

Walzer, Michael. 1994. *Thick and Thin: Moral Argument at Home and Abroad.* Notre Dame: University of Notre Dame Press.

Warren, Kenneth. 2004. "Ralph Ellison and the Problem of Cultural Authority: The Lessons of Little Rock." In *Ralph Ellison and the Raft of Hope: A Political Companion to Invisible Man,* ed. Lucas Morel. Lexington: University of Kentucky Press.

Weber, Eugen. 1976. *Peasants into Frenchmen: The Modernization of Rural France, 1870–1914.* Stanford: Stanford University Press.

Wellmer, Albrecht. 1996. "Hannah Arendt on Judgement: The Unwritten Doctrine of Reason." In *Hannah Arendt: Twenty Years Later,* ed. Larry May and Jerome Kohn. Cambridge: MIT Press.

White, Hayden. 1973. *Metahistory.* Baltimore: Johns Hopkins University Press.

———. 1978. *Tropics of Discourse.* Baltimore: Johns Hopkins University Press.

———. 1988. *The Content of the Form.* Baltimore: Johns Hopkins University Press.

———. 1992. "Historical Emplotment and the Problem of Truth." In *Probing the Limits of Representation,* ed. Saul Friedlander. Cambridge: Harvard University Press.

White, Stephen. 2000. *Sustaining Affirmation: The Strengths of Weak Ontology in Political Theory.* Princeton: Princeton University Press.

Young-Bruehl, Elisabeth. 1982. *Hannah Arendt: For Love of the World.* New Haven: Yale University Press.

Zagorin, Peter. 1990. "Historiography and Postmodernism." In *History and Theory: Contemporary Readings,* ed. Brian Fay et al. Oxford: Blackwell.

Index

Names

Ahmad, Aijaz, 181
Alcoff, Linda, 175
Allen, Danielle, 176
Anderson, Benedict, 5, 18
Anderson, Joel, 89
Ankersmit, Frank, 160
Anzuldúa, Gloria, 34
Arac, Jonathan, 95, 151
Arendt, Hannah, 15, 39, 104–123, 151,
    174, 175, 176, 177, 178
Austen, Jane, 132
Aylesworth, Gary, 161

Bakhtin, Mikhail, 53–54, 177, 181
Bartov, Omer, 39–40
Bauman, Zygmunt, 39
Benhabib, Seyla, 59–60, 62, 104,
    121–122, 151, 154, 155, 163, 164, 174,
    175, 176, 178, 180
Benjamin, Walter, 122, 163, 164, 178
Bhabha, Homi, 181
Blight, David, 149
Bohman, James, 171, 174, 175
Brandom, Robert, 156
Braudel, Fernand, 159
Butler, Judith, 7, 12, 54–63, 75, 89, 152,
    155, 169
Byers, Thomas, 151

Calhoun, Craig, 35, 151, 156
Carr, David, 161, 165
Carroll, Noel, 46
Caruth, Cathy, 62
Chartier, Roger, 68–69, 166
Chatterjee, Partha, 150
Chopin, Kate, 52
Clifford, James, 178
Code, Lorraine, 164, 171
Colebrook, Claire, 167, 178

Connolly, William, 168
Cooke, Maeve, 155

Dean, Carolyn, 173
Derrida, Jacques, 12, 30, 56–59
Descombes, Vincent, 151
Disch, Lisa, 175
Dole, Robert, 35, 158
Dosse, François, 161, 166
Dreyfus, Hubert, 66, 80–81, 166,
    169
Dworkin, Ronald, 33, 151, 183

Edgar, Walter, 149
Ellison, Ralph, 15, 28, 104–123
Euben, Roxanne, 181

Fanon, Frantz, 133
Ferrara, Alessandro, 154, 177
Fish, Stanley, 16, 81, 83–84, 141,
    144–147, 170
Fiss, Owen, 183
Fitzgerald, F. Scott, 94–95
Flaubert, Gustave, 6, 52, 89
Forter, Greg, 172
Foucault, Michel, 12, 13, 54, 55, 63–75,
    80, 93, 94, 96, 105, 125, 126, 129,
    152, 165, 166, 167
Fraser, Nancy, 62, 165
Friedlander, Saul, 37, 123
Friedman, Thomas, 174
Frye, Northrup, 80
Fullinwider, Robert, 149, 150

Gadamer, Hans-Georg, 52, 68, 69–70,
    114, 118, 154, 171, 173
Galston, William, 150
Gaonkar, Dilip, 150
Gauchet, Marcel, 182
Geertz, Clifford, 66, 82, 169–170